Kafka
Gothic and Fairytale

66

Internationale Forschungen zur Allgemeinen und Vergleichenden Literaturwissenschaft

In Verbindung mit

Dietrich Briesemeister (Friedrich Schiller-Universität Jena) - Guillaume van Gemert (Universiteit Nijmegen) - Joachim Knape (Universität Tübingen) - Klaus Ley (Johannes Gutenberg-Universität Mainz) - John A. McCarthy (Vanderbilt University) - Manfred Pfister (Freie Universität Berlin) - Sven H. Rossel (University of Washington) - Azade Seyhan (Bryn Mawr College) - Horst Thomé (Universität Kiel)

herausgegeben von

Alberto Martino

(Universität Wien)

Redakteure:
Norbert Bachleitner & Alfred Noe

Anschrift der Redaktion:
Institut für Vergleichende Literaturwissenschaft, Berggasse 11/5, A-1090 Wien

Kafka
Gothic and Fairytale

Patrick Bridgwater

Amsterdam - New York, NY 2003

Cover illustration: Giovanni Battista Piranesi, *Interior of a Prison*,
© National Gallery of Scotland

Le papier sur lequel le présent ouvrage est imprimé remplit les prescriptions
de "ISO 9706:1994, Information et documentation - Papier pour documents -
Prescriptions pour la permanence".

The paper on which this book is printed meets the requirements of " ISO
9706:1994, Information and documentation - Paper for documents -
Requirements for permanence".

ISBN: 90-420-1194-7
©Editions Rodopi B.V., Amsterdam - New York, NY 2003
Printed in The Netherlands

CONTENTS

PREFACE

There is a contradiction between Kafka's persona with its love of fairytale and his Ka or shadow with its affinity with Gothic. The extreme lucidity of his style is at odds with his alarming, tortured, 'Kafkaesque' narratives and the endless ambiguities in which they are clothed. His admiration for Goethe is only partly the admiration of a great artist for a greater; he was also drawn to the calm certainty of Goethe's blessedly uncomplicated nature, as opposed to the endless involutions and convolutions of his own almost invariably troubled self-awareness, which the protagonist of each of his novels comes to share. This inner contradiction drove him simultaneously to reveal his meaning and to seek to conceal it, and because he craved understanding, yet feared it, there is a further contradiction between the fact that he writes, in prose, a form of poetry of the first voice, expressing and addressing himself, often, like his 'starvation-artist' persona, seemingly indifferent to the public, and the infinite trouble to which he went to throw the reader off the scent.

What follows is a comparative study of Kafka's work, especially the novels and some of the related shorter punishment fantasies, in relation to the Gothic and fairytale conventions. His deployment of Gothic motifs contrasts with his use of fairytale ones, which he (like the German Gothic or 'black' Romantics and twentieth-century practitioners of the Gothic Fairytale) knowingly subverts, but in each instance what counts are less the parallels and affinities, than the use to which he puts Gothic and fairytale, and how and why he leaves them behind. Max Brod dismissed the problem of Kafka's shadow by denying his Gothic side. It would have been easy, in the present context, to dismiss it in the opposite way, by assimilating him wholesale to the Gothic tradition as it developed from 1764 to 1924, but when all is said and done it is precisely the mixture of Gothic and its opposites in Kafka that makes him so interesting.

The perennial problem in Kafka-criticism has been how to reconcile the general and the particular. I therefore first consider the nature of Gothic and fairytale, and the dreamlike nature of his writing, before moving on to an examination of the novels, as I understand them to be, and some of the major shorter texts in the Gothic and fairytale contexts. Within the confines of a relatively short study of this kind it is, of course, neither possible nor appropriate to give consequential close readings of three whole novels, one of which is far from short. In a separate book, *Kafka's Novels: An Interpretation*, currently in the press, the problems inherent in reading Kafka are discussed at some length. Here let it simply be said that his creative technique, described in Chapter 4 with reference to what Dilthey called the hermeneutic circle, is the key to understanding his writings, which are dreamlike in being governed by the alternative logic of dreams, so that 'normal' logic tends to be replaced by verbal association. Reading his texts means focusing on the secondary meanings of words and on metaphors which have been taken literally, for he was far too careful a writer to use words with irrelevant secondary meanings or which formed inappropriate verbal bridges. No analysis of his work is adequate that does not pay proper attention to the associations that he deliberately put in place and which constitute the deep structure and with it the meaning of his work.

A study such as this faces the risk not only of making Kafka's work seem more Gothic than it really is, but of making Gothic seem more Kafkaesque than it really was. I have tried to avoid both risks. It would have been easy, by mistaking the surface meaning of Kafka's work for its real meaning, and thus taking it as turning on an external conflict between the individual and an all-powerful public (as opposed to introjected paternal) Authority, to make it seem even more Gothic than it comes to seem in the following pages. In reality, however, the novels in particular are a classic example of how the surface meaning of a text serves to mask its real, 'unsayable' meanings, which in turn underlines the parallel between the creative process and what Freud calls the dream-work.

German text is quoted in translation unless the emphasis is on the meaning of individual words or phrases, in which case the words in question are quoted and their meanings discussed. The translations are mine unless specified otherwise. Since the book is not addressed to folklorists as such, I have generally translated 'Volksmärchen' by 'fairytale' (written as one word, as in *The Encyclopedia of Fantasy*, to emphasize that there are no fairies involved), although 'folk fairytale' and 'folktale' are occasionally used by way of emphasis.

For reading my first draft and making many useful comments I am much indebted to Alan Menhennet.

ABBREVIATIONS AND SIGNS

The following abbreviations are used in the text and footnotes:

BF   *Briefe an Felice* , ed. Erich Heller & Jürgen Born (Frankfurt a.M.: S. Fischer, 1967)

BM   *Briefe an Milena* , ed. Willy Haas (Frankfurt a.M.: S. Fischer, 1952)

Br   *Briefe 1902-1924* , ed. Max Brod (Frankfurt a.M.: S. Fischer, 1958)

BV   *Brief an den Vater,* in *Er. Prosa von Franz Kafka* ([Frankfurt a.M.]: Suhrkamp, 1963)

J   Gustav Janouch, *Gespräche mit Kafka* (Frankfurt a.M.: Fischer Bücherei, 1962)

T   *Tagebücher 1910-1923,* ed. Max Brod (Frankfurt a.M.: S.Fischer, 1949

KHM J. & W. Grimm, *Kinder und Haus-Märchen,* Ausgabe letzter Hand, ed.Heinz Rölleke (Stuttgart: Reclam,1997)

The signs → and ← and ↔ are used to denote verbal association including displacement along a chain of associations.

In the notes, all references to a given work after the first are given in the shortest intelligible form. Titles of journals are abbreviated in the usual way.

A German (or, occasionally, Czech or Italian) word which is not actually present in the text in question is italicized.

1. INTRODUCTION

1.1. Kafka's Gothic World

Kafka was a haunted personality, the dreams and day-dreams, of which his writing was the expression, filled with phantoms, the demons, or devils, as he generally called them, of self-doubt, self-accusation and self-judgment, fear of life and fear of death (to which he was inclined to ascribe his insomnia, although he also put it down to fear of his father). He saw the flames of Hell breaking through the very ground on which he stood (diary, 21 July 1913), an experience with which the poet Shelley would have sympathized. Shelley's own use of the image in his early and most Gothic phase, in a letter to Edward Graham in summer 1810 ('Persevere even though Hell [...] should yawn beneath your feet')[1] was conventional by comparison. But while the 'supernatural' in the form of all those plaguy demons by which he was tormented (see BM 25), and the 'supernatural assize' of conscience, whose agents they mostly were, was an everyday reality to him, he was, like Shelley, opposed to religious superstition, which he saw as dishonest and all too easy. God in particular he found implausibly abstract, although he believed in principle in the idea of a personal god and in the reality of a multiplicity of personal devils,[2] and was, to his misery, obsessed by the idea of the Fall, that ultimate superstition and *terminus a quo* of Gothic. Even without the pervasive Gothic iconography of his work with its theme of transgression against paternal power, he can immediately be seen to belong in the Gothic context. Writing was, for him, a transgressive act because of the weight of paternal disapproval it carried, and his novels, the subject of all three of which is transgression, are formally transgressive in being closer to the romance, to fairytale, to autobiography, and even to lyric poetry, than to the novel as such, of which he had a low opinion.

His *Brief an den Vater (Letter to my Father)*, written in 1919 and never delivered, must be the most damning indictment of 'paternal tyranny' ever written. Putting in the shade Shelley's similar but less fully articulated criticism of his father, who was both more trying and more tried than Kafka *père*, whose son lacked Shelley's explosive propensities, it shows with painful clarity that Franz Kafka lived in a world dominated by precisely those uncertainties about the nature of power, law, society, family and

---

[1]   *The Letters of Percy Bysshe Shelley*, ed. F. L. Jones, 2 vols (Oxford: Oxford University Press, 1964), I, 10.
[2]   An interesting parallel is Shelley's *Essay on the Devil and Devils* of 1819-20, in *Shelley's Prose*, ed. D. L. Clark (Albuquerque: University of New Mexico Press, 1954), 264-275.

sexuality that have been said[3] to dominate Gothic fiction. The fact that Herrmann Kafka, a self-made man, was in his not always obvious way a loving father, much concerned about the future of his vulnerable, 'disappointing' son, does not mean that he was not also, at times, a tyrant in his son's estimation. There are two issues here: how the father actually was, and how his son, whose self-esteem was low, sometimes perceived and felt him to be. Recently published correspondence[4] shows more clearly than before that the father's heart was in the right place, but it does not, and cannot, unwrite the *Brief an den Vater*, or indeed *Das Urteil* and *Die Verwandlung*, in all three of which the father-son relationship has, however, been subjected to differing degrees of fictionalization. Even in the objective-seeming *Brief an den Vater* the real-life relationship has been subjected to poetic license, being exaggerated in the process, and, what is more important, it has been subjected to dream-distortion, so that the father not only represents the father as the son saw him, which is not how the father saw himself, but arguably stands as much for the writer's super-ego as for his 'old man'. Writing, as Kafka knew very well, of its very nature involves falsification. Feelings are not verbally perfect; once the expression is perfected, they are arguably no longer true. The *Brief an den Vater* is particularly 'stagey', but all Kafka's writings involve an act or fictional performance to which they self-consciously, if hermetically, draw attention. The sense of guilt that drove him to write was in the final analysis more the product of his own hypersensitivity than of his father's occasional unthinking insensitivity.

These important points made, Kafka spent much of his life as a 'slave'[5] in the household of a 'master' who was a law unto himself, recognizing only his own rules, laws and opinions, so that the son's every move was liable to be construed into a transgression against paternal law. He grew up with the ideas of tyranny, a term he uses repeatedly in the *Brief an den Vater,* and heresy, meaning, as always, disobedience vis-à-vis the patriarch's 'commandments'. No wonder, then, that he claimed that all his work was about his father. One should, of course, be wary of one who was more inclined to throw his critics off the scent than to abet them, as he would have seen it, in an act of intellectual voyeurism or rape, but these particular words need to be taken seriously. They do not mean that only a Freudian interpretation of the work is valid, just that this has a psychological dimension that no sensible overall reading can afford to ignore; that goes, above all, for Freud's account of the 'dream-work', which is tantamount to a description of the creative act that Kafka wisely left others to describe. There is no need to read Freud on the Devil as a

---

3   Fred Botting, *Gothic* (London & New York: Routledge, 1996), 5.
4   Franz Kafka, *Briefe 1900-1912*, ed. Hans-Gerd Koch, 5 vols (Frankfurt a .M.: S.Fischer, 1999-).
5   Hence the name of Raban (a self-projection) in *Hochzeitsvorbereitungen auf dem Lande* (cf. Czech *rab*, slave).

substitute for the father[6] to realize that Kafka *père*, who was given to referring to his ascetic son as a 'devil', himself gave him the devil of a time. Kafka's identification with the Devil, and with witches and vampires, derives from this bedevilled relationship. The world in which he lived, reflected as it is in the world of which he wrote, is very much a Gothic world, although its ruling tensions are those of fairytale too, for his father is also, as the *Brief an den Vater* makes clear, that archetypal projection of another's fear, the ogre of fairytale, the bogeyman of childhood. Given that Kafka, whose name *(kavka)* means 'jackdaw' in Czech, was in the habit of using the *Rabe* (raven) as an emblematic self-reference, it is appropriate, if not entirely fair, that the fairytale type of the *Rabenvater* (cruel father) can be construed as 'Kafka's father'. It is just the sort of linguistic nicety the son appreciated.

In coming to see his father as an ogre, Georg Bendemann, the protagonist of *Das Urteil* (see 9.1), was re-enacting his creator's similar perception, for Kafka was at times intellectually and emotionally overwhelmed by his father, 'that huge man [...] the ultimate authority' (BV 140): 'You were so gigantic, a giant in every respect' (BV 151), he wrote, flinching as he described 'the sense I have of your magnitude' (BV 186). When the son was deemed to have failed, notably in not being a replica of his father in some particular respect, he would find 'a great voice thundering at him' (BV 146), a childhood experience that is echoed in Chapter 9 of *Der Proceß* when the Priest calls out to Josef K. in a tone of voice that will brook no disobedience. The father, that is to say, was an ogre not only in the sense of being an intimidating physical presence, but in a moral sense as well. Describing himself - in his usual self-deprecating way - as a weakly, timid, wavering person, Kafka found his father 'too much' for him, too vehement, too domineering. His approach to those he regarded as inferiors (his son, his employees) was liable to be confrontational. Like Ann Radcliffe's Montoni, he seemed the very incarnation of the domestic tyrant: 'From your armchair you ruled the world. Your opinion was correct, any other being mad, hare-brained, crackpot, not normal' (BV 142). As a result, the father took on, for his son, 'the enigmatic quality that all tyrants possess whose rights are based not on reason but on their person' (BV 142). Kafka was devastated by the force of his father's personality, hectoring temperament and tyrannical nature, to say nothing of the loudness of his voice and the hotness of his temper.

In one form or another this relationship resting on what Nietzsche had dubbed the dual morality of master and slave lies behind works such as *Das Urteil, Die Verwandlung, Der Verschollene, Der Proceß* and *In der Strafkolonie*, all of them dreamlike self-punitive fantasies turning on Kafka's father-complex. Pointing to *Das Urteil*, he writes of 'your judgment of me', and goes on: 'you don't charge me with

---

6 See 'A Seventeenth-Century Demonological Neurosis' (iii. 'The Devil as a Father-Substitute'), in Sigmund Freud, *Art and Literature* (London: Penguin, 1985), 397-408.

anything downright improper or wicked' (BV 136), which takes the reader back to the first sentence of *Der Proceß*. The 'parasitism' with which the son was to imagine himself being charged by his father (BV 191, cf. T 23f) first appears in symbolical form in the 'Ungeziefer' (with which Kafka had identified since 1910) of *Die Verwandlung*. What was particularly difficult to bear was 'that awful hoarse undertone of anger and utter condemnation' (BV 147), 'the words of abuse flying around me in swarms' (BV 148). As a child Kafka cringed before his father, hiding from him and only daring to emerge when he was so far away from him that his power could no longer reach him (BV 148). For the child the orders barked at him were tantamount to 'a heavenly commandment' (shades, here, of the autocratic, quasi-divine Old Commandant, a variation on the universal dream figure of the 'old man').

To make matters worse, the father did not keep the commandments he imposed on his son, for whom the world was thus divided into three domains:

> One, in which I, the slave, lived under laws that had been invented for me alone [...] then a second world, infinitely remote from mine, in which you lived, concerned with governance, the issuing of orders and [the venting of] your annoyance when they were not obeyed; finally, a third world where everybody else lived happily, free alike from orders and having to obey them. (BV 145)

From his father's intemperate condemnation of him and all his works the son acquired an intense sense of guilt that never left him. When he said that all his writings were about his father, he meant they were about the boundless sense of guilt that, he sometimes felt, formed his paternal inheritance, for the authority of the father was inevitably introjected, becoming a tyrannical inward monitor. He goes on to write of 'this terrible trial that is pending between us [Franz and Ottla, the youngest sister who was similarly demonized by their father because of her independence of spirit] and you [...] a trial in which you keep on claiming to be the judge' (BV 164). The relevance of this to *Der Proceß* is obvious, although the situation described in the novel is more complex, having been fictionalized in multiple ways. Given the father's constant complaint that his commandments were not being obeyed, 'heresy' became, for his son, an inescapable personal condition. No wonder it looms so large between the lines of *Der Proceß*. At a very early stage the son was forbidden to speak in the sense of answering back: '"Not one word of contradiction!" you would say, and the raised hand that accompanied your words has been with me ever since' (BV 147). It can be seen to this day on the first page of *Der Verschollene*, where it is, ironically, attributed to the Statue of 'Liberty'.

Even the portrait of Diana, goddess of the hunt, in *Der Proceß* is, among other things, a reflection of the state of affairs in the Kafka household in those fatally formative years, in which, as Kafka put it in the letter to his father, his mother unconsciously played the part of a beater during a hunt, so that the concept of the hunt with himself as prey was a part of the psychological burden he carried forward. He even suffered imprisonment at the 'tyrant's' hands, describing the 'extraordinary feeling of terror' when he was carried off to the balcony and locked out from the family: the sense of exclusion left its mark, as did the ogre's threat to 'tear him apart like a fish' (BV 149; tearing someone to pieces is, of course, a fairytale motif)[7]. The negative feelings engendered by being browbeaten as a child, and well into adulthood, are commonplace in the Gothic novel. I mean the feelings of being disinherited, of despair, guilt, and terror. The inner world of which Kafka wrote was in many ways a Gothic one because he spent virtually all his life in such a world. 'Gothic', in his case, is more than a literary kind; it is an existential condition.

1.2. Kafka and Gothic

Given the manifold ways in which it has been read (and misread, the latter far outweighing the former), it is astonishing that Kafka's work has not already been placed in the context of literary Gothic, which has a strong Bohemian side stretching from the anonymous *The Secret Tribunal; or, The Court of Winceslaus. A Mysterious Tale* (chapbook, 1803) to Heinrich Zschokke's *Drakomira mit dem Schlangenringe oder die nächtlichen Wanderer in den Schreckensgefängnissen von Karlstein bei Prag. Eine Schauergeschichte aus Böhmens grauer Vorzeit* (1847) and Marion F. Crawford's *The Witch of Prague* (1891), which even has a character named Israel Kafka, and thence to the successive versions of *The Student of Prague* (film, 1913, 1926, 1935). Aside from Kafka's Gothic side having been denied by Brod, the main reasons for this are probably the fact that Gothic, for all its supposed German origins, is essentially an Anglo-American and Anglo-French phenomenon, and that what passed as its German equivalent, the so-called *Schauerroman* (chiller or thriller), was long considered too 'sub-literary' to be worth serious critical attention. Until comparatively recently German censure of 'popular' literature even extended to Tieck's *Abdallah*, a work with some literary pretensions.

Far from being a reason for excluding him from the Gothic context and pantheon, the fact that Kafka is one of the jewels in the crown of high modernism is all the more reason for placing him in it, for modernism with its subversion of existing forms goes back precisely to the period of high Gothic at the end of the eighteenth century. This is when most of the modernist revolutions and revaluations began, the intertextualities between Kafka's novels and the Gothic novel being just one aspect of a fundamental pattern of cultural and intellectual parallels between the turn of the eighteenth century and the turn of the nineteenth.[8] The modern, post-Richardsonian novel began with the Gothic novel, and the idea of playing with existing literary forms is as much a feature

---

[7]   See Stith Thompson, *Motif-Index of Folk Literature*, 6 vols (Copenhagen: Rosenkilde and Bagger, 1955-58), VI, 783.

[8]   See Patrick Bridgwater, 'Backdating Modernism', *Oxford German Studies*, 30 (2001), 107-132.

of Ludwig Tieck's early work as it is of high modernism as described by the Devil in Thomas Mann's *Dr Faustus*. The leitmotif of that novel, that 'everything seemed to have been done', was first voiced by the Marquis de Sade (to whom I return in 2.4) in his *Idée sur les romans* a century and a half earlier.

So long as the German equivalent of Gothic was thought to be the preserve of literary adventurers like Grosse and Kahlert, Spieß and Weber, it would have seemed neither appropriate nor useful to consider Kafka in that context, although the truth is that Grosse's *Der Genius. Aus den Papieren des Marquis C. von Grosse*,[9] better known outside Germany as *Horrid Mysteries*,, inspired both Tieck's *William Lovell* and the novel Hoffmann wrote in 1795-96 and then probably destroyed after it had been turned down by a publisher, *Cornaro: Memoiren des Grafen Julius von S.* Tieck revelled in *Der Genius*, the first two parts of which he and his friends Schmohl and Schwinger read aloud to one another in a mammoth ten-hour session back in the heroic days of Gothic (and enthusiasm) in June 1792, and Hoffmann's most (and most influentially) Gothic work, the novel *Die Elixiere des Teufels* (1814-15), is reminiscent of *Der Genius* in respect of its 'constant sense of characters being manipulated by powers outside their control'.[10] To speak of Grosse's work as 'low-brow' and Hoffmann's as 'high-brow' is to over-simplify, and in any case writers like Grosse represent only the marginally literary fringes of Gothic, for in Germany the early Gothic novel in the form of the *Bundesroman* of, say, Veit Weber, was appropriated by the Romantic novelists, for instance by Tieck in his *William Lovell*, who took over much of its ultimately explained supernatural and gave it a psychological basis[11] which is important in the present context in that in Kafka the dark imagery of spectral terrors appears in psychological guise.

Whereas in England the novel, for a time, gave ground to the Gothic romance, in Germany both the Gothic romance and the Romantic novel lost ground, at much the same time, to the fairytale, for the literary part of the German Gothic romance was appropriated by the German Romantic novel, which quickly yielded the high ground to the *Märchen* (and to the *Novelle*, which need not concern us here). Kafka is thus the inheritor not only of the German Romantic view of the novel as poetry, and of the internalized 'Gothic' of the German Romantic novel as such, but also of the *Märchen*. How very close the relationship is between fairytale and Gothic will become ever clearer as we proceed. Veit Weber was seen at the time as a *schauerlicher Märchenerzähler* (a teller of horrific fairytales), and Tieck's recipe for a Gothic novel ('Giants, dwarfs, ghosts, witches, a touch of murder and violent death, moonlight and

---

[9] The title is imitated from that of Schiller's *Der Geisterseher*.
[10] Eric A. Blackall, *The Novels of the German Romantics* (Ithaca & London: Cornell University Press, 1983), 231.
[11] Blackall, 64.

dusk, all this sweetened with love and sensibility to make it more palatable'[12]) is scarcely less applicable to fairytale than it is to Gothic. The weird fairytales Shelley used to tell his sisters were very much of a piece with his Gothic tales.

As Tieck pointed out as long ago as 1795, in the foreword to his *Peter Lebrecht*, 'horridness' (in Jane Austen's sense) is a characteristic not just of the likes of Grosse, but of the whole German early Romantic phenomenon that we now know as the Sturm und Drang, which corresponds to English-language Pre-Romanticism and Gothic Romanticism. German readers at this time expected to have their hair made to stand on end: 'The reader is happy so long as the events served up are as ghastly as they are ghostly'. Besides, once literary labels and evaluative preconceptions are set aside, and German Gothic is seen to include not only the early work of Schiller (notably *Der Geisterseher. Aus den Papieren des Grafen von O.* [1787, incomplete], but also the banditti-tragedy *Die Räuber* [1781], which so impressed the English Romantics) and Tieck (*Abdallah* [1795], *Der blonde Eckbert* [1797] and *Liebeszauber* [1812, translated by that Gothic dark horse Thomas De Quincey in 1825]), but the anonymous *Die Nachtwachen des Bonaventura* (1804), Hoffmann (*Die Elixiere des Teufels* [1814-15], translated by De Quincey's friend R. P. Gillies in 1824) and Achim von Arnim (notably *Der tolle Invalide* [1818], a tale of diabolical possession, and *Die Majoratsherren* [1820]; Heine rated Arnim's evocations of terror above those of Hoffmann[13]), the case for considering Kafka in the Gothic context suddenly looks more reasonable. However, the point is academic since the parallels, which mostly concern the non-German Gothic novel as such, will be seen to speak for themselves.

Exactly how much Kafka knew of the Gothic novel is not clear. Notwithstanding some parallels between his work and Grosse's *Der Genius*, there is no particular reason to think that he came across any of the *Schauerromane* as such. On the other hand he greatly admired the work of Heinrich von Kleist, especially *Michael Kohlhaas*, which contains elements of Gothic, has been shown to be indebted to E. T. A. Hoffmann, and may also have been familiar with works such as *Das Zauberschloß* and *Der Geheimnisvolle* (a copy of which was owned by Scott) by Ludwig Tieck, that earlier master in the exploration of anguish and anxiety, although much of Tieck's earlier work in particular has always been relatively inaccessible, buried alive in the twenty-eight volumes of *Ludwig Tieck's Schriften* (1828-54). Like Tieck's *Abdallah* and *Der blonde Eckbert*, Kafka's novels are fantasies of guilt with their literary roots in Gothic and fairytale, which they play off one against the other. Like Hoffmann's *Die Elixiere des Teufels*, and like some of Dostoevsky's early work, they feature aspects of personality acting as characters. Because of the issues they raise, parallels

---

12 *Ludwig Tieck's Schriften in 28 Bänden* (Berlin: Reimer, 1828-54), XIV, 164. Brentano, in his *Chronika eines fahrenden Schülers* (1803), used the word 'gotisch', linking it with 'modisch'.
13 S. S. Prawer, *Caligari's Children. The Film as Tale of Terror* (Oxford: Oxford University Press, 1980), 18.

between Kafka's work and that of Hoffmann and Tieck, which overlaps with what in English literary history is called Gothic Romanticism, are discussed (in 5.5.1) in the context of the *Kunstmärchen*, and parallels between Hoffmann and Kafka are also discussed (in 3.4) in the context of the uncanny. 'Romantic' and 'Gothic' do not, of course, mean the same thing, for Romanticism is a literary period and mode, whereas Gothic is a literary form, but much Gothic writing was produced in the Romantic period, and not a little Romantic literature is, in England as in Germany, Gothic. There are overlaps in that both mode and form favour the romance (imaginative, non-mimetic fiction) and share a concern with dreams and nightmares, the supernatural, and the figures of Cain, the Wandering Jew and the Satanic hero-villain. Romantic-period Gothic is marked by the internalization of early Gothic motifs and thus, in Maturin and Brockden Brown, an increasing emphasis on the psychological, the development of which Kafka is, via Dostoevsky, the distant heir. *Melmoth the Wanderer* has rightly been seen[14] as a forerunner of Dostoevsky, who admired Maturin's work, and of Kafka, who, despite his engagement with the Wandering Jew, is not known to have read it.

For the present we therefore pass from Hoffmann to two of his many Russian admirers, Gogol and Dostoevsky (who claimed to have read, in both Russian and German, every word that Hoffmann ever wrote), both of them among Kafka's favourite writers from university onwards. Gogol he read repeatedly. *The Nose* offered him a model for a tale of metamorphosis, while the fact that Gogol starved himself to death may have given him, on one level, the idea for the starvation-artist and its echo in *Forschungen eines Hundes.* Gogol's Ukrainian tales abound in devils and fairy-tale elements, as do Kafka's works, in which the devils in question are internalized and disguised. However, interesting though the parallels between Kafka's work and Gogol's are, they belong in the context of the grotesque, of which Gothic may be an effect, rather than the Gothic as such. With Dostoevsky it is a different matter.

Fyodor Mikhailovich Dostoevsky's[15] early works in the Gothic mode stand as a monument to the once overwhelming impact of Hoffmann on writers from Anton Pogorel'sky (*The Double,* 1828, a tale which spawned a host of others, most of them similarly named), to the Gothicist and so-called 'Russian Hoffmann', Vladimir Fyodorovich Odoevsky (*The Salamander*, 1841-4), and thence to Dostoevsky's *The Double* (1846). Jessie Coulson wrote of this that it 'might have cropped up as one of

---

14 See C. R. Maturin, *Melmoth the Wanderer*, ed. Douglas Grant (London: Oxford University Press, 1968), iii-xiv.

15 One probably need look no further for the origin of the name of Oberportier Feodor in *Der Verschollene*, whose name represents a German version of the Russian spelling (Fëdor[Fyodor]) of Theodor(e).

the tales of the still popular Hoffmann',[16] but in reality this study of 'a man haunted or possessed by his exact double' is closer to Hoffmann than that: its starting-point is *Die Elixiere des Teufels*. From the 1820s to the 1840s Hoffmann was a celebrity in Russia, his *Die Elixiere des Teufels* a cult novel in every sense. Looking east as well as west, Kafka learned from Hoffmann at second hand as well as first.

Dostoevsky, whom Kafka regarded as one of his 'real blood relatives',[17] grew up, imaginatively, on the novels of Ann Radcliffe. In his *Winter Notes on Summer Impressions* (1863) he recalled how, on long winter evenings, before he could read himself, he would listen, spellbound, as his parents read to him, at bedtime, the novels of Radcliffe, and how he would then rave about them in his sleep. By the age of eight he had read them himself. Before long he was reading Maturin as well; impressed, he later read him to his fellow-students. It therefore comes as no surprise to find that his own early works of the 1840s are Gothic, and that in his writings he, like Dickens, deploys Gothic themes, plots and characters. Indeed, Leonid Grossman has argued that 'there is not a single feature of the old [Gothic] novel that Dostoevsky does not use,[18] and as he does so, he, like Kafka after him, 'raises the themes and techniques of the Gothic novelists to new heights, for he forges a metaphysical system out of a language that in the hands of lesser novelists remains merely a style'.[19] Dostoevsky, whose convoluted, Gothic inner world anticipated and helped to shape Kafka's similar world, made an important contribution to the development of later psychological Gothic by focusing on what Kafka was also to explore, his heroes' tortuous, labyrinthine mentalities. Kafka's early *Beschreibung eines Kampfes* (1904-8)[20] reflects his reading of Dostoevsky's equally early *The Double* (1846): the first-person narrator's discovery of and relationship with his 'new acquaintance', with whom he walks as far as the riverside railings on the Franzensquai (Nábřeží Frantisku) beside the Vltava, parallels Mr Golyadkin, Senior's, discovery of his shadow in the guise of Mr Golyadkin, Junior, as he is leaning against the parapet of the wall beside the river Fontanka in St. Petersburg.[21] The detail is probably a tribute to Dostoevsky, whose hero-view perspective in *The Double* left a permanent mark on Kafka's narrative technique. Of course, *Beschreibung eines Kampfes* is no more typical of the later

[16] In the 'Translator's Introduction' in Fyodor Dostoevsky, *Notes from Underground [&]The Double,* tr. Jessie Coulson (Harmondsworth: Penguin, 1972), 7f.

[17] See R. S. Struc, 'Kafka and Dostoevsky as "Blood Relatives"', *Dostoevsky Studies*, 1981, 111-117.

[18] Quoted from Robin Feuer Miller, 'Dostoevsky and the Tale of Terror', in *The Russian Novel from Pushkin to Pasternak*, ed. John Garrard (New Haven & London: Yale University Press, 1983), 116.

[19] Feuer Miller, 104.

[20] The dating of this work is still disputed.

[21] Kafka's copy of Chamisso's *Peter Schlemihl*, it should perhaps be said, postdated *Beschreibung eines Kampfes* by three years. Dostoevsky's passage probably involves an echo of Hoffmann's *Kater Murr* (II, 2), where Kreisler, leaning over the bridge, sees his double in the mirror of the water.

Kafka than *The Double* is typical of the later Dostoevsky, for doubling as such, arguably a dysfunctional attempt to cope with mental conflict,[22] tends to be used before the writer has learned to live with his self and its creative neurosis. Twenty years later, Golyadkin Senior's neurotic feeling of being surrounded by enemies is paralleled in *Der Bau.*

Back in 1904 Kafka was deliberately emulating Dostoevsky, but living, as he did, in the Freudian era, he quickly outgrew such nineteenth-century studies of the double, preferring, instead, to explore the newly revealed subconscious in ways that did more justice both to its complex, multifaceted nature and to its own mode of expression. More typical of his work are the novels and punishment fantasies in which the protagonist's personality is not split into two, but is 'decomposed' into multiple fragments. In *The Interpretation of Dreams* (1900) Freud re-established a point made by Schubert, that dreams are peopled by figures variously representing the dreamer. By 1908, in 'The Relation of the Poet to Day-Dreaming', he was commenting on 'the tendency of the modern writer to split up his ego, by self-observation, into many part-egos, and in this way to personify the conflicting currents of his own mental life in a number of different figures.'[23] As Ernest Jones was the first to remark, in 1910, this process of 'decomposition' is the opposite of the process of condensation that is also found in dreams. In *Das Urteil* (1912) Kafka's self is decomposed into the figures of Georg Bendemann, his 'friend in Russia', and the father's images of both, but within the next few years he went on to write two novels in which, as also in a later third novel, the protagonist is subject to a more radical decomposition. What we see in Kafka's novels, as in *The Brothers Karamazov*, in which all four brothers represent different aspects of their creator, is what Rogers calls 'doubling by division' (but is better called by its proper name of decomposition), as opposed to 'doubling by multiplication'.[24] The self, that is to say, is not reduplicated but fragmented.

That it was to Kafka's Gothic or shadow self that Dostoevsky appealed is confirmed by his enthusiastic subjective reaction - also during his student days - to one of the Russian novelist's most involved works, *A Raw Youth* (1875, in German *Ein Halbwüchsling*).[25] His Russian kinsman remained an inspiration to him, helping, among other things, to inspire *Die Verwandlung*. At the beginning of *The Double,* Golyadkin awakes from 'disordered dreams' to find the 'dull, dirty, grey autumn day' peering in at him; it would be a fine thing, he thinks, if 'something disastrous had happened' in the night. On going to see Doctor Rutenspitz (!), he is told that he needs 'a radical transformation' of his whole life; he gets it when he subsequently encounters his double. Having gatecrashed a party, Mr Golyadkin Senior feels 'an utter insect' -

---

22 Robert Rogers, *The Double in Literature* (Detroit: Wayne State University Press, 1970), vii.
23 Freud, *Art and Literature*, 138.
24 Rogers, 5.
25 See Max Brod, *Über Franz Kafka* (Frankfurt a. M.: Fischer-Bücherei, 1966), 46.

the feeling that is taken literally in *Die Verwandlung* and in *The Brothers Karamazov*. In the 'Confession of a Passionate Heart' (*The Brothers Karamazov*, I.3.3l) Dmitri Karamazov speaks of 'the insects to whom God gave "sensual lust"', and goes on: 'I loved vice, I loved the ignominy of vice, I loved cruelty; am I not a louse [or bug], am I not a noxious insect?' He speaks of 'the insect [...] in my soul'. Kafka goes beyond Dostoevsky, for while Dmitri Karamazov merely feels himself to be no better than a louse, Gregor Samsa actually becomes a kind of cockroach. One wonders whether Kafka knew the preposterous piece of doggerel in *The Devils* (Part I, ch. 5) in which Lebyatkin likens himself to a cockroach. In the second section of *Notes from Underground*, the nameless anti-hero admits that he 'wasn't even capable of making an insect' of himself.

In Dostoevsky, then, there are several possible starting-points for *Die Verwandlung*, at the beginning of which Gregor Samsa awakes - or appears to awake, for there is room for doubt - from uneasy dreams to find himself transformed into a gigantic insect, that is, into his own double or other, the reality of his former, human existence gradually fading from memory as grey sky and grey land shade one into the other. Gregor Samsa's discovery of and reaction to his beetle-self is reminiscent of Golyadkin's discovery of and reaction to his double: in each case it is a matter of seeing oneself for what one is, and in each case the closeness of dream to reality is underlined. Is Golyadkin day-dreaming (hallucinating) all the time? Does Gregor Samsa really awake, or is his whole experience a nightmare? Josef K. too awakes to find himself involved in a nightmare situation from which, in one version of the ending, he was to have awoken, the clear implication being that the whole novel is a dream. Before gatecrashing the party Golyadkin wondered 'why did I shilly-shally when there was nobody there? I should have simply barged in'. Years later Kafka made his man-from-the-country shilly-shally in just that way, and the repeated references to Schiller's Gothic *Die Räuber* in *The Brothers Karamazov* include the dagger-in-the-heart motif which also surfaces at the end of *Der Proceß*.

Pasley has shown that Kafka was indebted, in *In der Strafkolonie*, to Dostoevsky's letters (a 1914 German translation of which he possessed) and *[Memoirs from] The House of the Dead*, and, in *Der Bau*, to Dostoevsky's *Notes [Letters] from Underground*.[26] *The House of the Dead* is a fictionalized account of Dostoevsky's experiences as a convict and exile in Siberia. Goryanchikov, his mouthpiece, in describing his ten-year spell of hard labour in the penal colony or prison fortress at Omsk, after which he retired to K. (Kuznetsk), is describing the four years of penal

---

26 See *Der Heizer, In der Strafkolonie, Der Bau*, ed. J. M. S. Pasley, 30-32, and L. Dietz, *Franz Kafka*, 2nd edn (Stuttgart: Metzler, 1990), 158. Josef K's feeling of being seasick on dry land echoes a letter (*Briefe*, tr.. A. Eliasberg [Munich: Teubner, 1914], 43) in which Dostoevsky wrote to his brother that he had often had the feeling that the floor was going up and down and that he was sitting in his room as in the cabin of a steamer.

servitude at Omsk followed by five years of compulsory military service at Semipalatinsk, to which Dostoevsky was condemned for circulating anti-government writings. Goryanchikov is a forerunner of Raskolnikov, the hero of *Crime and Punishment* (of which Kafka possessed a 1908 German translation), which also features a number of motifs that appear in Kafka's work,[27] including the 'denunciation emanating from malicious persons' and the motif of building castles in the air. Besides, what is *Der Proceß* if not an internalized and therefore inverted study of 'crime' and 'punishment', on which Kafka has put a highly personal spin? The Dostoevsky whom Kafka recognized as a 'blood-relative' was surely the one described by Freud shortly after Kafka's death: the neurotic self-punitive with a paradoxical hatred of and identification with his father. What is missing in Kafka is 'the trope of forgiveness, whereby the harshness of the Law is reinscribed and transformed through regaining faith in an originary benevolent parent figure.'[28] In identifying with Dostoevsky and his protagonists, Kafka will, of course, have reflected that their sufferings were more real than his own partly imaginary and frequently exaggerated ones. This is no doubt one of the reasons why he distances himself from his protagonists, by means of irony, in a way that Dostoevsky does not.

Notes from Underground, for its part, is a rambling study of a neurotic introvert who seeks to 'prove to himself that he is a man [...] by becoming a troglodyte' (§ 8); its isolated, nameless anti-hero is in many ways Dostoevsky-like and in some ways not unlike Kafka, who differed from him, however, in being able to 'make himself an insect', to say nothing of making himself a species of giant mole. Dostoevsky's anti-hero says 'I tell you solemnly that I have often wished to make an insect of myself', and we have seen that Kafka identified with Dmitri Karamazov in perceiving of himself as a noxious insect. He possessed a 1914 German translation of *The Brothers Karamazov*, that 'Gothic pile of a novel'[29] that contains a trial scene in which *The Mysteries of Udolpho* is mentioned, while 'not a few' of its themes and central characters have been shown to be traceable to *The Castle of Otranto*.[30] Chapter 3 of *Der Proceß* has the same title as Part 3, Book 9, of *The Brothers Karamazov:* 'The Preliminary Investigation'. And then there is the parable of the 'Grand Inquisitor', told by Ivan Karamazov to his brother Alyosha, to 'make him think twice about surrendering to a religion [Christianity] against which he, Ivan, rebels',[31] which may

---

27 See M. Church, 'Dostoevsky's *Crime and Punishment* and Kafka's *The Trial*', *Literature and Psychology*, 1970, 47-56.
28 Elizabeth Wright, *Speaking Desires can be Dangerous. The Poetics of the Unconscious* (Oxford: Polity, 1999), 6 (and see 48-50). Freud's essay is in his *Art and Literature*, 435-60.
29 See Ignat Avsey, 'Gothic in Gogol and Dostoevskii,' in *The Gothic-Fantastic in Nineteenth-Century Russian Literature*, ed. Neil Cornwell (Amsterdam: Rodopi, 1999), 219.
30 Avsey, 217-24. On Gothic elements in *The Brothers Karamazov*, see also R. F. Miller, 'Dostoevsky and the Tale of Terror', in *The Russian Novel from Pushkin to Pasternak*, ed. John Garrard (New Haven: Yale University Press, 1983), 103-21.
31 H. Politzer, *Franz Kafka, Parable and Paradox* (Ithaca: Cornell University Press, 1962), 85.

well have given Kafka the idea for the Parable of the Doorkeeper, which turns on the same issue, and is told by the Priest, whom I show to belong in the context of the Inquisition, to Josef K., who refuses to surrender to what he sees as superstition resting on a lie. Dostoevsky's Grand Inquisitor not only stands behind the figure of the Old Commandant in Kafka's penal colony; he also personifies the Spanish Inquisition and with it the whole machinery of power resting on the notion of transgression that is the engine of Gothic. Dodd has drawn attention to parallels between, on the one hand, Ivan Karamazov's 'Legend of the Grand Inquisitor' and Ippolit Terentyev's 'Necessary Explanation' and, on the other hand, Kafka's *In der Strafkolonie*.[32] The parallels with the Parable (Legend) of the Doorkeeper, in which Josef K. rejects the Priest's 'necessary explanation', are no less significant, and earlier in the novel the Gothic figure of the 'Prügler' was very likely inspired by Dostoevsky's 'palach' (whipper, flogger), although Kafka puts the figure to totally different, symbolical use.

What makes Dostoevsky so important in the present context is that his work, like Dickens's, represents a *Stoffreservoir* or source of Gothic motifs with which Kafka is known to have been familiar. It was also from him that Kafka learned to give his shadow free rein. The involuted, labyrinthine mentalities of Josef K., K., and the Burrower bear the unmistakable imprint of Kafka's great Russian precursor.

So far as English-language literature is concerned, Kafka's admiration for Dickens is clear from the diaries, in which he declared 'Der Heizer' to be a straight imitation of Dickens, and the novel *Der Verschollene* even more so. What matters here is not his knowledge of Dickens's work and the relationship between his own work and Dickens's work in general terms, which has been more than adequately explored by Mark Spilka, but the fact that there is in Dickens's work, as much recent research has shown,[33] more than a little of Gothic, which Dickens, like Kafka, is given to subverting for his own comic ends; the tragic in Kafka is so obvious that the comic is too often overlooked. Dickens is therefore another indirect source for Kafka's knowledge of the Gothic. If Dickens's fiction is 'studded with Gothicism, [...] like a Christmas pudding [...] with plums',[34] Kafka could well have pulled out some Gothic plums from Dickens' work, which he, like Dostoevsky, knew well and greatly admired. *Little Dorrit* (*T*, 746), for instance, has been shown to contain rather more than the 'traces of Gothic fear and power' that Botting rightly found there.[35] That 'Der Heizer', as the first chapter of *Der Verschollene* is also known, is indebted to *David Copperfield*, a novel with a clear Gothic subtext, for instance in the matter of

---

32 W. J. Dodd, 'Dostoyevskian Elements in Kafka's Penal Colony', *GLL*, 37 (1983-1984), 15-21.
33 See, especially, Julian Wolfrey's 'Notes toward a Reading of the Comic-Gothic in Dickens', in *Victorian Gothic*, ed. Ruth Robins and Julian Wolfreys (Basingstoke: Palgrave, 2000), 31-59.
34 Benjamin F. Fisher, in *The Handbook to Gothic Literature*, ed. Marie Mulvey-Roberts (Basingstoke: Macmillan, 1998), 45.
35 See Fred Botting, *Gothic* (London: Routledge, 1996), 126, and David Jarrell, 'The Fall of the House of Clennam: Gothic Convention in *Little Dorrit*,' *Dickensian*, 73 (1977), 155-61.

David's/Karl's box, is obvious, although Kafka goes way beyond Dickens in exploiting the symbolism of the box. Pasley has commented that

> Like the young David Copperfield or Oliver Twist, Karl Roßmann is thrown out harshly upon the world and [...] exposed defencelessly to the irrational judgments of authority [...] What is peculiarly Dickensian [...] is the fusion of social and family difficulties, the way in which the odyssey of an innocent through a mainly hostile and authoritarian society is tacitly understood as a series of re-enactments of a father-dominated family drama.[36]

This apt comment also points, implicitly, in the direction of Gothic. Conversely, *Bleak House* is not only a largely Gothic work, but also in some ways a proto-'Kafkaesque' one. Such points are well documented. *Pickwick Papers* boasts, among other things, a troubled father-son relationship and a haunted castle, Miss Havisham in *Great Expectations* is a positive model of *Verschollensein* or figurative live burial, and there is also the residual vampirism of that novel. No matter whether he connected them with Gothic, Kafka will also have found in Dickens the foregrounding of the 'Gothic' side of familiar things, the labyrinth image or maze metaphor that is basic to his own work, and a mastery of the macabre, to say nothing of the gloom that readers often wrongly attribute to Kafka, which is present in Dickens in full measure. Insofar as Ann Radcliffe, as a pioneer of modern psychological fiction, was a formative influence on Dickens, as on Dostoevsky, both of whom cultivated the tale of terror, she is *ipso facto* a distant ancestor of Kafka. The ending of *Der Verschollene* (see 6.2.1) suggests that he was not only familiar with *The Mysteries of Udolpho*, which had been available in an excellent German translation ever since 1795, about which he also knew from Dostoevsky and probably from Poe (see 2.3.) as well, but, more to the point, that he had read it.

Whether he knew the work of William Godwin (see 7.2.1) and/or Charles Brockden Brown (see 3.5), is not known. Nor is he known to have read M. G. Lewis's *The Monk*, Mary Shelley's *Frankenstein* or her father's *St Leon*, Percy Bysshe Shelley's *Zastrozzi* [37] (discussed in 4.5), or even Bram Stoker's *Dracula*, although there are many intriguing parallels between *Das Schloß* and *Dracula*, some of them suggesting that Kafka, who was an admirer of the Sherlock Holmes stories of Conan Doyle, who finished his schooling at a Jesuit-run school in Austria and has in recent years been placed in the Gothic context, may also have known Stoker's Gothic classic, which first appeared in German (translated by H. Widtmann, and published in Leipzig by M. Altmann) in 1908. He certainly knew of that 'foul German spectre',[38] the Vampire, which was very much at home in Moravia (as well as in Moldavia), that is,

---

36 Franz Kafka, *Der Heizer*, ed Pasley, 10.
37 He possessed Alfred Wolfenstein's translations of a selection of Shelley's poetry.
38 Charlotte Brontë, *Jane Eyre*, ch. 25. On vampires and vampirology, see Christopher Frayling, *Vampyres* (London: Faber & Faber, 1991), and *Von denen Vampiren*, ed. Dieter Sturm and Klaus Völker (Frankfurt a. M.: Suhrkamp, 1994).

is the south-west of his own country, where his favourite uncle lived, and which he often visited. He may also have known Jan Neruda's 'The Vampire'.[39]

Someone who has read *The Mysteries of Udolpho* and has a good knowledge not only of Hoffmann, but of Dickens and Dostoevsky, and, as we shall see, some knowledge of Poe, must be granted to have some knowledge of Gothic, even if it appears to have been less extensive than his exceptional knowledge of fairytale.

[39] See *Czechoslovak Stories*, tr. & ed. Sárka B. Hrbkova (London: Duffield, 1920; repr. New York: AMS Press, 1971), 75-80. Neruda's *Spisy* (collected works) appeared in 41 volumes between 1906 and 1915.

2. LANDMARKS

2.1. Kafka and Harriet Lee

That Kafka felt guilty not only as his father's son, but as writer and human being, brings us to the first of four landmark parallels which begin to place him in the Gothic context. Karl Rossmann, the hero-as-victim of Kafka's first novel, *Der Verschollene*, in being alienated from his father, and Josef K. in his second novel, *Der Proceß* (here normally named in full to avoid confusion with K. in *Das Schloß*), who is arrested and eventually obliged, like Kafka himself, to admit himself guilty 'without having done anything wrong', are reminiscent of the protagonist, Kruitzner, in one of the most impressive of the early Gothic novellas, Harriet Lee's *The German's Tale: Kruitzner* (or *Kruitzner. The German's Tale* - both forms of the title are found) of 1801.[1]

This little-known tale is quasi-Kafkaesque in that Kruitzner, when relieved of his command as a young man, is guilty not because of any particular transgressive act, but because he refuses to accept the undoubted fact of his guilt,[2] which consists in invariably putting self-indulgence before anything else. This is also Josef K.'s position until, finally acknowledging the authority of the moral monitor within, he makes his belated confession in the final chapter of the novel. The parallel becomes even more striking when joined by others linking *Kruitzner*, set in Silesia and Bohemia in 1633, with all three of Kafka's novels, but especially with *Der Proceß* and *Das Schloß*. These novels and the related stories are what Harriet Lee, in 'The Author's Address to the Reader' of *The Canterbury Tales* (5 vols, 1797-1805), declared her own (and her sister's) tales to be, 'day dreams'; but, as the products of what Kafka called his 'dreamlike inner life', they are more precisely and continuously dreamlike than Harriet and Sophia Lee's tales, which are rêveries, products of the imagination rather than the unconscious. The hypnagogic element, so strong in Kafka, is absent in the Lee sisters.

Frederick Kruitzner, whose oddly spelled name, assumed in his disgrace by the later Frederick Count Siegendorf (named after the village of Siegersdorf in Lower Silesia), may have been suggested by Clara Reeve's *The Exiles, or Memoirs of the Count de Cronstadt* (1788),[3] in which Cronstadt for a time borrows the name of his

---

[1] See Harriet & Sophia Lee, *Canterbury Tales,* 2 vols (London: Colburn & Bentley, 1832), II, 134-56, esp. 134-43, 155-76, 224, 232, 247-75 .

[2] See Robert Miles, *Gothic Writing 1750-1820. A Genealogy* (London & N. Y.: Routledge, 1993), 216. The parallel with Kruitzner is closer than that with Kleist's Michael Kohlhaas, who is simultaneously guilty and guiltless, although Kafka learned much from Kleist's style.

[3] A promiscuous borrowing of names is a feature of the Gothic novel and tale.

servant Albert Kreutzer), bears the same initials as Franz Kafka and is, like him, a native of Prague; he even develops a consumptive malady. However, more significant than these purely coincidental details are the parallels linking Kruitzner and Josef K., likewise a native of Prague, who shares Kruitzner's selfishness, pride and life of 'self-indulgence and voluptuous dissipation'. More especially, he too is given to indulging in a 'licentious debauch' (with Elsa and others) at the wrong time. To Josef K., at the beginning of the novel, may be applied the words written of Kruitzner: 'A confused sense of shame, blended with a suspicion of error, passed rapidly across his mind; but it was a troublesome sort of feeling, and he dismissed it as such.' His sense of guilt, like Kruitzner's, changes from a stubborn refusal to countenance the very idea of it into a slow, reluctant acceptance of its ineluctable reality. Like Josef K. after him, Kruitzner 'never yet made [it] a part of his character to contend with any passion', his imperious temper directing him to constitute himself sole judge of his actions. Josef K., for his part, in the suppressed fragment of the novel dealing with his reiterated transgression in the form of weekly visits to Elsa's bed, deliberately flouts his conscience: 'Refusing to be led astray by the court he went where he wanted to go.' Perhaps because he shares Kruitzner's *hauteur*, it takes Josef K. a long time to come to the humbling realization that he is his own sole judge in a more positive sense. As their sense of past transgression grows, both men lose their self-love and capacity for self-deception, until Josef K. too, in the *Rumpelkammer* scene (*Der Proceß*, ch. 5), experiences what Harriet Lee (quietly quoting from Shakespeare's *Julius Caesar* [II,i.63]) called a 'phantasma, or a hideous dream', so that we may say of him, as of Kruitzner, that 'it was at the very climax of his worldly prosperity that the spectre, conscience, first appeared to him.'[4] Nor is it only Kruitzner who eventually finds himself in a 'horrible gloom peopled with frightful and distorted images, which presented to him the spectres of a guilty mind even in the moment of innocence'; so too does Josef K., whose heedlessly hedonistic life is arrested by conscience at just such a time. Indeed, Josef K., who comes to be haunted by conscience just as much as his predecessor, is even challenged by name in the same Cathedral as Kruitzner.

If *Der Proceß* parallels *Kruitzner* in many ways, so too does *Das Schloß*. Kruitzner, when we first meet him, is the mysterious stranger of Gothic, his identity a matter for speculation. K., likewise a native of Bohemia, who resembles him in both respects, is, like Kruitzner, travelling (and, in English, though not in German, heading) west; both men's identity is assumed. What is Kafka's Castle but 'a small number of ill-built houses confusedly huddled together, and dignified with the title of a Bourg',[5] in which the proud poor are described as living in arrogance and sloth? Kafka actually writes of his Castle as 'a huddle of village houses'. Kruitzner and K.

---

4   Sophia & Harriet Lee, *Canterbury Tales* , II, 156, 159, 158, 166, 224, 246, 232 (order of quotation).
5   *Canterbury Tales*, II, 134.

are therefore associated with much the same initial image, and the Castle, personified in Klamm (who, like its supposed owner Count Westwest, and like the Prince de T. in Lee's tale, is, as it were, an apparition who never appears), may be compared, even in incidental detail, with the Prince de T.'s dubious 'palace'. The idea of gaining admittance to a forbidden 'castle' (Schloß Siegendorf, Schloß Westwest) looms large in both works.

Kruitzner also prefigures aspects of *Der Verschollene* and the related *Das Urteil*. Kruitzner brings shame upon his family by debauchery in his native Prague, which he, like Rossmann, leaves in disgrace. Kruitzner is, figuratively, 'buried alive' at the beginning of Lee's tale, as is Karl Rossmann at the beginning and end of *Der Verschollene*, the title of the novel implying, in German, both the idea of being buried alive and the idea of going missing. Kruitzner and Rossmann have to live with the wanton follies of the past, though Rossmann's are tame compared to Kruitzner's. Both transgress repeatedly, albeit in different senses, Rossmann too being haunted by 'the ghosts of [the] departed joys' of his previous cosy (in Austrian German, *heimlich*) existence, so unlike his present *unheimlich* (uncanny) one in which the immediate past keeps on catching up with him. Karl's relationship with his father is similar to Kruitzner's, which also parallels Georg Bendemann's in *Das Urteil*. Paternal authority is a major topos in both works, for the Gothic generation of 1789-1820 shares with the generation of a century later an unwillingness to accept authority as such, whether divine, ecclesiastical, paternal, patriarchal or political; it was the idea of authority, undermined by the Renaissance and the Reformation, that was decisively challenged by the French Revolution. The usurpation of the Count by his father, and by the Count of his son, is paralleled in Kafka's story by Georg's supposed usurpation of his father's power and position. Georg's father, like Kruitzner's, condemns his own son to death. The traffic crossing one of the Moldau (Vltava) bridges in Prague at the end of *Das Urteil* takes the reader straight back to the image of the nobility crossing it in *Kruitzner*, but what a contrast there is between Prague as experienced by the aristocracy in the seventeenth century and described with considerable élan by Harriet Lee, and that experienced by Kafka and his personae.

Kafka is unlikely to have known Harriet Lee's work unless he learned of it via Byron, whose *Werner*, dedicated 'To the Illustrious Goethe by one of his humblest admirers', was based on *Kruitzner*, which Byron, who read it at the age of fourteen, described as containing the germ of much that he went on to write. Given that Kafka possessed a German translation of a selection of Byron's diaries and letters, and was keenly interested in the Cain figure, it is not impossible that he knew *Werner*, and, through it, *Kruitzner*. Be this as it may, these close parallels show that Kafka's work is, on the face of it, close to early Gothic in terms of ambience, externals, machinery and motifs, although they make it seem more Gothic than it really is. The difference, and it is a crucial one, is that Kafka's works are self-punitive fantasies in which the protagonist is a persona of the author, whereas Harriet Lee's work is fantasy pure and simple. From this point of view Kafka has more in common with William Beckford.

2.2. Kafka and Beckford

Surprisingly, perhaps, Kafka's novels stand comparison with Gothic at its most imaginative, as in Beckford's *Vathek* (1786; German translations 1788 [three different ones], 1842, 1907, 1921, 1924), although one should naturally not expect to find in them the exotic oriental mode and partly subterranean setting, inspired by *Vathek* and *The Arabian Nights*, of Tieck's *Abdallah* (1795), for whereas *Vathek* is written in eighteenth-century orientalizing mode, the literary equivalent of the artistic and decorative *chinoiserie* of the time, Kafka's novels are composed in the minimalist mode that he shares with Robert Walser and Samuel Beckett. The perceptions and the iconography in each case are, however, typically Gothic.

Their brilliant imaginations apart, Beckford and Kafka may appear to have little in common, but they both write fables of the self: 'though the novel [as such] has its roots in the reality round us[,] it regularly aspires to the condition of fantasy, which is what *Vathek* is. But it is a fantasy still rooted in the perception of the real, for Beckford's story [...] is a statement in fable of the author's own dominant impulses.'[6] The same is true of *Der Proceß* and *Das Schloß*, which are autobiographical and realistic in the sense of having a controlling model in the reality of Kafka's inner life, but are otherwise far removed from realism. *Das Schloß* in particular resembles *Vathek* in combining writing of the highest imaginative quality with a view of life in which 'reality' is disconcertingly dislocated or displaced, which is why Kafka, like Beckford, has been associated with surrealism; Max Ernst again and again painted images with the same basic meaning as *Das Schloß*, and his 'Forest' series (images of the sun behind a forest which is blocking the viewer's imaginative way to it) could be an illustration of Kafka's best-known aphorism ('There is a goal, but no way'). The fact that Beckford overplays his hand as narrator, while Kafka underplays his, serves to underline the similarity of the hands in question. Vathek and K. both seek knowledge and the power that comes from knowledge, but there is more to it than that, for *Vathek*, often not considered Gothic at all, in fact provides a context in which the Gothicity of Kafka's novels can begin to be assessed.

In a short, cogent essay Frederick S. Frank has isolated four generic characteristics of Beckford's orientalized Gothic which may be applied to all three of Kafka's novels. They are:

1. 'the pattern of the demonic quest or perverse pilgrimage'

---

6   Walter Allen, *The English Novel* (London: Phoenix House, 1954), 86

2. the notion of (Vathek's) 'heroic' villainy

3. 'the preference of the characters for diminishing enclosures and [...] forms of architectural sequestration [...] such [...] as towers, grottos, caverns, contracting corridors and subterranean theatres of hellish anguish', and

4. 'the evocation of a hypothetically malignant cosmos, an ontologically unreliable and ambiguously deceiving Gothic universe in which all moral norms are inverted or twisted, where disorder is far more likely than order, and where universal darkness can bury all without warning and at any moment'[7]

Like *Vathek*, Kafka's three novels are quest-novels, the quest in question being in each case a perverse one. Karl Rossmann quests for his lost innocence, Josef K. for his non-existent innocence, and K. for his non-existent *raison d'être*. To quest for the impossible is Romantic, to quest for that to which one is specifically not entitled is Gothic, but it is perverse to quest, as the 'man from the country' does in the Parable of the Doorkeeper in *Der Proceß*, and as Josef K./K. does in both *Der Proceß* and *Das Schloß*, for that in which one does not even believe. The most famous of all Quest romances and paradigm of the Demonic Quest is, of course, the legend of the Holy Grail, which Kafka's two K.-novels reference, *Der Proceß* explicitly and *Das Schloß* implicitly and by analogy. What Josef K. and K. seek, respectively the legendary wonder of acquittal and the talismanic certainty which K. believes to be represented by the Castle, is tantamount to the Holy Grail of legend.

Though not exactly 'heroic villains', Karl Rossmann and Josef K. are highly ambiguous figures, at once heroic and unheroic, innocent and guilty. Josef K.'s sense of guilt is associated with ever smaller spaces, in which he feels more and more ill at ease; the modern equivalents of Gothic towers, caverns, corridors and subterranean vaults are everywhere in evidence, all of them internalized. The typical dark, rambling corridors of Gothic are found alike in the ship and in Pollunder's extraordinary Gothic mansion in *Der Verschollene*, where, their roles reversed, Klara and Karl rehearse the roles of 'pursuing hero-villain' and 'fleeing maiden',[8] in the ubiquitous attics in *Der Proceß*, in the Herrenhof in *Das Schloß*, and, not least, in the underground world of *Der Bau*. The Gothic and folkloric spaces of *Das Schloß* include the 'forbidden chamber'[9] in the form of Klamm's room at the Herrenhof and, in a more general sense, of the Castle as a whole, which K. wishes to penetrate and violate, knowing it to be forbidden territory. In a Freudian sense the forbidden chamber is personified in

---

7   F. S. Frank, 'The Gothic *Vathek*: The Problem of Genre Resolved', in *Vathek and the Escape from Time. Bicentenary Revaluations*, ed. K.W. Graham (New York: AMS Press, 1990), 157.

8   Frank, 'The Gothic *Vathek* ', 160.

9   On the motif of the forbidden chamber, so important in folklore, see E. Sidney Hartland, 'The Forbidden Chamber', *Folk-Lore Journal,* 3 (1885), 193-242. On Bluebeard, see Mererid Puw Davies, *The Tale of Bluebeard in German Literature* ()xford: Clarendon Press, 2001).

women-figures like Johanna Brummer *(Der Verschollene)*, Fräulein Bürstner *(Der Proceß)* and Frieda *(Das Schloß)*.

The ascent and descent imagery of *Vathek* is paralleled in *Der Verschollene*, the difference being that whereas ascent into his Faustian tower and descent into Eblis are both signs of Vathek's perverted aspirations, in *Der Verschollene* Karl's continued ascents mark his Sisyphean attempts to climb back to innocence, while his continued descents indicate his irretrievably fallen condition. The endings of the two romances, though different, are less different than they seem, for if Vathek goes to Hell (Eblis) and Karl merely goes missing, in reality they both go to the Devil, which is what Eblis (Devil) and *verschollen sein* (to go to the devil) actually mean. The Gothic downward journey of no return is symbolically iterated in Karl's last journey, which is by Freudian definition and narrative logic alike a journey into the underworld of death. Vathek's 'linear descent' - 'psychologically, from wish-fulfilment to frustration; and metaphysically, from a vision of humanity as unlimited potentiality to humanity as finite actuality in an alien world'[10] - is replicated in both *Der Verschollene* and *Das Schloß*.

In the end Beckford, like Kafka after him, is concerned with what he calls 'the condition of man upon earth'.[11] Like Kafka, he uses his Gothic novel to confront 'the moral ambiguities of an inexplicable universe'.[12] His characters are not free; like Kafka's, they merely 'delude themselves with a dream of freedom',[13] for at issue throughout *Vathek* is what has been called 'the contradiction between the illusion of man's freedom and the reality of his imprisonment in a necessitarian universe'.[14] Kafka, in the person of his 'ex-ape' Rotpeter in *Ein Bericht für eine Akademie*, explicitly made the point that freedom is a subject on which human beings all too often delude themselves. Josef K. and K., for instance, may appear to be 'free', even all too free, but in reality they are determined in what they are, and, being what they are, are not free. Nor could they be, given the inexplicability and unaccountability of the universe in which they exist. There are no fixed moral modalities there to explain and justify the notion of freedom, which is in any case incompatible with the idea of man's fallen nature: if one is not free to rise, one is not free. Nor, as we shall see, can there be any certainty on the subject of guilt, the burden of which is no less great for being self-assumed.

The early Gothic novelists portray an irrationally determined universe, challenging the efficacy of rationalism both as an outlook and as a response to existence.[15] Kafka does so too. In his novels we are confronted with the paradox of an eminently lucid, if

---

10 Frank, 'The Gothic *Vathek*', 168.
11 *Vathek*, ed. R. Lonsdale (London: Oxford University Press, 1970), 120.
12 Frank, 'The Gothic *Vathek*', 158.
13 Frank, 'The Gothic *Vathek*', 158f.
14 K. W. Graham, 'Beckford's *Vathek*: A Study in Ironic Dissonance', *Criticism*, 14 (1972), 252.
15 See Frank, 'The Gothic *Vathek*', 160.

hermetic, narrative which at every point undermines belief in a rational world order: the - in poetic terms - exceptionally logical narration is the very denial of what commonly passes as logic. It is no chance that Gothic was born in an age of revolutionary change and enjoyed a rebirth in the 1890s, which saw reprints of so many Gothic classics; nor is it simply that 'the Gothic romance is a genre that in its historical development, as well as in individual texts, moves from a stable modality of clearly defined conventions and forms toward an unstable and deliberately indeterminate modality',[16] but that 'characters in Gothic fiction are forced to ask their questions and seek their answers in a sort of intellectual vacuum without the support of stable value systems to affirm any answers their quest might lead them to'.[17] Nothing is more basic to Kafka's work, and to the novel of the time,[18] than this particular vacuum, which *In der Strafkolonie* illustrates very clearly, and the *horror vacui* to which it leads. The *ancien régime* of the Old Commandant was tyrannical but clear-cut. Since then, under the New Commandant, those monstrous certainties have been replaced by an era of empty formalism, hollow routine and far-fatched exegesis, in brief, moral confusion and no less monstrous uncertainties. In the old days law was law; following the death of its only begetter there is a multiplicity of laws that in societal terms is tantamount to no law at all. It is this lack of certainty surrounding the status of the law under the New Commandant that is the unkindest cut of all from the point of view of those ritually disempowered by it. Even if K., in *Das Schloß*, were to obtain answers to his questions, we can be sure that they would be not only ambiguous, but wholly subjective. *Vathek* can therefore be read as a prototype of the subjective and subversive Gothic tendencies that were in effect to come to a head in Kafka. In *Das Schloß*, as in *Vathek,* the conventional romance's 'pattern of achievement and self-fulfilment'[19] is reversed, and Gothic, the night-side of romance and fairytale, is revealed to be 'a region of total ontological distress, where the mythology of the imaginative self as an agent of control gives way to the nightmare of a supreme and malignant "otherness" which cannot be escaped or transcended'.[20]

2.3. Kafka and Poe

This malignant 'otherness' informs the work of Poe, about whom Kafka remained strangely silent, and Dostoevsky, whom he idolized. He knew of Poe's work, which was so influential in the German-speaking Europe of the time that it would have been

---

[16] G. R. Thompson, quoted from Frank, 'The Gothic *Vathek',* 170.
[17] Frank,'The Gothic *Vathek* ', 158.
[18] I am thinking here of Hermann Broch's *Die Schlafwandler* (1931-2) with its interleaved, counterpointed passages on the 'Zerfall der Werte'.
[19] Frank, 'The Gothic *Vathek* ', 167
[20] Frank, 'The Gothic *Vathek* ', 169.

difficult to avoid, and seems to have read some of it, but when Gustav Janouch[21] told him that a friend of his had called him 'a second, profounder and therefore more praiseworthy Edgar Allan Poe', he reportedly had no time for such a notion (J, 29). In this he was, of course, reacting to Janouch's naive, over-insistent questions. If he had expressed any interest in the subject, there was a real danger that it might have been exaggerated and maybe misconstrued. His silence served its purpose. On the other hand, a comparison of 'The Pit and the Pendulum' with *Der Bau* and *In der Strafkolonie* shows that he had some knowledge of Poe's work, which was similar enough to his own to attract his attention, yet so different as to make it the object of curiosity rather than lasting interest.

On the human level, of course, he and Poe were opposites, the Ascetic and the Cannibal respectively, though Kafka shared Poe's view of 'demoniacal impatience', and both men were given to seeing or invoking demons. One simply cannot imagine Kafka entering West Point or marrying (for, like the narrator of Poe's 'The Oval Portrait', he already had a bride in his art) or taking to drink; temperamentally he was an altogether cooler character than Poe. Unlike Poe, he was not given to dissimulation. Without going into detail, Heinz Politzer wrote that 'The reality in *Der Verschollene* is secondhand material. [Some of] it is [perhaps] taken from the beginning of [...] Poe's "The Narrative of Arthur Gordon Pym".'[22] This might seem far-fetched if the motif of the Verona salami in Karl's box were not so strongly reminiscent of that of the Bologna sausages in Augustus's box. In that same narrative Poe used the name Block, which was to reappear in *Der Proceß*. By the same token, Kafka's torture-machine in the penal colony of life has a precursor in Poe's Pendulum (in 'The Pit and the Perndulum'), a no less 'remarkable piece of apparatus', into the wooden framework (Poe) or bed (Kafka) of which the prisoner is strapped in readiness for the execution in which the blade(s) of the contraption (the Pendulum, the Harrow) descend to cut into the living flesh; execution complete, the victim's body is consigned to the pit. Both pieces of apparatus are described in a chillingly matter-of-fact way, but the tales in question differ in that whereas Poe's is horror pure and simple, Kafka's is as ambiguous as it is multi-dimensional. 'The Pit and the Pendulum' is a study in terror; *In der Strafkolonie* turns on the, in the context, questionable notions of transgression and punishment. Titorelli's 'Heidelandschaften' *(Der Proceß)* depict a panorama as 'deplorably desolate' as any described by Poe. What Poe calls the 'ignes fatui of superstition' are seen in Chapter 9 of the same novel, and what do the extraordinary candle-bearers in Pollunder's Gothic mansion bear if not also 'ignes fatui' in the most literal sense? These are, however, incidental points.

---

21 Although 'discredited' as a biographical source, Janouch's *Gespräche mit Kafka* contains some important and entirely credible material; it is better used judicially than not used at all. In the present instance there is no reason to doubt Janouch's word.
22 Heinz Politzer, *Franz Kafka. Parable and Paradox*, 120.

While it would be unwise to suppose Kafka imaginatively empowered by Poe in any particular way, the idea of constructing a castle-in-the-air could have come from Poe's story of Hans Pfaall, and Gregor Samsa's flat, dry remains are reminiscent of the 'shell which falls in decaying from the inner form', with death as the final, painful metamorphosis in Poe's 'Mesmeric Revelation', for the beetle's elytra amount to a kind of carapace or shell. Then there is the more general point, made by Wolfgang Kayser, that in planning its underground structure, Kafka's Burrower exhibits 'a mathematical imagination reminiscent of [...] Poe's',[23] meaning the ingenuity analysed by Poe at the beginning of 'The Murders in the Rue Morgue'. Otherwise Kafka's imagination works quite differently from Poe's. Though Poe too was concerned with the exact meanings of words, his imagination was not excited by their multiple meanings in the way in which Kafka's is. The Burrower may seem to be identifiable with what Poe calls 'the intellectual or logical man', as opposed to 'the understanding or observant man', but Kafka himself belongs to the latter type, and I would argue that the Burrower does too. Poe's work is based on mathematical logic, Kafka's on poetic logic. On the other hand, Kafka shares with Poe a poetic imagination which automatically concentrates on concrete particulars, and he too disapproves of simile, though for a different reason, preferring literal symbolism.

Like Hoffmann, Poe does, however, sometimes take metaphors literally in a way that points forward to Kafka. In 'The Gold-Bug', for instance, the idea of being 'bitten by the gold-bug' (the old dream of finding gold) is taken literally to the point where Legrand becomes so 'absorbed' by the bug that he comes to resemble it. To write, as Benjamin F. Fisher has done, of 'the weight [Poe] so often gives to physical description as the means of entrance into corridors of the mind or as symbols of those corridors',[24] is, in effect, to point forward to Kafka. Both Poe and Kafka, like the early American Gothic writers, and like Tieck and Dostoevsky, set out to explore the mind and its Gothic recesses, but if Kafka, in *Der Bau*, portrays the mind under intolerable pressure, he is less directly concerned with psycho-pathology than Poe. Although he shares Poe's horror of the pit, his burrow was inspired not by Poe, but by the underground den of the similarly nameless, neurotic anti-hero of Dostoevsky's *Notes from Underground*. Kafka's tales may, at times, feature the 'sickening clarity' of Poe's tales,[25] but they lack Poe's 'overwrought intensity', which is simply not Kafka's style. As to the means of portrayal, 'legalistic precision' is a term that may properly be applied to both men's styles, and the names of Kafka's figures involve what Poe calls 'a kind of punning or hieroglyphical signature'.

---

[23] Wolfgang Kayser, *Das Groteske* (Oldenburg: Stalling, 1957), 161.
[24] In *The Handbook to Gothic Literature*, 180.
[25] Rictor Norton, *Mistress of Udolpho. The Life of Ann Radcliffe* (London & New York: Leicester University Press, 1999), 256.

The fact that in Kafka's work, as in Poe's, the outward trappings of Gothic are turned inwards, does not mean that the ambience of their work is the same. With the exception of the Burrower, for instance, Kafka's characters are not anxiety-ridden in the same sense as Poe's. Josef K. is a prey to anxiety, certainly, but *Der Proceß* is not a study of anxiety in the manner of Poe. Kafka, it is true, shares with Poe a sense of demon-ridden existence, and, judging by his personae, he too was haunted by death as by a fiend, but his work has more to do with metaphysics proper than with what Poe calls 'metaphysical science' (meaning psychology) and with the morbidity of spirit and narrative presentation approaching melodrama of Poe. Though his work has a significant psychological dimension, Kafka's central concern - unlike Poe's - is not psychological or physical horror as such. There are exceptional passages that prove the rule, but for the most part we look in vain in his work for the exaggerated horrors of Poe's tales. While nightmare - Poe's 'nightmare of the soul' - looms large in both men's work, Kafka generally focusses on metaphysical terror and the terrors of religion rather than physical horror. With the exception of the demented Burrower, Kafka's protagonists, unlike Poe's, are not threatened by madness. Whereas Poe's 'The Pit and the Pendulum' is an unbearably graphic analysis of the nightmare experience of falling to one's death, *Der Verschollene* is a no less graphic adumbration of the Fall of Man. The difference of focus of the two writers is obvious.

Max Brod went out of his way to stress that Kafka was not at home in Poe's world:

> Poe needs this morbid world of his [...] Kafka lives in a similar world to Poe, but he doesn't need Poe's world. He doesn't feel comfortable in it; he knows he doesn't belong there. He's not interested in the portrayal of such a world unless he's the one doing the portraying. He was not in the habit of reading Poe-type books.[26]

What Brod meant by Poe-type books ('Bücher vom Typus Poe') is not clear, but the fact that Kafka was not in the habit of reading such books means, in general terms, that he found Poe's world uncomfortable and depressing. Although Brod was right to emphasize that Kafka was not at home in Poe's world, his determination to suppress Kafka's Gothic self or shadow meant that he was obliged to argue thus, and the many parallels betweeen Kafka's work and Poe's show that he exaggerated. There is, however, when all is said and done, a gulf betwen the work of the two men as regards both spirit and style. Kafka, unless I misread him, will have found Poe's work distasteful: its emphasis on horror, violence and brutality, on death and the fear of death, was not to his taste. As well as being too close to the knuckle for comfort, Poe's world was too negative, too overwrought, too hopeless and humourless for Kafka to be able to dwell, imaginatively, in it. He needed to cut horror with humour.

---

[26] Max Brod, *Über Franz Kafka* (Frankfurt a. M. & Hamburg: Fischer Bücherei, 1966), 309.

2.4. Kafka and the Marquis de Sade

When Kafka described the Marquis de Sade as the godfather of the modern age, he was probably thinking of the fact that Sade had put into words the monsters within that Fuseli had intuited and which Goya subsequently painted. In the present context, however, this is less important than Sade's attitude towards the novel of his time. Whatever the precise pedigree of the 'modern novel', the term as such was first used in 1800 by Sade (well described by Leslie Fiedler[27] as standing 'almost emblematically at the crossroads of depth psychology and revolution') to characterize the Gothic romance as opposed to the eighteenth-century novel in which 'everything seemed to have been done'. In arguing thus, Sade anticipated by a century and a half the Devil's thesis in Thomas Mann's *Doktor Faustus*.

Strictly speaking a form of romance, the Gothic novel can best be regarded as a revolutionary sub-genre of the novel. In terms of its popularity, though not of its origins, it was the product of the French Revolution, which, coming on top of the Inquisition (which did not end until 1772 in France and continued until 1834 in Spain and until 1859 in Italy), so shook and shocked the European imagination as to cause it to mutate. Without the Terror, the vogue for the novel of terror would not have grown as it did, although this was, of course, revolutionary in other ways as well in that it subverted the idea of the Richardsonian novel and the bourgeois ideology on which it was based, to say nothing of being opposed to realism and the claim of reason to explain reality. 'What ardent imagination', Schedoni asks in Ann Radcliffe's *The Italian*, 'ever was contented to trust to plain reasoning?' Confronted with a reality more traumatic and terrifying than ever, the novel for a time reverted to the older romance and indeed to fairytale: the ultimate ogres are the Grand Inquisitor and Robespierre, both of them more than adequate avatars of the Devil.

In a general way the Gothic novel was inspired by what Michael Sadleir, writing in 1927, called 'the instinct to liberty'.[28] Although the earliest Gothic novels and their immediate precursors went back a generation, the craze for the Gothic was one of the consequences of the French Revolution and, more distantly and less directly, of the English Puritan Revolution that fed into it. It may seem ironical that the storming of the Bastille, that most Gothic of Gothic castles, built to house heretics, in which 'le citoyen S[ade]' wrote his *Aline et Valcour* (1793),[29] should have triggered such a proliferation of imaginary castles, and that the Terror of 1793-4 should have spawned

---

27 Leslie A. Fiedler, *Love and Death in the American Novel* (Normal, IL: Dalkey Archive, 1997), 33.
28 M. Sadleir, *The Northanger Novels* (London: English Association), 1927, 20.
29 At the same time time Hubert Robert ('Robert des ruines'), formerly Keeper of the King's Pictures, was imprisoned at Saint Lazare, painting the dark prison corridor (see W. Gaunt, *Bandits in a Landscape* [London: The Studio, 1937], 108-118) that casts its shadow into Kafka's novels.

so many imaginary terrors, but the novel of terror is surely the appropriate novel of the age of Terror. This at all events was the view of Sade, who described the early Gothic novel as the inevitable outcome of the French Revolution and its aftermath. From *The Monk* (1796) onwards the Gothic novel holds up the mirror to post-revolutionary Europe, it being perhaps only thus that novelists could hope to move their readers, who expected the novel to reflect and explain society. The inherent instability of the Gothic novel is a reflection of the instability of European society at the time, which was to be repeated a century later, when the next old order was approaching its end, hence the new vogue for Gothic from the 1890s onwards and a similar vogue almost a century later. Literary Gothic is thus associated with historical change, *Spätzeitlichkeit*, and, in that sense, decadence.

That Kafka possessed the instinct to liberty is shown by all his best-known works and confirmed by the statement in his diary (18 Oct. 1916) that he had a boundless desire for freedom. By 'freedom' he meant, of course, the freedom that comes from commitment, the freedom that is meaningful because it is limited. He knew better than most that freedom is the subject of much self-delusion, and that what counts is the use to which it is put. Kierkegaard's 'either/or' was important to him because he was painfully aware that every moment of life is a decisive moment in which either the right or the wrong decision is made, if, that is, it is possible to know, in the absence of a fiercely unambiguous moral code like (that of the Old Commandant) which the right decision is.

It is, however, in the negative form of 'neither/nor' that the central problem of the Gothic novel faces each of Kafka's 'heroes' in turn, by which I mean that they reach the point where they can neither prove their own innocence or meaningfulness as individual human beings, nor live with their guilt and/or lack of meaning. Their only certainty is that of the grave, what the author of the *Nachtwachen* calls 'absolute Death' as opposed to the non-stop dying that passes for life. Gothic shares with medieval Gothic, and with Kafka, a preoccupation with death. Well might Virginia Hyde, in an important study of the eschatological tradition of medieval Gothic art as reflected in the iconography of Kafka's work, write that

> In his morally equivocal positions, as in his customary focus upon the labyrinth regardless of his apparent subject, Kafka has deep affinities with the aesthetics of gloom associated with the Gothic Revival in literature, and he takes his place unmistakably in a tradition centering, like it, upon the dark and infernal nether regions and the fearful prodigies issuing from them.[30]

Her comparison of Kafka with Bosch is a good one; a further parallel would be Kafka's friend Kubin, the iconography of whose work is more obviously eschatological than Kafka's own. As Virginia Hyde has shown, a fundamental feature

---

[30] Virginia M. Hyde, 'From the "Last Judgment" to Kafka's World: A Study in Gothic Iconography', in *The Gothic Imagination: Essays in Dark Romanticism*, ed. G. R. Thompson (Pullman, WA: Washington State University Press, 1974), 136.

of Kafka's Gothic world is the Apocalypse with its Seat of Judgment that is to be seen both in Prague's Cathedral of St Vitus and in Castle Karlštejn. Maybe that is why Heinrich Zschokke entitled his last novel *Drakomira mit dem Schlangenringe oder die nächtlichen Wanderer in den Schreckensgefängnissen von Karlstein bei Prag. Eine Schauergeschichte aus Böhmens grauer Vorzeit* (1847).

The early Gothic novelists had a variety of reasons for writing as they did. They were concerned not only to discredit the essentially feudal *ancien régime* with its state-sponsored superstition and 'pulpit-terrorism' (Peter Pindar), but also to subvert and transcend the mainstream novel of the time, and, in the case of the American early Gothics, to distance themselves from what was by then perceived as the colonialist English novel. More mundanely, the average Gothic novelist also wrote in order to give the reader a pleasurable (because safe) *frisson*. Some, of whom M. G. Lewis is the best-known, were literary *banditti*, aiming to evoke horror and shock the Philistines, relieving them of their material prepossessions in the process.

Kafka's aim, when he began writing four generations later, was more subtle and infinitely more complex. His concern with *Angst*, for instance, is more metaphysical than 'aesthetic'; in this respect his work belongs not with Radcliffe or Lewis, but, in its low-key way, with metaphysical Gothic as represented by Maturin's *Melmoth the Wanderer*, where fear is 'exalted into a hideous cloud over mankind's very destiny'.[31] More particularly one thinks of 'those 'pits of agony [...] where lie the souls of those who feel an involuntary pollution darkening their minds and dread lest their natures should conform to those of their persecutors'[32] since this points to the self-loathing with which Kafka sometimes weighed the fact that his 'cannibalistic' father's and paternal grandfather's blood ran in his own veins. While many early Gothic novelists sought to take advantage of the reader as the form rapidly became a cult, there were some, William Beckford, Charles Brockden Brown and Mary Shelley among them, who had more personal and valid reasons for writing. When Ann Radcliffe, on the other hand, reveals herself, as she does in her rhapsodic descriptions of landscape, the self-revelation is unintentional; and Shelley, in *Zastrozzi*, surely did not intend to reveal his own neurotic personality quite so clearly.

Above all Kafka is concerned to placate his inner demons. The reader is far from being his prime concern in the normal sense, although he came to control the reader more successfully than any other novelist has ever done, proof of this being the boundless secondary literature that has long since engulfed his writings like an ever stronger *Verschanzung* (defensive fortification) as an army of critics has made his work not more but less accessible. Not for nothing did the Great Wall of China catch

---

[31]   H. P. Lovecraft, *Supernatural Horror in Literature* (Chislehurst: The Gothic Society, 1994), 8.

[32]   J. M. S. Tompkins, *The Popular Novel in England, 1770-1800* (repr. London: Methuen, n.d.), 259.

his imagination. He saw writing as a form of prayer and a form of 'necromancy',[33] a word which conjures up the idea both of summoning spirits and of banishing them; in his case the emphasis is on exorcism. He is opposed to the inanity and gross materialism of the low-mimetic mode of aesthetic naturalism, but also to any form of literature that deviates from being the simple, honest expression of an inner reality. He had no time for literary exhibitionism of any sort. The fascination which his work has for his readers has more to do with his skill in expressing and universalizing his state of mind at any given time, than with any narrowly literary aim as such. What he most values are integrity and lucidity.

Like the Gothic Romantics before him he sees literature as the expression of inner reality. On the metafictional level his novels are about his own feelings of guilt, inadequacy and nonentity as he sought, first, to explore and express his own inner life in the form of his dreams and day-dreams, night- and daymares; and, second, to communicate what matters to him most, which he tends to call 'truth' or 'spiritual reality'. However, before he could do any of this to anything like his own satisfaction - he was fiercely self-critical as a writer - he had first to seek a point of 'absolute' vision from which to view reality and a universal language adequate to his individual expressive needs. He eventually found both in the perspective, style, and symbolical language of dreams, myth and fairytale, the archetypal symbolism of which is also present in Gothic. The implication of this for our reading of his work is addressed in Chapter 4. Focusing on his 'dreamlike inner life' and how it was expressed in his dreams and daydreams, and on fairytale, was the making of him as a writer, for together they prevented his work from being the mere private construct that he continued to fear it might prove to be. His writing was always basically self-exploration, but in the years between *Der Proceß* and *Das Schloß* he gave a little more thought to the reader in a more positive sense, while continuing to live in his own inner world. In his final years, while working on *Das Schloß* and *Der Bau*, and slowly dying, he was once more motivated by the desperate and entirely poetic impulse to banish on to paper the demons within him, until eventually writing was the only means of communication open to him as advanced tuberculosis of the larynx denied him speech. He refers to his protagonist in *Der Proceß* and *Das Schloß* as K. (the conventional use of an initial, ostensibly to mask identity, was adopted by the early Gothics from the novel of the time; it is a feature of Schiller's *Der Geisterseher. Aus den Papieren des Grafen von O**** [1787-9], but also, long before that, of Gellert's Richardsonian but backward-looking novel *Leben der schwedischen Gräfinn von G**** [1747: *The Life of the Countess of G ****, translated by a Lady, 2 vols, 1747]) both because K.'s identity is challenged in the novel and because the

---

[33] Janouch, 32.

autobiographical reference is important to him, although it must again be emphasized that while K.'s problems are Kafka's, his responses to them are not.

So while the context in which Kafka writes is the relativistic, sceptical, secular modern world, what he writes about is his own self-punitive dream-world. The idea of transgression against patriarchal power, central to the Gothic novel, is fundamental to his work, although we shall see (in 3.3) that it is by no means clear whether what is in question is a real transgression or not; most of Kafka's 'transgressions' against his father were, after all, imaginary. That one can go too far both in refusing to do one thing and in doing another brings us to the Sadian story-within-a-story in *Das Schloß*, in which Amalia is led by her own and her father's conscience to believe that she has done wrong in denying her fate by rejecting Sortini's seigneurial advances, while her sister Olga is similarly convinced that she was right to give herself to the minions of the Castle as a placatory offering; but the whole point of the inset tale is that what Amalia and Olga do and don't do is, in each case, both right and wrong. Whereas for Amalia a transgression is what she is expected to do, for Sortini it is what she fails to do; behind this clash of values lies the clash between Kafka *père et fils* (for Kafka a transgression is what he is expected to do (join the family business; not write; be his father's son), for his father it is what his son fails to do. It is at this point that Kafka's interest in Sade finally makes sense, for the story of Amalia and Olga appears to echo Sade's story of Justine and Juliette and their respective moralities in illustrating the Misfortunes of Virtue and the Prosperity of Vice. This does not mean, of course, that Kafka is adopting a crassly immoralist position by inverting conventional morality; on the contrary, his position is amoral, for at a time when 'the parish priest is sitting at home rending one vestment after another' (see *Ein Landarzt* [1916/17]), the old moral certainties are no longer available. In the early twentieth century, as in the early nineteenth, all is relation, all antinomies unresolved, at least in the context of Gothic. In *The Italian* (1796: II, ch. 4) Ann Radcliffe made the deplorable Marchesa di Vivaldi speak of the need to 'discriminate the circumstances that render the same action virtuous or vicious'. Although in weighing them the reader needs to remember who is speaking, her words show that the modern ('Gothic') era of moral relativism has arrived. At the time of writing *Das Schloß* Kafka was torn between the passive, traditional Judaeo-Christian morality and the assertive new Nietzschean one, so that he was in effect subject to the same uncertainties as the authors of the early Gothic novels, which, with the exception of a few precursors, appeared at a time of boundless uncertainty and the resurgence of the irrational. It is time that we addressed these and other Gothic ideas.

3. THE GOTHIC CIRCLE

3.1. Introductory

Kafka's work shares with Gothic what can only be called an infernal circularity: from projection into the world at birth as literal outcast, to transgression and consequent further loss of control, to the search for self which ends as it began, the vicious circle pervades every aspect of the lives of Kafka's protagonists, most challengingly and claustrophobically in *Der Bau* and *Der Proceß*. In the absence of transcendence, fairytale magic, or any kind of exit to meaning, existence is, in all three novels, as in *Die Nachtwachen des Bonaventura*, portrayed as circular. There is no point at which the increasingly vicious circle yields to linear meaning. Even in *Der Verschollene* the circle continually reasserts itself in the form of Karl R.'s recapitulated fall, and in the K.-novels, for all the shadows of Christian iconography, hints of an inaccessible earlier and other creation, existence is seen in post-Christian, neo-pagan terms. There is no teleology, no transcendence, no redemption, no grounds for hope, just a process comparable to the weary, sorrowful circle of Nietzsche's doctrine of identical recurrence.

Whether the protagonist is seen as trapped in the centre of the labyrinth, as in *Der Bau,* or as going round it seeking in vain for an entrance that does not exist, as in *Das Schloß*, this infernal circularity turns existence into a nightmare of meaningless experience. Far from being able, eventually, to break out from the vicious circle of meaningless existence, Kafka's protagonists are finally sucked into the black hole of non-existence that lies at its centre. The experience is, as in *Die Nachtwachen des Bonaventura*, that of Nothingness.[1] Because the structure of Kafka's novels is not teleological, but fractal, the order of their chapters used to be seen as scarcely less controversial than the logic of the events described in them. Such logic is circular: nothing is ever proved except cumulatively or by default. Even Josef K.'s guilt is not proved; it is merely deduced. The Gothic prison-cell (however transparently disguised as 'Bau' [burrow], 'Kasten' [crate]] or 'Pension' [boarding-house], all of which mean a prison or lock-up, or as 'Kabine' [cabin], 'Zimmerchen' [little room], and so on, which stand for the same thing) therefore becomes a metaphor for life itself. No matter whether the fate of Kafka's protagonists is defined in terms of imprisonment, or of exclusion, there is no exit this side of the final defeat. Whereas in the earlier Gothic

---

[1]   My argument at this point is indebted to Manuel Aguirre's admirable *The closed space: Horror literature and western symbolism* (Manchester & N.Y.: Manchester University Press, 1990).

novel disorder gave way to order, with Kafka disorder has become the norm. Normality as such no longer exists. Abnormality has become normative.

Each of Kafka's protagonists receives the 'mysterious message' that is as much a part of the stock-in-trade of the Gothic novelist as the speaking tube is of pantomime. Indeed, with characteristic logic, humour and literal-mindedness he even invents, in *Das Schloß*, a self-appointed castle messenger in the figure of Barnabas, named after the biblical 'Son of Consolation' who inspired hope that turned out to be misplaced in that the 'Letter of Barnabas' was spurious. Karl Rossmann, the pariah-protagonist of Kafka's first novel, receives a strangely challenging and ominously high-handed missive from 'Onkel Jakob', who in symbolical terms represents a reassertion of patriarchal authority. In *Der Proceß*, Josef K. receives a typically Gothic bolt from the blue ('You are under arrest'), and his successor, K., receives not only a summons to the Castle, to which he is then denied entry, but also, early on in *Das Schloß*, the infamous letter from Klamm that says one thing and means another, this being followed, later in the novel, by a second letter that is equally ominous, given its inaccuracy and the dubiousness of its claim to be what it purports to be. The mysterious messages in *Das Schloß* in particular raise the question of the identity both of the sender and of the addressee, for the protagonists of the novels and tales alike find themselves, as a result of a typically Gothic challenge, in doubt about their very identities.

3.2. The Alienated Hero

Kafka's Gothic is a reflection of his identity problem. However he looked at his genetic inheritance and position, and therefore at his own identity, he could not get away from a sense of alienation. Because his paternal genetic inheritance involved unacceptable characteristics and weaknesses, while his own individual characteristics (and the weaknesses into which he construed them) were rejected by his father, self-definition became a major preoccupation. Rejected by his father, a stranger in his native city, writing in the impoverished language of its non-native minority, blaming himself for outliving two brothers who died in infancy, Kafka is in many ways the archetypal Cain-like outcast of Gothic.[2] Karl Rossmann and his fellow-protagonists may lack the burning cross on the brow of Lewis's Exorciser, but inwardly they bear Cain's mark. Kafka originally planned to write his first novel on the Cain-and-Abel or 'hostile brothers' theme that had loomed so large in German Pre-Romanticism (Sturm und Drang), most notably in Schiller's *Die Räuber*, one of the two works, the other being *Der Geisterseher*, that caused Schiller to be regarded, in the Anglo-American

---

[2]   In the Romantic *Umwertung der Werte,* Cain, like the Devil, becomes a heroic figure; see Lowry Nelson, Jr., 'Night Thoughts on the Gothic Novel', *Yale Review,* 52 (1962), 237.

and French world, as a father of the Gothic, and was also a common fairytale motif (cf. the Grimms' 'Die zwei Brüder' [The Two Brothers]). Kafka's diaries and letters make it abundantly clear that he, like Byron, saw himself as a Cain-like and therefore devilish marked man; it is this fact that accounts for his interest in Byron's letters and journals, a selection from which he possessed. Early Gothic, it is worth adding, had a maritime branch, the pirate-pariah combining the bandito and the accursed wanderer (Flying Dutchman); in Scott's *The Pirate*, his female enthusiast and pretender to supernatural power, Norna of Fitful Head, inhabits Hoy Island, which rises from the sea for all the world like a Gothic castle. Kafka's *Der Verschollene*, which continues this convention, opens with the floating Gothic world of the ship (a version of the pirate-ship) arriving in a New York harbour of the imagination dominated by a gigantic figure on Manhattan Island (a deformed version of the Statue of Liberty) whose upheld sword threatens the transgressive new arrival.

Kafka's personae are, like the typical Gothic hero/villain, social outcasts with no hope of regaining the lost paradise for which they yearn, and as such versions of the Wandering Jew,[3] to whom Kafka likened himself. Not villainous enough to count as criminals of the imagination in the usual sense, they nonetheless belong with Goethe's Faust, Byron's Manfred and Maturin's Melmoth among the great outcast-heroes of world literature. Their expulsion from the childhood or fool's paradise in which they had been living prior to the opening of the novel represents the sudden slippage or change for the worse that sets Gothic novels in motion. They are typical Gothic subjects in being alienated from themselves, this being indicated, as in dreams, by means of literal symbolism: Karl Rossmann and K. appear as literal aliens in an unknown environment, and Josef K. is repeatedly shown as a stranger to the environment of conscience, and therefore ill at ease within it. Indeed, Josef K. seems to have been unaware that the realm of conscience - reified in the form of the omnipresent courtrooms in general and the *Rumpelkammer* in particular - existed. In Kafka's work the Gothic theme of pursuit takes the form of the haunting and hounding of a man - they are predominantly male self-projections - by his conscience. Haunted consciousness is as central to all three of his novels as it is to *The Mysteries of Udolpho*. In *Der Proceß* the pursued becomes the pursuer (as in Godwin's *Caleb Williams*, translated into German in 1795 and 1798; and in *Frankenstein*, not translated until 1948): Josef K. is first pursued by the Law, and then, in the second half of the novel, himself pursues it to the bitter end, hounding himself to death in the process.

Moral purist that he was, Kafka believed one mistake to be enough to destroy a life: common to the Old Testament, Jewish folklore and his own first novel is the idea

---

3   Whether Kafka knew Christian Schubart's *Der ewige Jude* (1783), which caught P. B. Shelley's attention, or Hans Andersen's novel *Ahasverus* (1848), is not known.

of paradise being lost on account of a single sin. When he said there are no fairytales nowadays (diary, 22 July 1916), he was referring to fairytale endings. Knowing the age of miracles with its ideas of atonement, reconciliation, redemption, and the deus ex machina to be past, he found his own burden of psychological guilt crushing. His protagonists, for their part, like their Gothic predecessors, are part victim and part villain, the victims alike of universal guilt and their own all-too-human weaknesses. Lacking Kafka's own obstinate, saving belief in the presence of something indestructible in himself, they founder helplessly in guilt and inadequacy, bedevilled by transgressive desire. The psychological sophistry by means of which we delude ourselves into thinking that what we want is right is illustrated as much by the protagonists of Kafka's novels as it is by Lewis's Ambrosio. Are we not told of Josef K. that 'The woman really attracted him, and on mature reflection he could find no valid reason why he should not yield to that attraction'? The 'fleeting suspicion that she might be trying to lay a trap for him', which was wholly justified, he 'had no difficulty in dismissing from his mind'. Josef K. is a fool.

We have seen that Kafka regarded himself, with whatever degree of justification, as the hapless victim of patriarchal power. Georg Bendemann's father in *Das Urteil*, who condemns his son for supposedly trying to usurp his power and position, is substantially the same as his model in the *Brief an den Vater*. The story's themes (patriarchy, usurpation, disinheritance, the inter-generational power struggle, filicide) are all Gothic ones. Given that Kafka wrote of himself as 'in truth a disinherited son' (BV 174), it is not surprising that disinheritance, one aspect of the patriarchal abuse of power, is, in one form or another, a major theme in each of his novels, all three of them late Gothic precisely in turning on control, on the usurpation and abuse of power and its corrupting influence: 'Gothic fiction [...] conjures a shadow world wherein power is simultaneously unveiled and veiled, it is both explicit and naked in its effect, and inaccessible and mysterious in its sources. Gothic fiction explores power mythologized.'[4]

It may seem strange, then, given his strong views on the subject of patriarchy, that his attitude to women is so unambiguously patriarchal. His female figures mostly involve pastiches of the demonic feminine, woman as the 'Enemy' of mankind in a gendered sense. It is to this that the aphorism 'Women are snares waiting to drag man down into the merely finite' (J 123) - a reversal of the folktale idea that the first man caught woman in his snare[5] - applies. In the continuation of that aphorism he wrote of 'all the female varieties of man-trap [Fangeisen]', a viciously visual image which presupposes woman as she-devil (cf. the fairytale figure of the Fänggin, an associate of the Devil), huntress (Diana) or, since transgression against patriarchy is involved,

---

4   Mary E. F. Fitzgerald, 'The Unveiling of Power: 19th-Century Gothic Fiction in Ireland, England and America', in *Literary Interrelations*, ed. H. Kosok & W. Zach (Tübingen: Narr, 1987), II, 15.
5   Stith Thompson, *Motif-Index*, A1275.10.

poacher (a perversion of the classical image). This is why, when Titorelli paints the goddess of Justice, the image he produces looks like 'a goddess of the Hunt in full cry'. Either way, the victim is man, and more specifically Kafka, who grew up with the idea of the hunt, with the Devil - his father - as huntsman and himself as prey, cast in the same role as the witch in late medieval society. When he wrote of 'Women's monstrous sexuality, their natural uncleanness' (diary, 23 July 1913), he was reading Gustav Roskoff's *Geschichte des Teufels* (1869) with its lengthy account of witchcraft. He projected his own problems on to woman because his position in the power-relationship with his father was, stereotypically, that of a woman confronted by patriarchy. His clinical dissection of patriarchal authority and values allies him with female Gothic, and his symbolical use of space has more in common with female Gothic as delineated in, say, Ann Radcliffe's *A Sicilian Romance* than with male Gothic. Thus the attic, by Kafka's time long since encoded as a space of female interiority, becomes, in *Der Proceß*, the space of Josef K.'s challenged interiority, although it does so via the German language (*Schädeldach, Dach*, head; *Dachboden*, mind) rather than through the intermediacy of female Gothic as such.

3.2.1. The Devil as Gothic Hero

Like the Gothics, Kafka emphasizes the power of the irrational by showing the inability of reason to plumb the depths of the soul. What Block says of the Court in *Der Proceß*, that 'in these courts things keep on coming up for discussion that are simply beyond reason', chimes with Gothic. While the inquisitional and other excesses of the Catholic church were rightly regarded with abhorrence as part of the *ancien régime*, the irrational spirit of the late eighteenth century was such as to encourage belief in an alternative form of superstition in the shape of the supernatural, with the result that the Devil once again became an important, albeit mostly invisible, presence in literature, as he had been in the sixteenth century, the source, in literary terms, of so much in Gothic. It is ironical that this happened at a time when belief in the Devil had finally come to be regarded, in theological terms, as superstition. In Germany, as in England, the Devil was a major link between the Gothic world of the sixteenth century and the literary Gothic revival (and its renewal in the late nineteenth century). Lest, however, it be supposed that Kafka is in the tradition initiated by M. G. Lewis, with whom 'the Gothic novel [...] began to dedicate itself to the revelation of [...] a malign cosmos where the devil, not God, is the only authority and prime mover',[6] it must be emphasized that he, unlike Lewis, set out to prove the impossibility of existence in such a world, and therefore the need for a residual faith such as his own belief in what he followed Goethe and Schopenhauer in calling 'the indestructible'.

---

6   Frank, in *Horror Literature: A Reader's Guide*, ed. N. Barron (New York & London, 1990), 7.

Der Proceß shows, above all, what it was intended to show: that Kafka himself could not live as Josef K. does. He was very clear about this, writing in aphorism 50 that 'Man cannot live without an enduring belief in the presence of something indestructible in himself, even though both the indestructible and his belief in it may remain hidden from him. One of the ways in which this may be expressed is through belief in a personal god.' The situation was, however, complicated by the fact that for him devils were a deal more real than any belief in a personal god, which, however desirable it might in theory be, was at best difficult and at worst impossible, whereas devils were, by contrast, a fact of life, impossible to ignore.

From Cain, that 'Satan clad in human flesh',[7] we therefore pass to Satan *in propria persona*, a major figure in Gothic and fairytale alike, who in the form of the increasingly internalized demonic Other will lead us to the Fall and thence to transgression as such. Kafka's reading of Roskoff[8] speaks for itself. If Maturin's Melmoth is 'an amalgam of various Romantic avatars: Satan, Faust, Gothic hero/villain, Wandering Jew, Cain',[9] then so too is Kafka's protagonist in his successive incarnations (Karl R., Josef K., K.). Josef K., who gives in to every temptation for the entirely diabolical and Gothic reason that he can see no reason why he should not, resembles the Gothic hero in his Faustian desire for knowledge,[10] while Karl R. and K. are not only pastiches of the Gothic Romantic type of the Mysterious Stranger; as part-autobiographical figures, they are also figurations of the Accursed Wanderer or Wandering Jew (cf. Lewis's Exorciser; Frankenstein and his monster; Dracula), a figure with whom Kafka identified ('I am as old as [...] the Wandering Jew': J 108). The fact that the Wandering Jew was said to fall into a trance once every hundred years, and to wake up a young man of about thirty, may help to explain Josef K.'s symbolical age, which also corresponded to Kafka's own age at the time. Like Melmoth, then, Kafka's personae all embody not only the Cain-figure, but also, more specifically, the 'devil' that he had come to feel himself to be.

The prototype of the 'heroic villain' of the Gothic novel is Milton's Satan, celebrated by Edmund Burke for his sublimity and heroized by the Gothics for his resistance to patriarchal power:

> the hero of *Paradise Lost* (1667-1674) is none other than Satan [...] The ridiculous Devil of our [medieval] ancestors has become in Milton's hands a giant and a hero [...] an epic, majestic figure, a Promethean character [...] During the period of the Romantic revolt in all European countries

---

7   M. Rudwin, *The Devil in Legend and Literature* (London: The Open Court Company, 1931), 305.

8   Gustav Roskoff, a compatriot (in the Czechoslovak dispensation) of Kafka, was born in Bratislava in 1814. In 1850 he was appointed to a chair in Old Testament Exegetics in the University of Vienna. His Satanology is his main work.

9   Rosemary Jackson, *Fantasy: The Literature of Subversion* (London & New York: Routledge, 1995), 104.

10   Faustianism had been a part of Gothic from Godwin's *St Leon* of 1799 onwards.

> Satan was considered [...] a Prometheus of Christian mythology. He was hailed as the vindicator of reason, of freedom of thought, and of unfettered humanity.[11]

Though Satan is in reality not the hero but the God-sized villain of *Paradise Lost*, the personification of the sublime of evil, he is the ultimate hero of many Gothic novels in which diabolical possession is an important motif, as in a figurative sense it is in Kafka's novels. This extraordinary anachronistic vogue was started, so far as late eighteenth-century England is concerned, by a romance by Veit Weber (ps. of [Georg Philipp Ludwig] Leonhard Wächtler), *Die Teufelsbeschwörung* (1790), translated by Robert Huish as *The Sorcerer* (1795), to which Lewis was indebted for the dramatic ending of *The Monk* (1796). In early Gothic (*Lenore, Otranto* and *Vathek* for example) God was a presence, and if in the course of Gothicism 'the Deity disappears though the Devil remains',[12] the fact should not be misunderstood. The early Gothic novelists, whose work mostly ends with order restored, did not so much seek to break down order as to flirt intellectually with the chaos that was already in the air and, in France at least, on the streets. Kafka, by contrast, takes things to their logical conclusion.

Notwithstanding the fact that between *Paradise Lost* (1667) and *Der Verschollene* (1912) the Devil passed from being seen as a part of the divine creation to being recognized as a creation of the human mind, Milton's belief in a personal Devil was shared by Kafka, whose identification with the arch-rebel derives in large measure from that bedevilled relationship with his father. On the Freudian view spelled out by Ernest Jones, the Devil is simply the personification of the repressed, unconscious instinctual life. Belief in the Devil, said to be attributable, as in Kafka's case, to 'infantile experiences of fear', represents

> in the main an exteriorization of two sets of repressed wishes, both of which are ultimately derived from the infantile Oedipal situation: the wish to imitate certain attributes of the father, and the wish to defy the father; in other words, an alternating emulation of and hostility against the father.[13]

The Devil, that is to say, represents unconscious aspects of the Father-Son complex. More specifically he represents both the father against whom hostility is felt, and the son who defies the father, each party seeing the other as diabolical. From the son's point of view, Kafka *père* was the very devil to live with: he exhibited to the full the diabolical characteristics of arbitrariness, unjustness, petty tyranny and general unreasonableness, all of them documented to the full in the *Brief an den Vater*. He mocked his son's endeavours and derided his literary ambitions and achievements. Kafka therefore had a double reason for identifying with the 'devil' his father declared

---

11 M. Rudwin, 10, 15.
12 Dorothy Scarborough, *The Supernatural in Modern English Fiction* (New York: Lethe Press, 2001), 7.
13 Ernest Jones, *Nightmare, Witches and Devils* (New York: W. W. Norton, n.d.), 155.

him to be: because in reacting against and defying his father he was performing the rôle of the Devil as arch-rebel that he felt was expected of him, and because he could not help letting his father's unjust censure get to him, coming to see himself, in the upshot, as in some way diabolical, whereas in reality he was closer to being saintly. It could even be argued that he was, in psychological terms, imitating his father when he set out to be as unlike him as possible. All the special characteristics of the giants of old having been transferred to the Devil, when Georg Bendemann refers to his father as an ogre, he is, at least on a subconscious level, recognizing his diabolical status, and the wish that fathers the thought 'if only he would fall and break in little pieces' is also a devilish one. At the same time it has a folktale ring to it (cf. the motif, common to Iceland and India, of the ogre who bursts, as well as the homelier echo of 'Humpty-Dumpty' [Wirgele-Wargele]), to say nothing of also being typical of dreams.

Given that it is about its protagonist's recapitulated Fall, it is appropriate that Kafka's first novel is peppered with references to the Devil. Leaving the German title aside for the moment, the story starts with the Stoker, for 'the stoker' (*Brendly* in German,[14]) is one of the Devil's many euphemistic appellations, as is Blackman or the Black One (cf. Karl's chosen pseudonym of 'Negro', the nickname he has in his last post, from which he is dismissed for being an 'absolute devil'; the chosen name makes clear his subconscious self-perception). The novel thus begins and ends with the Devil, and a Freudian Devil at that. *Brendly* (cf. 'brenzlig', hot [as in: it's getting too hot for me]; in Austria, smelling of burning; figuratively, ominous) connects by verbal association with 'Brenner', the obviously symbolic name of the Pension in which Karl is said to have visited Therese on three occasions, and to which he was supposed to go after being dismissed from the Hotel Occidental. It is present in the word 'Spiritusbrenner' (primus stove); the usual word is *Spirituskocher*, so Kafka clearly attached importance to the word *Brenner*, which also connects with *brennen,* to burn, cf. the way in which Frieda's 'little body burned in K.'s hands' in Chapter 3 of *Das Schloß*; and *sich brennen,* to burn one's hands, to make a serious mistake (*Brandmal* means mark of shame). *Brennen* also means to distill, which, via the demon drink (*Branntwein*, brandy), points back to the Devil. Kafka *père*, it should be said, was fond of a drink. The diabolical and infernal connotations of this whole complex of words and ideas are interwoven throughout the narrative of *Der Verschollene* in particular. Since 'Brenner' also points, via a verbal bridge, to Brunelda, it seems that on a symbolical level the Pension Brenner (to which Karl does not go) is identical with Brunelda's flat (to which he does go). In doing so, he is going to the very source of his condition: he who was intoxicated by the flesh is going to live 'with' Brunelda (cf. *beim Teufel sein*, to be lost), the very symbol of his engulfment by it; he who, in

---

[14] 'Among [the Devil's] many appellations [is] *Brendly* (meaning in German: 'the stoker') for tending to the furnaces and keeping the fires of hell burning' (Rudwin, 27).

the guise of Robinson, became drunk on brandy is going to live at its very source (cf. the keg of brandy, no less, which is kept behind the trunks in Brunelda's flat).

Brandy as a sign of the diabolical reappears in *Das Schloß* when K. invades what he imagines to be Klamm's official sledge and helps himself to the brandy that represents his own and Klamm's diabolical nature, leaving it dripping from the footboard, whence it runs under the sledge (*unter den Schlitten kommen*, literally to run/get under the sledge; figuratively, to come to grief, the reference being to K. coming to grief thanks to the brandy). As Kafka probably also knew, brandy, in the form of the idea of making a knot of spilled brandy, is associated with the 'impossible task' of folklore.[15] Brandy is replaced by rum in Chapter 18, when K. drinks a small bottle of rum, left for him by Frieda; the effect is no less disastrous since it makes him fall asleep when Bürgel, or so the reader probably fancies, is offering him the key to his castle. To argue that since he has a sledge Klamm must be a real figure, would be to miss the point, which is that the sledge is itself symbolical, standing for the metaphor 'mit jemandem Schlitten fahren' (' to ride roughshod over someone, to give someone hell'), which is precisely what K.'s conscience does after the episode involving 'Klamm's sledge'.

In the case of *Der Verschollene*, such references confirm that Karl, who identifies with the Stoker, has gone to the Devil. This is shown literally: Karl makes for the cabin of the Stoker, who is said to have 'bewitched' him, meaning that he is 'a devil' ('ein teuflischer Mensch', a Hoffmannesque cliché), as Kafka was evidently called by his father. When Robinson gets drunk on brandy (ch. 6), Karl invokes the Devil, saying 'Zum Teufel' (figuratively 'what the devil', literally 'to the devil'), but there is more to it than that, for *zum Teufel gehen* (to get lost), a synonym of *verschollen sein*, means literally to go to the Devil; although the English figurative meaning is not normally present in German, Kafka is clearly aware of it (he had a reading competence in English), and uses the title *Der Verschollene* to mean, among other things, 'The Man who went to the Devil'. Josef K. makes a similarly revealing remark to the warders in the first chapter of *Der Proceß* when he says 'Laßt mich, zum Teufel' ('Leave me, dammit', but with the comma removed the German words mean 'let me go to the Devil', which is what he does). Colour-symbolism points in the same direction, compare the use of the colour red (the colour of the Austrian Krampus, a devil-figure), which links the Klara and Brunelda episodes. When Klara is playing the part of Johanna, the servants, each bearing a huge candle, can be seen as Lucifer-figures pointing the way to Karl's recapitulated Fall.[16] It is symbolically appropriate that the

---

[15] Stith Thompson, *Motif-Index*, H1021.4.
[16] In Latin *lucifer* means light-bearer.

Nature Theatre of Oklahoma[17] features men dressed as devils, for in signing on and heading for Oklahoma, Karl is going west (the English metaphor, non-existent in German, is equivalent to *verschollen sein*).

The Devil has often been represented with a long beard like those associated with the Court in *Der Proceß*, or with a red beard like the onlooker at the time of K.'s arrest and the student Bertold, and as walking with a limp, like the lame student and sacristan in the same novel,[18] in which Josef K'.s Luciferian folly is fully revealed in the Cathedral when the lamp the Priest had given him to carry goes out. Of K. in *Das Schloß* it may be said that 'a great Devil has taken possession of him and a multitude of little ones has come to serve the great one' (aphorism 10). The great Devil is Klamm; the little devils or demons include K.'s so-called assistants (the 'helpers' of folktale) with the dark skins and goatee beards of their kind, who do everything short of assisting him, and the peasants in the Herrenhof, mirror-images of the (d)evil within K., who is finally brought down to their level. The more we learn about Klamm, the clearer it becomes that he represents the (D)evil in K., his pride, moral incontinence, lack of concentration, and so on. It is the very fact that he is possessed by him that makes K. mistake the devil within for the god without. Klamm is so named (Czech *klam*, delusion) because K. seeks him as though he were God, when all the time he is the Devil and is egging K. on in his futile, vainglorious quest. It is appropriate that Kafka's own name, *kavka*, denotes, in Czech, a dupe or gullible person, and that K. bears Kafka's initial. The implication is that K. is duped into thinking Klamm real. When K. 'sees' the Devil, he mistakes him for God, because he wants to believe in God. There is no need for him to believe in the Devil, for 'Once one has given house-room to the Devil, he no longer insists that one believe in him' (aphorism 28; I have substituted 'Devil' - the personification of evil - for 'Evil' as better illustrating my point). The whole world of *Das Schloß* is corrupt because it exists under the sign of (the) (D)Evil (the English pun also exists, as Kafka, an eager reader of the Grimm brothers' dictionary, will have known, in Low German: (D)Üwel); to adopt aphorism 100, it cannot be more diabolical than it already is. The deep, impersonal, authoritative voice that calls out as K. is proving his diabolical credentials by making the love of the damned to Frieda among the pools of beer outside Klamm's room is, of course, the voice of Klamm himself, the great Devil within K. and projection of his licentiousness and concomitant spiritual pride; that is why it is as it were a travesty of the voice of God.

---

[17] I avoid the obvious translation (Oklahoma Outdoor Theatre) in order to draw attention to the prefix Natur-, which both implies that this travelling theatre stands for the theatre of the world and refers back to Karl's Fall ('Natur' also means private parts and, in Austria, semen).

[18] See Stith Thompson, *Motif-Index,* G303, which lists other characteristics of the Devil that correspond to details of the novels.

The second letter K. receives from Klamm is clearly from this same Devil. Viewed thus, it makes excellent sense. It is addressed to the 'Herrn Landvermesser', that is, the *vermessen* or Luciferian K., and to the symbolically appropriate address - the Brückenhof Wirtshaus, the reification of his confused mind. It gets to the right address too. In commending K. for the surveying work he has carried out thus far, which has been nil, Klamm is in reality commending him for the damnable, diabolical pride - in German, *Vermessenheit* - with which he has behaved. When he goes on 'Lassen Sie nicht nach in Ihrem Eifer!' ('Keep up the good work'), he is surely using the word 'Eifer' in its original sense of *Eifersucht* (jealousy) and *Zorn* (anger), urging K. not to cease his guilty questing, not to give up his angry pride. In being brought Klamm's letter, K. is being tempted in the wilderness (cf. Matth. IV, 1), for the letter is in effect a diabolical echo of the words spoken to Christ immediately before he was led into the wilderness: 'This is my beloved Son, in whom I am well pleased.' K. has succumbed to precisely those temptations Christ is said to have faced in the wilderness: he has lived by bread alone, without a thought for higher things, and has tempted one whom he wrongly thought his god, for Klamm has from the beginning been invested (by K.) with a godlike aura intended to deceive the unwary (K.).

That K. is now being tempted by 'his devil', is a matter of poetic justice. When he arrives back at the schoolroom chilled through as a result of the 'böses, böses Wetter', this is a sign of the evil *(das Böse)* to which he, like Josef K. before him, has allowed himself to become all too attached, and therefore confirmation that he too is possessed by the Devil, who causes him to transgress further in breaking down the door of the wood shed, which K. does as it were in the Devil's name. When he is consequently dismissed by the Teacher, K. is appropriately told to go to the Devil ('scheren Sie sich sofort [...] aus dem Haus' is an elaborate euphemism for the more usual *scher dich zum Teufel!*), this being what K. does at the end of the novel when he identifies with the 'Pferdeknechte'. The diabolical nature of the Castle is clear enough. Sortini may be able to avoid the shaft ('Deichsel') of the horse-drawn fire-engine when he jumps over it, but K. is unable to elude the Devil (*Deixel*).

The idea of the Devil is therefore internalized in Kafka's work: the Devil as Gothic personage is replaced by the devil as a non-Gothic subjective concept, one's *own* devil, this being externalized in the person of Klamm. The Devil's entourage, the demons of inner space, of the mind, are likewise externalized in an attempt to understand and in some measure contain them. The extent of Kafka's obsession with the Devil in the form of his own supposed diabolical weaknesses, is shown by the aphorism 'There can be knowledge of the diabolical, but not belief in it, for things cannot be more diabolical than they already are' (aphorism 100), and perhaps by the way in which he has K. fall asleep when Bürgel appears to be revealing the Castle mysteries to him, for it is written in the *Malleus Maleficarum* that 'The devil often tempts us to give way from very weariness.'[19] Kafka was plagued by the demons of self-doubt, possessed by the diabolical, because wholly unjustified, idea of his own guilt, the terms in which this was put by his father being revealed by the father's condemnation of his son in *Das Urteil* as 'a diabolical person'. Like the anonymous author of *Die Nachtwachen des Bonaventura*, Kafka was motivated by what is there called 'this poetic Devil inside me', for he also associated the Devil with the for him guilty act of writing. In 1912 he wrote to Felice of 'the Devil, who always has a hand in the desire to write' (BF 184), and five years later described writing - the activity for which he lived and for which he had by then begun dying - as 'the reward for service to the Devil', adding 'This descending to commune with dark powers, this release of spirits which in the nature of things are kept bottled up, dubious embraces, and whatever else may happen down there [...] Perhaps there is a different kind of writing; I know only this one' (Br 384).That was written in 1922. In 1931, seven years after Kafka's death, Maximilian Rudwin went further in writing of 'the Fiend' as 'the fountain-head of all fiction'.[20] By service to the Devil, Kafka meant service to the devil of self.

This obsession and identification with the Devil was powerfully reinforced in summer 1913, when he read the Viennese theologian Gustav Roskoff's *Geschichte des Teufels* (1869), quoting from it in a letter to Felice dated 14 August 1913 (BF 444), in which he again likened his writing to service to the Devil, adding: 'Of course, one would need to be a pretty canny graphologist to be able to deduce that from my handwriting'. In addition to reinforcing Kafka's view of woman as she-devil - the Lilith-figure is ubiquitous in European culture from 1880 to 1920[21] - Roskoff's book confirmed his already distinctly medieval view of the Devil: he saw himself as being plagued by a multiplicity of devils. A year before, on 9 July 1912, he had noted in his diary, apropos 'the invention of the Devil', that 'It is [...] the multiplicity of devils that constitutes our unhappiness in this world [...] the many devils within us'. The whole long paragraph confirms that the idea of the Devil/devils had by that time already become a central feature of his inner life; in May 1914 a day-dream features fifty little horned devils.

Roskoff also discussed a number of related ideas, several of them ones which loom large in Kafka's work, notably the ideas of the scapegoat, of the Fall, and of Woman as 'the mainspring of sensuality', to say nothing of demons' role as pestilential spirits - compare the coven of horrid little girls outside Titorelli's studio in *Der Proceß*, female

---

[19] *Malleus Maleficarum*, Part II, ch.1.
[20] Rudwin, 273.
[21] See Bram Dijkstra, *Idols of Perversity* (New York & Oxford: Oxord University Press, 1986), 306-9.

imps of Satan one and all[22] - and of cannibalism, an important idea in his work (see 9.4).

3.3. Transgression

Whether any of Kafka's works are deemed interpretable as a whole in terms of Gothic, as opposed to containing a variety of Gothic motifs, will depend on one's view of Gothic and of the meaning of the works in question, but if the emphasis is put, as much recent criticism of Gothic has put it, on the notion of transgression against patriarchal power, then core works such as *Das Urteil, Der Verschollene, Der Proceß, In der Strafkolonie* and *Das Schloß* turn, as the *Brief an den Vater* shows, on just that.

The whole story of Amalia's Secret, for example, which is an *exemplum*, a story told as a case in point, normally, as in the previous instance, the Parable of the Door-Keeper, in the course of a sermon, turns on the idea of transgression, as do *Das Urteil, In der Strafkolonie* and *Der Proceß*. Olga is horrified by the would-be 'seigneurial' abuse of power practised by Sortini, and it is clear that figures such as Klamm alias Momus alias Sortini, the father in *Das Urteil* and, more explicitly, the Old Commandant in the penal colony of life, exercise precisely the arbitrary patriarchal power that is challenged in so many Gothic novels. However, this abuse of power, which can only be properly assessed if the identity of Sortini (with K.) is borne in mind, has another, post-Gothic dimension. Josef K., who is unable to prove his innocence, and Amalia's father, who is unable to prove his guilt, are both victims of the abuse of power, the power in question being what it began to be in the course of high Gothic, namely, the power of the mind, for neither the innocence of the one nor the guilt of the other exists in any objectively verifiable sense. Josef K. in trying to prove his innocence, when he is guilty, and Amalia's father in trying to prove his guilt, when he is innocent, are abusing their moral selves. As, of course, is Sortini.

At this stage we need to distinguish between different levels of fiction, for when a creative process analogous to Freud's 'dream-work' (see 4.4) has taken place, and the latent content has been disguised by the subconscious, it looks as though Kafka's work shares the Gothic obsession, most in evidence in the German *Bundesroman* (secret-society or Rosicrucian *[Rosenkreuzerroman]* novel) with the ways in which one individual exercises power over another. It looks, for instance, as though Klamm, and through him the whole Castle-administration, is controlling K. in a more refined version of the way in which Kafka *père* controlled his son, and yet what is really controlling K. is his own wayward imagination, of which Klamm and his understudies are projective figments. The protagonists of all three novels appear to fall foul of

---

22   That 'die Bucklige' (hunchback) is 'barely thirteen' may reflect Kafka's knowledge, gleaned from Roskoff, that women were required to abjure heresy from the age of twelve onwards.

patriarchal power and its control mechanisms, foremost among them the very notion of transgression (cf. the disobedience of which Kafka, like Shelley, was accused by his father). Karl Rossmann is repeatedly expelled from 'paradise' by an autocratic father-figure, and Josef K. and K. are ostensibly controlled by systems representing power pure and simple, but in reality all three of them are controlled by their own lack of self-control, notably in the context of sexual self-indulgence, and, once it is too late, by conscience. At this point the vicious circle again comes into play, for we have seen that Kafka's conscience was shaped by his father's disapproval. The whole apparatus of the Court in *Der Proceß* is real enough, in the way in which dream imagery and events are real, but take away the mummery, and its significance, as the internal tribunal of conscience, is scarcely less clear. It is the same with *Das Schloß*, in which the story of Sortini and Amalia, the fictionality of which is stressed both in that Sortini is a figure in a fiction within a larger fiction and in that his reality is questioned through the confusion surrounding his identity, is another version of the story of Klamm and Frieda, K. and Frieda, and K. and the girl from the Castle, inserted into the main text as a parable on the subject of transgression.

Background to the novels is the author's sense of transgression against a conscience provoked into hyperactivity by a lifetime of paternal fiats and interdictions. In the first two novels the apparent transgression against patriarchal law stands for the real one against conscience. What is ultimately most important in *Das Schloß*, as in the two earlier novels, are the protagonist's transgressions against his own better judgment, since this is where the would-be land-surveyor is most in need of the moral yardstick which he literally and figuratively lacks. We have already seen this to be the issue that underlies the story of Amalia and Olga. It is wrong to apply Judaeo-Christian moral values and judge Amalia's self-denial to be right and Olga's self-surrender wrong, for are not Judaeo-Christian values by definition patriarchal? Are there not other ways of looking at Amalia's behaviour, other codes, other values? Is self-denial invariably right? May not this virtue become a vice if practised too assiduously? May it not equate with fear of life? Is that right? Is self-surrender to life always wrong? Is not life for living? And so on. The point of the parable is to provoke such questions, to indicate that 'transgression' is a far from simple concept, given that the 'Law' or 'system' or 'authority', or whatever, is ultimately simply that of the isolated, faithless self, for the corruption of the Castle authority, like that of the Court in the previous novel, is simply a reflection of K.'s corrupt human nature, which is in turn a reflection of what Kafka, on the whole wrongly, thought of as his own moral weakness. The real issue is human fallibility, and there is a further point to be borne in mind: that land-surveyor is clearly a metaphor for writer, so that Kafka is himself the self-appointed surveyor of his domain, challenging himself as to his credentials, wondering all the time whether his writing, a matter of life and death by now, is informed by judgment or misjudgment. He is wondering, that is, whether his creative life's work consists of meaningful structures or meaningless constructs.

To conclude, with reference to any of the works under discussion, that everything is ultimately a matter of conscience would, however, be to bypass the real issue, which is that the conscience or moral immune system, like the brain as a whole, starts off blank and has inscribed on it in course of time various notions and precepts of greater or lesser validity. Kafka himself was, much of the time, puritanical to a degree, building up the slightest transgression into a 'cardinal sin', although his values are, for the most part, humanistic rather than dogmatically or orthodoxly religious. Indeed, his work challenges the power over an individual such as himself of a value-system like the Judaeo-Christian moral code, in which that individual may or may not believe, and, what is more important, which may or may not be valid. I refer to Judaeo-Christianity because, while he was increasingly conscious of his Jewish heritage, the iconography and religious background of his work, as of his native city, reflects the eschatological tradition of the Catholic middle ages, which is never out of sight for long in the parts of the 'old city' of Prague in which he lived and worked. Wherever he went in Prague, he was reminded of patriarchy and, with it, of sin, hence his belief that 'irrespective of any [other kind of] guilt, we [humans] are guilty of sin'. By definition sin means transgression against the law of the father.

The moral of the original Gothic novel, Walpole's *The Castle of Otranto,* that 'the sins of the fathers are visited on their children', underlies all Kafka's work in the psychologically explicable, theologically fundamentalist form of an obsession (if it had merely been an idea, he would have rejected it) with the idea of original sin. This precludes the idea of redemption, which he would have classed as a fairytale, or as one of the legendary wonders, beautiful maybe, but unproveable and therefore incredible, of which Titorelli tells. Athough he was neither an orthodox Jew nor a Christian, Kafka inherited from Judaeo-Christianity a disastrous legacy in the form of what became, at times, an obsession totally at odds with his own moral lack of dogma. Original sin, the transgression to end all transgressions, means, as Schopenhauer, whose view surely shaped Kafka's, saw so clearly, that our very existence is a transgression: we ought not to exist, so that, existing, we are guilty. Kafka's experience of life was tragic in the sense that he wanted to believe, but found it always difficult and often impossible to do so, and because what he derived from religion, far from being consolatory, was unremittingly disheartening. His troubled religiosity made him liable to dwell on the negative. The divine being simply that in which Josef K., unlike Franz K., fails to believe, a matter of legend, what remains is the negative sublime of terror, once the source, according to Burke, of everything sublime, but now, in a godless age, void of such meaning, and therefore merely that 'grim phantasm, fear' (Poe).

Because Kafka wanted to believe in God, but was obsessed by the Devil, his work contains elements of a Gothic-style travesty of religion in which God is replaced by the Devil, but the underlying problem is the validity and relevance of Christian concepts and the Christian moral code in the work of a non-Christian writer in the post-Christian early twentieth century. The paradox of Gothic, that it became the expression of a post-Christian outlook but was locked into the medieval Christian 'conception of guilt-laden, sin-ridden man',[23] is illustrated nowhere more clearly than in Kafka's novels. In this sense he is the very personification of Gothic.

Transgression, in Kafka, which ranges all the way from presumption to the 'licentious enactment of carnal desire',[24] is often the result of misjudgment or hubris, hence K.'s personification of the misjudger in *Das Schloß*. K.'s supposed profession of *Landvermesser* derives not from the verb *vermessen*, which means to measure, but from the reflexive form of the verb, *sich vermessen*, which means to mismeasure and to presume. All three meanings are relevant to K.'s supposed profession, but the fact that he is not actually a land-surveyor at all means that the ideas of mismeasurement and presumption are all the more important. The normal German word for land-surveyor is *Landmesser*. In opting for the less common, alternative form, 'Landvermesser', Kafka was foregrounding the idea of mismeasurement, of misjudgment. So far as his challenged identity is concerned, K. is no 'land-surveyer', but figuratively speaking he is, for he is given to misjudgment (not a very desirable trait in a surveyor), of doing what he knows to be wrong, and particularly of going too far in his obsession with self-justification, which at a given point shades over into self-righteousness and thence into pride (in German, *Vermessenheit*, for which K.'s *Landvermesserarbeit* stands). How fine, but crucial, is the line between judgment and misjudgment, between being right and being self-righteous, between self-worth and self-importance.

The reason why Kafka's novels, unlike the average Gothic novel, have neither hero nor villain in the normal sense, is, of course, that there are no valid criteria by which to identify them as such. The fact that Josef K. and K. are ostensibly heroic in persistence, but, judging by results, wrong in persisting, subverts the notion of heroism. Josef K., who persists too long in proudly proclaiming his innocence, and in the end judges himself unworthy of living, seems, on the surface, to be innocent of any specific 'transgression' in the Gothic sense, but the fact that the idea of transgression is beset with problems complicates the issue. What is a 'transgression' in the early twentieth century, when more or less hermetic references to medieval Christianity echo away into a void? A matter of perspective, of judgment without a yardstick. The very word distances the concept from modern reality. Basically it

---

[23]   G. R. Thompson, in *The Gothic Imagination: Essays in Dark Romanticism* , ed. G. R. Thompson (Pullman, WA: Washington State University Press, 1974), 6.

[24]   Botting, 6.

means going too far in crossing some forbidden liminality or boundary, but the paraphrase lacks the appeal, the transgressive edge, of the term that is now so widely used in the context of Gothic. However, when discussing the novel as such (ch. 7), we will see that, beneath the surface, it is precisely in the Gothic sense that Josef K. is guilty. The Priest's argument that it is the guilty who go around proclaiming their innocence is as astute as it is fatuous: quite apart from the fact that there are no characters in the novel who are not projections of himself (the Priest represents K.'s moral self), Josef K. is the only person who is competent to assess his own innocence or guilt, although readers find themselves challenged by Kafka's exegesis, which is provocatively inconclusive, to arrive at their own verdict, and readers of *Das Schloß* too must by the same token judge for themselves whether K.'s persistence is morally great or merely foolish. In the text, of course, it is described as neither, for the basis for making a clear moral judgment is lacking.

The points made in a recent survey of Gothic are therefore readily applicable to all three of Kafka's novels:

> Gothic engages us by showing us a world in which evil is stronger than good, and disorder more likely than order. Homes and other places of former security are forbidding, unsafe or deserted; once revered figures of authority [...] are sinister and despotic; motives are malign and devious; even children are fiendish and malicious.[25]

These are fundamental points. Karl Rossmann is forbidden his childhood home and its symbolical replications, Josef K. is arrested in the once unchallenged privacy of his rooms at Frau Grubach's *Pension* (which just happens to mean 'prison cell', so that his arrest was inherent in his way of life),[26] and K., like Karl Rossmann before him, is challenged in and expelled from one domicile after another. The Priest in *Der Proceß* serves the Court as the typical Confessor of Gothic serves the Inquisition; indeed, he turns out to be the Prison Chaplain, the church being, as it was throughout the Inquisition, which is thereby invoked, in cahoots with the court. It is in what would once have been the sanctuary of the Cathedral that Josef K. meets his third and final challenge, and Georg Bendemann, Gregor Samsa and the Burrower are others who meet their greatest challenge precisely where they might have fancied themselves in least danger of having to face a challenge of any sort, let alone a fatal one. On the verbal level it is *Der Bau* that makes my point most clearly, for the 'Burgplatz' at the centre of the burrow has the connotation of being a citadel or place of womb-like security *(Burg ↔ Geborgenheit)*, and yet this counts for nothing, for what is contained or hidden *(geborgen)* deep within this *Satansburg*, like death within life, is

---

25 F. S. Frank, *Guide to the Gothic: An Annotated Bibliography of Criticism* (Metuchen, N.J., & London: The Scarecrow Press, 1984), xii.

26 She is more than the commonsensical figure she seems, for her name points to Czech *hrobař* (gravedigger) and *chrobák* (dung-beetle), these serving to suggest that she too is a projection of Josef K.

the fear that undermines and destroys any sense of security. The Castle authorities, leaving aside for the moment their purely fictional nature, appear to be a self-serving power for evil, although even on this there is no absolute certainty, for if all were not relation in the post-Nietzschean moral sphere, the novel would not exist in its present form. Indeed, if *Das Schloß* shows anything, it is that moral valuations and the judgments to which they lead are relative and therefore unsafe. It often seems as though the reader can only make an unambiguous judgment in the foreknowledge that it will necessarily be unfounded and simplistic. In brief, Kafka goes beyond transgression in the Gothic sense to a concern with the genealogy and meaning of moral values as such, the undermining of moral preconceptions being one aspect of the loss of control faced by protagonist and reader alike.

3.4. Loss of Control

If the Gothic novel deals with 'control [...] and with the uncontrollable: lust, greed, fear, death',[27] all of which dominate Kafka's work, with death, which preoccupied and terrified him as the invisible but ever-present factor in the equation, what is quintessentially Gothic is the loss of control that is the product of the weakness at the heart of human nature, and in that sense of the malignity of human fate. One recent overview of Gothic writing has seen it as evincing a 'new metaphysical paradigm, where belief in providence persists, but not faith in its benevolence'.[28] With Kafka, as in Gothic, the reader is faced with a vision of life as nightmare, for Gothic tales gave literary expression to the metaphysical anguish and anxiety which, like so much in the Gothic world of the Romantic period, were re-experienced a century later.

Kafka too depicts a world out of control. No matter whether the mask it wears is paternal, patriarchal, ecclesiastical, or whatever, the apparent abuse of power facing Kafka's protagonists serves to bring home to them their total inability to control their destinies. From the outset they are disempowered. They may seem to live in a world too well controlled, but appearance, as so often, misleads; in reality their troubled inner world is the product of their own lack of self-control. Properly seen, the world of the K.-novels, too, is 'dark, disordered, threatening and fallen',[29] a world in which, following the Gothic logic of disaster, things go from bad to worse. Slipping from a safe and orderly universe into a looking-glass, uncertain one beyond the simplifications, consolations and falsifications of reason and rational discourse is the most basic Gothic experience, and if there is any single Gothic emotion, it is the

---

27 Lucien Jenkins, in the Introduction to P. Teuthold [sic!], *The Necromancer* (London: Skoob Books, 1989), iii.
28 Miles, *Gothic Writing 1750-1820*, 3.
29 Frank, *Guide to the Gothic [I]*, xi.

apprehension that is thereby engendered. All this applies to Kafka's novels and tales, which in this respect differ from most earlier Gothic mainly in that the sudden loss of control, the shift from security to vulnerability that triggers a Gothic-style metamorphosis, is, typically, their starting-point. Thus Karl Rossmann's life is totally changed by his moment of weakness, compare the moral of *Ein Landarzt:* 'Mistake the sounding of the night-bell just once, and it can never be made good'. In general terms, Kafka means that a single mistake is enough to destroy a life, but his metaphor, which recalls *Die Nachtwachen des Bonaventura* (1804), carries the more specific meaning that mistaking night for day, dream for reality, can prove fatal.

In his work, as in Gothic, all pre-existing or perceived certainties are undermined, and there is, as there already was in *The Monk*, a pattern of false leads and real and apparent contradictions. From some leads the protagonist draws the wrong conclusions; from others he fails to draw any conclusion, and when he is offered what might be supposed to be the right conclusion, as K. is by Bürgel, he also fails to draw it, although I hasten to add that there is in reality no reason to think that there is a right conclusion, or that, if there were, K. would be capable of drawing it; he is simply at his most human and vulnerable when exhaustion prevents him from hearing Bürgel's message. The only certainty is therefore that there is a myriad of false conclusions (in German, *Fangschlüsse*) waiting to be drawn, and the same applies to *Das Schloß* as a whole. At issue here is our inability to understand not so much the outside world, which to the romantic mind is but a projection, a figment (*pace* Schopenhauer) of will and imagination, as ourselves. Kafka seems to enable readers by showing them the conflicting motivating impulses of which Josef K. himself remains unaware. Being, necessarily, governed by one dominant emotion, impulse or thought at a time, Josef K. cannot see himself as the reader is able to see him, and since we are in a similar position when it comes to viewing ourselves, and there is no conscious central controller of his and our manifold impulses and the selves they seem to spawn, self becomes a fluid concept and identity problematical.

It is, however, not only imagined certainties that slip out of control as they are transformed into sites of danger; so too do places hitherto considered secure, for the challenge inherent in Gothic operates on both inner (figurative) and outer (spatial) levels. Proof of this is *Der Bau*,[30] where the creative burrower finds his womb-like citadel of security transformed into a Gothic prison-vault-cum-tomb, for in the German language the idea of the grave (*Grab*) is contained in that of digging (*graben*); there could hardly be a better example of how *das Heimliche* (the familiar) is transformed or perverted into *das Unheimliche* (the uncanny). Kafka shows the individual's long-cherished positive ideals being destroyed one after another as he is

---

30 The reader is referred to Kafka's 'Der Riesenmaulwurf' (in *Beschreibung eines Kampfes*) and also to Richard Dehmel's 'Märchen vom Maulwurf' of 1896.

driven into an inner world of his own creation, until in the end, back to the wall, all that remains is the defensive ideal of trying to protect this inner world against his worst enemy, himself, in the form of the death that he carries within him like a malign second self. Both the bewildering suddenness of change - Karl Rossmann's seduction and his receipt of Onkel Jakob's missive; Josef K.'s arrest; K.'s reception in the village - and the slow encroachment of the irrational upon the rational, especially in the K.-novels, are notably prefigured in Gothic, and these changes in his environment signal a change or metamorphosis in the protagonist himself.

Metamorphosis, in the literal sense a feature of fairytale rather than of Gothic, is, with Kafka, more often figurative or psychological than literal. Karl Rossmann, Josef K., the Man-from-the-Country, K., Amalia's father, the Country Doctor and others are changed out of all recognition by what happens to them at a fateful moment as a result of misjudging a situation or misreading a challenge. Most literal and visible of the many metamorphoses in Kafka's work is that of Gregor Samsa in *Die Verwandlung* (see 9.2). In historical terms Kafka's bug is merely one of the fearful prodigies issuing from the Gothic imagination. What makes it both unique and other than Gothic is its multivalency and the self-loathing it represents.

The uncanny, through which Kafka is linked with the German early Gothic master E. T. A. Hoffmann in a way that goes to the heart of both men's work in that 'What is experienced as the uncanny is an objectification of the subject's anxieties, read into shapes external to himself',[31] is an important agent of the loss of control. Hoffmann believed in demons that work in and through the mind and in the mind's ultimate ability to withstand them; Kafka shared the former belief but lacked the latter. In Hoffmann's *Der Sandman* of 1816/17, Freud's paradigm of the uncanny in literature, the experience in question derives from the taking literally of a metaphor (in this case that of the 'sandman'), the technique that is at the very heart of Kafka's work, as it is also at the heart of fairytale. In Kafka, as in Hoffmann, it is the premise or half-suppressed opening metaphor that is weird or supernatural, not the story as such, which is normally but a consequential elaboration of the opening. Granted, for instance, the weird opening of *Die Verwandlung*, the development of that situation could not be more matter-of-fact. It is the grounding of their fantasies in reality, or rather in what looks like or passes for reality, that makes the work of Hoffmann and Kafka at once so compelling and so disconcerting, in other words, so uncanny, for it is the essence of the uncanny that it verges on the homely or cosy *(das Heimliche* for an Austrian writer like Kafka; in standard German the word would be *das Heimelige*, which lacks the direct resonance with *das Unheimliche)*, but veers away from it in a disconcerting, scary way. Hoffmann, like Goya, reveals what is normally hidden, and may be better left so, and at the same time transforms the familiar into the alien and

---

[31] Jackson, *Fantasy,* 66f.

therefore alarming. In Kafka's work we see both this and its opposite. In *Die Verwandlung*, for instance, he makes the alien overwhelmingly familiar.

A further form of uncanniness is also relevant: the sense of empty space which according to Heidegger is produced by the loss of faith in divine images (cf. the 'empty crucifixes' of the great pulpit and the 'empty niche' of the small pulpit in the Cathedral in *Der Proceß*, but also the god-forsaken empty space of Titorelli's heathscapes, and *Das Schloß* as a whole; it is that same empty space that the would-be surveyor K. surveys). In the first chapter of *Der Verschollene*, the crucifix in Johanna Brummer's cell-like bedroom, and the Madonna on the wall of the Stoker's no less cell-like cabin, are, in seeming empty of any transcendental meaning, more like pin-ups than icons, and something similar could be said of the empty Cathedral in *Der Proceß*, which Josef K. approaches as a work of art and leaves as an adjunct of the Court. Of the numinous as such there is everywhere a chilling absence. Given the way in which the uncanny challenges the moral order, it is true to say that the process begun by the early Gothics is finally complete in Kafka. I mean the separation of action and morality and therefore the putting into question of the nature of right and wrong. In the works of Kafka the uncanny stands, as Siegbert Prawer has written, naked and as it were 'unassimilated into any recognizable transcendent or ethical scheme'.[32] It is this that makes him the great master of the uncanny in twentieth-century literature and at the same time, properly defined, the greatest master of the Gothic form.

3.5. The Search for Self

In an international perspective Kafka can be seen as a successor to the cerebral Gothic of Charles Brockden Brown and the little-known Richard Henry Dana, Snr. There are curious parallels between Brockden Brown and Kafka, both of whom, racked by the conflict between their 'legal' careers and their literary enterprises, disavowed their work before dying of tuberculosis at much the same age. Brockden Brown complained that the 'rubbish of the law' left him listless and melancholy, which was also the gist of Kafka's complaint as a law student. Brockden Brown ceased to be a creative writer when he married; Kafka, fearing this might happen to him, could never bring himself to marry. Both drew their inspiration from their own company. Brockden Brown, going further than Kafka in this, wrote his four main novels at the same time. Both produced haunted, dreamlike, projective, mythopoeic fiction, 'explorations in the borderlands of consciousness',[33] although the fact is misleading,

---

32 Siegbert Prawer, *The 'Uncanny' in Literature* (London: Westfield College, 1965), 17, 21.
33 Ernest Marchand, in the Introduction to his edition of Charles Brockden Brown, *Ormond* (New York: Hafner, 1962), xxi.

for Brown, unlike Kafka, was at bottom a Godwinian novelist of ideas. Like Brockden Brown's *Edgar Huntly*, Kafka's novels are as much dreamed as written. Mervyn, in *Edgar Huntly*, a lonely, guilty individual à la Kafka, is, like Karl Rossmann, a 'country boy'[34] who leaves home to seek his fortune. In *Wieland*, in which the names of Carwin and Clara seem, no doubt fortuitously, to anticipate those of Karl and Klara in *Der Verschollene,* Brown confronts his characters with the problem of drawing reliable inferences from unreliable sense data. Brown's *Wieland* and *Edgar Huntly* both explore the dark side of the human psyche through symbols of enclosure,[35] as Kafka was to do in *Der Proceß* and *Der Bau.*

Kafka's work is, however, even closer to that of Dana, who, like him, 'explored the darkness within the Gothic castle of the mind'; Paul Felton, the hyper-sensitive main character of *Paul Felton* [36] is a prisoner of the 'Castle of self'[37] and comes to be a man possessed. At least two of Kafka's personae (the word is used in the double sense of dramatis personae and mask), K. and the burrower of *Der Bau* are prisoners of that same Castle. The horror of self-encounter, most memorably treated in Hoffmann's *Die Elixiere des Teufels*, is one of the central themes of American Gothic (Brown, Dana, Poe), and is ubiquitous in Kafka, where it ranges from the protagonist's encounter (inspired by Hoffmann via Dostoevsky) with his double in *Beschreibung eines Kampfs*, to the takeover of the persona by the Gothic or lower self (shadow) in *Die Verwandlung*. In the two K.-novels it is the lower self that is challenged, and, in *Der Proceß*, condemned, as a result of encounters with the higher self, the significance of which is, however, negative and its function destructive. Whereas Dostoevsky presented figures who, like Gregor Samsa, no longer 'coincide with their "ideal" selves',[38] Kafka, in his novels, depicts fragmented personalities: the subsidiary figures in the novels are not the protagonist's alternative selves, just aspects of his personality, ideas in his mind (his pride, feeling of guilt, distractibility), and so on. They are not his 'doubles' as such; the parallel is with fairytale, not with Gothic.

Kafka's writings are conditioned by the breakdown of order and therefore of certainty and security, and with it the loss of stable identity, that ultimately derives from that archetypal Gothic event, 'the mythic expulsion of man from Eden',[39] for the Gothic tradition, we are told, 'replays with almost infinite variations the myths both of the temptation and fall in Eden and of the perilous experience of the post-lapsarian

---

34   Karl is a country-boy in the Jewish sense of an ignoramus.
35   See *American Writers before 1800*, ed. J. A. Levernier & D. R. Wilmes (Westport, CT, & London: Greenwood Press, 1983), 217.
36   See Richard Henry Dana, *Poems and Prose Writings,* 2 vols (New York: Baker & Scribner, 1850), I, 270-374.
37   F. S. Frank, in *Horror Literature: A Reader's Guide*, 21.
38   Jackson, *Fantasy,* 135.
39   See *The Gothic Imagination*, ed. G. R. Thompson, 3, 2, 5f (order of quotation).

wilderness.'[40] That wilderness, marked by a sense of emptiness and non-identity, is the setting of all three of Kafka's novels. From the moment of his half-innocent transgression Karl Rossmann no longer has any reassuring sense of self; he no longer knows who and what he is, and in the end, when he adopts one of the Devil's appellations, is forced to adopt the identity of the other that has usurped him. He faces a typically Gothic challenge when the 'doom of exile' is pronounced upon him. His expulsion from his childhood Eden, as it seems in retrospect, is like a second birth, an idea that Kafka carefully plants before the reader at the beginning of the second chapter, and to which he also alludes in the guise of Karl's 'Rauferei' (romp) with Klara, the most important, untranslatable aspect of which is the underlying metaphor ('geworfen', thrown, also means born, a meaning which in English is restricted to domestic animals), that has, in Kafka's usual way, been taken literally. This second birth, like the first, is a birth into otherness and death. To the extent that Karl is seeking to regain his former innocence and the identity and security that went with it, *Der Verschollene* can be defined as a quest-romance. Karl seeks to regain his lost paradise, but finds only false paradises; he can never regain the apparently absolute innocence he once enjoyed, but which never really existed since he was, if guilty of original sin, born guilty. Take away the idea of original sin, and Karl is more or less innocent, but - and this is the whole point - not absolutely innocent. By Kafka's strict logic, he who is not absolutely innocent is by definition guilty. He has no time for the morality of evasion.

The supreme embodiment and exemplification of the 'demonic quest-romance, in which a lonely, self-divided hero embarks on insane pursuit of the Absolute' (Thompson) is not *Der Verschollene*, but the Parable of the Doorkeeper in *Der Proceß*, and the text to which it most clearly applies, which is, paradoxically, *Das Schloß*, an almost endless elaboration of the Parable. The lonely, foolish Philistine who seeks that in which he does not believe because, in the theological terms that have lost any validity they once had, he lacks the grace of faith, is, it may be argued, palpably involved in an insane pursuit of the Absolute. This much seems to be indicated by the 'everlasting radiance' emanating from the doorway to the Law, although this arguably bears more resemblance to the maw of Hell as depicted by Alfred Kubin than to any more positive image from Hebrew myth. The man, a country bumpkin or (in folklore terms) numskull and (in Biblical terms) a Philistine, may, of course, be mistaken, in that what he glimpses before his death may be no more than the shadowy semblance of the once-divine, a kind of ghost-image or ghostly afterglow, and therefore ultimately no more than a reflection of his own lack of faith, for Kafka at this point echoes Plato's 'Simile of the Cave', which turns on the

---

40 Stephen C. Behrendt, in his Introduction to Shelley's *Zastrozzi and St Irvyne* (Oxford & New York: Oxford University Press, 1986), xiv.

difference between truth, belief and illusion. He is, axiomatically, mistaken in thinking that the door will open for him: it is already standing wide open, so all it can do is close. Which it does. The one certainty as regards the meaning of the parable is that the man-from-the-country's attitude of idle curiosity is of itself sufficient reason for the failure of his quest, which is no more than a pale shadow of the demonic quest of Gothic and its models in medieval romance. There is not even any firm reason to suppose that the object of his quest exists in any objective sense: the door in question is his door, and for him it proves to be not a door to the Law, in which he does not believe, but merely a final milestone on the way to death, a threshold he has no need to cross. He lacks the 'belief in a personal god', of which the Law is an analogue.

Otherwise it is K.'s quest for certainty about his appointment as land-surveyor that best illustrates the Gothic quest. K., like his earlier incarnation, Josef K., personifies the 'tormented condition' of which G. R. Thompson has written.[41] He seeks his own reason for being, and through it being as such, but is surrounded by nothingness, which closes in on him remorselessly, turning him into the Accursed Wanderer of fantastic convention, unable to reach his destination. The 'Absolute', object of the Gothic demonic quest, does not exist in the world of Kafka's protagonists save as an unattainable ideal, and even if it did, it would be something to which human beings have no right, not because it would be identical with the divine, but because there is no such thing as an intrinsic right in such a world. Gothic became the literary embodiment of absolute uncertainty, absolute loss of control, absolute loss of a right to anything, absolute lack of security, absolute lack of resolution even as regards one's own self-image and identity. This uncertainty, and the existential anguish it engenders, is more basic than the idea of transgression because, as we have seen, there can be no certainty that what is in question actually is a 'transgression', whereas the anguish is all too certain.

It is therefore hardly surprising that, of the ten constituent elements of the high Gothic novel isolated in a different context by Frederick S. Frank,[42] most feature in these three novels, including claustrophobically confined space, the pursuit theme, the suspension of rationality and (within the limits discussed above) morality, the presence of spectral or demonic 'machinery', the predominance of 'evil' and of psychopathic emotion in the sense of extreme apprehension, together with 'genealogical complications' in the shape of paternal or avuncular villainy. More important, Frank's basic definition of 'the most effective Gothic novel in any period' as 'a fantasy of the multiple self in which various hypothetical personalities or repressed and undesired identities are projected into an architectural dream collage where anything might happen and normally does' is immediately and exactly applicable to

---

[41] In *The Gothic Imagination*, ed. G. R. Thompson, 5f.
[42] See *Horror Literature: A Reader's Guide*, ed. N. Barron, 8f.

Kafka's novels, the iconography of which is as Gothic as their geography; indeed, the definition fits them better than it fits any early Gothic novels. There may be in Kafka's novels, as opposed to some of the tales, none of the physical horrors of, say, *The Monk* or *The Necromancer*, for the horrors of Gothic have been removed from the physical to the metaphysical and psychological spheres, but so far as the tales are concerned, the idea of someone drowning himself at his father's command, or having the wording of the commandment against which he has supposedly transgressed cut deeper and deeper into his flesh by a machine manned by a torture-operative who, like the hangman of the Inquisition before him, preens himself on his art, is Gothic enough by any standard. Both events have, moreover, precedents in the early Gothic novel in the shape of Maturin's *Melmoth* and St-Cyr's *Pauliska*. The presence of these horrors notwithstanding, what is so notably absent in either case is any sensationalism of treatment. Kafka's treatment is always chillingly matter-of-fact. This is what makes *Der Proceß* and *Das Schloß* into *Schauerromane* in the most literal sense. Whether that is also a Gothic sense, is considered in Chapter 10.

4. NOVEL AND DREAM

4.1. Text and Subtext

No matter how Gothic his work may seem in terms of its surface content, Kafka is at the same time a high modernist who renewed the romantic novel by inventing a new form of symbolical novel incorporating autobiography and fairytale; indeed, his novels, in which the various characters are aspects of a single being, as Jung believed the characters of fairytale to be, are strictly speaking romances. As such they join all those other instances that go to prove that the best novels are more than and other than novels. His mode of narration, which reflects the basic contradiction between persona and shadow already noted, is marked by a tension between (i) simplicity and complexity, (ii) surface meaning and sub-surface meaning, (iii) modes of narration proper to the fairytale (which has a crystal-clear narrative technique, but a fantastic or mysterious content) and the novel, and (iv) different kinds of logic. On the level of words and phrases what counts is the logic of verbal association, this being the engine that drives the text, but within the narrative as a whole there is a contrary process in operation, so that there is also a logical development from episode to episode. As in the fairytale, then, there is a tension between transparency and non-transparency, lucidity and inexplicability. Above all there is a tension between text and subtext.

Notwithstanding the deadly seriousness of his whole literary endeavour, Kafka retains, as narrator, an ironic, often shyly and slyly humorous distance from his work. He, unlike his reader, is always in total control of his narrative and its linguistic registers. Very few other writers have paid so much attention to the secondary and tertiary meanings of words and therefore been able to keep so many fictions going simultaneously. To do justice to his work in translation is absolutely impossible, to do justice to it in critical terms well-nigh impossible, for we are few of us such skilled jugglers with words, and it is a strange fact that these totally open texts often have the effect of causing critics to close their minds to every meaning except one, that one, because single, inevitably wrong. A partial truth is no truth at all.

That every Kafka text has a subtext is indisputable, but while each of his texts says precisely what it means, it does not follow that it means what it seems to say, or that it means only what it says or seems to say. On the contrary, it means not only what he consciously and subconsciously intended it to say, but also what he intended it to conceal, for, like the dreams and fairytales they so closely resemble, his texts have both a manifest (or surface) and a latent (or masked) meaning, these reflecting his dual intention at any given time of simultaneously revealing and concealing his meaning. Text and dream alike are the tip of an iceberg. As in a dream, the inner, intensely personal meaning of his text is displaced and thereby concealed beneath the surface of the text, which masks its 'unsayable' deeper meaning(s) by offering the reader a beguilingly simple (and of course misleading) surface reading that steers clear of the issues which Kafka, for all his devastating honesty, does not wish to be seen washing in public. Since the issues he conceals in the subtext are precisely those censored in dreams at the behest of the moral censor or super-ego (that internal monitor, represented in Freud's *Introductory Lectures* of 1916-17, as a 'door-keeper' who vets unconscious thoughts before deciding whether to let them through to consciousness), it follows that most of the meaning of a Kafka text is to be found beneath the surface, where ambiguity and displacement of emphasis hide it from view. The subversion of the apparent meaning, achieved by a masterly use of ambiguity which takes full advantage of the unstable and contradictory nature of language as such, and more especially of the web of secondary meanings that his chosen words so often possess (the critic's job is to expose these, not pretend they are not there), is made necessary by the psychological imperative to hide his meaning. The real, underlying meanings of his work are conditioned by his psychic, psycho-linguistic and psycho-sexual compulsions, and thus by the power-relationship of domination by his father that obtained when it was written, although the element of sheer verbal play, the play and interplay of meanings, is also exceptionally strong. Verbal play should never be overlooked, but neither should it be taken at face value; when Kafka puns, as he frequently does, he does so in order to sustain secondary levels of meaning and thereby reinforce the maze of the text.

The novels can best be compared with the burrow of *Der Bau* with its maze of passages, many of them (including some of the many literary references) blind alleys which lead nowhere, being intended to mislead or to lead round in circles. They are thus 'ways out' only for the author/narrator, not for the inquisitive critic, whom Kafka enjoys baiting, and who is as surely trapped in the labyrinth of the text as the burrower is entrapped and prematurely inhumed in his burrow. The 'dangers of being duped by the deceits of narrative' that have been said[1] to be demonstrated by one of the '*Northanger* horrid novels', Regina Maria Roche's *Clermont,* were built into his narratives by Kafka, who goes further than Gothic in this respect too. If his works seem like puzzles, they are puzzles without a solution, for any 'solution' can only be achieved at the expense of the text, by limiting it to one meaning or by restating it in different terms. It is easy to mistake the text's subjective significance (to the reader/critic) for its objective meaning. Although, as with fairytale, the text is 'its own best explanation [,] its meaning [...] contained in the totality of [...] motifs connected

---

[1]   Botting, 72.

by the thread of the story',[2] one of the most significant ways in which Kafka's texts differ from the fairytale whose motifs they are given to borrowing lies in the multiplicity of meaning of so many of the individual words of which they are constructed.

These texts are in fact the clearest possible illustration of what Dilthey called the hermeneutic circle, that is, the idea that the meaning of the constituent parts of a text can only be understood if one has an intuitive prior sense of the meaning of the text as a whole, while the meaning of the whole can be known only if one has a prior knowledge of the meaning of its constituent parts. The need for a 'mutually qualifying interplay between our evolving sense of the whole and our retrospective understanding of its constituent parts'[3] is fundamental to Kafka criticism, in which the problem has always been how to reconcile the general and the particular, given the self-evident importance of the latter. No one has ever written more lucidly than Kafka, and yet he has been more misunderstood than perhaps any other writer. In the final analysis this is less because of the brilliant way in which he combines multiple layers of meaning in apparently simple, and, it might - wrongly - be thought, unambiguous words, than because his very manner succeeds in tempting critics into interpreting a text of their own construction. It is easy to generalize about Kafka, so long as one does not delude oneself that one is thereby explaining his meaning. When it comes to that, it is true to say that *der Teufel steckt im Detail* (it's the detail that causes all the problems, literally: the Devil is in the detail).

That the last two paragraphs have necessarily moved away from Gothic is a reflection of the fact that Kafka's work has a complexity and a metafictionality that go beyond anything in Gothic, so that the many Gothic or ostensibly Gothic motifs are deployed in texts which are finally non-Gothic. The same goes for fairytale motifs.

4.2. Gothic and Dream

Gothic is essentially a dream literature, its hallmark the realized nightmare. While there is no etymological link between *Märchen* and nightmare, there is a conceptual one, for 'Wishes and fantasies may come to life in the fairy tale, but fears and phobias also become full-blooded presences'.[4] Ludwig Laistner, writing in 1889, argued that fairytale motifs derive from dreams; the motifs he discussed in trying to prove his point were nightmare ones.[5] A tale like 'Der Räuberbräutigam' is clearly closer to nightmare, and to Gothic, than to dream.

---

2   Marie Louise von Franz, *Interpretation of Fairytales* (New York: Spring Publications, 1970), 1.
3   M. H. Abrams, *A Glossary of Literary Terms,* 7th edn (New York: Harcourt Brace, 1999), 128.
4   Maria Tatar, *The Hard Facts of the Grimms' Fairy Tales* (Princeton, NJ: Princeton University Press, 1987), xv.
5   See Marie Louise von Franz, 5.

The Inquisition, which features in many Gothic nightmares, was so concerned about the heresies expressed in dreams, that it sought to control them,[6] and the literary Gothic Revival was preceded and accompanied by a preoccupation with dreams in general and the nightmare in particular. J. Bond published *An Essay on the Incubus, or Nightmare* in 1753, and Adam Friedrich Wilhelm Saalfeld's *A Philosophical Discourse on the Nature of Dreams* (1764) came out, appropriately, in the same year as *The Castle of Otranto*, which was said to be based on 'the very imperfect recollection of a dream'. Saalfeld's work prepared the way for Fuseli's 'The Nightmare' (1781, parodied in 1794 in Richard Newton's 'A Night Mare'), which in turn opened up the way for further dreams in art, including Fuseli's own 'An Incubus Leaving Two Sleeping Girls' (*c.* 1793), in which the iconography of the dream is tinged with eroticism. Percy Shelley wrote a related horror tale, 'The Nightmare', subsequently lost, which he had wanted Fuseli to illustrate. The rather literary picture of the nightmare painted by R. Macnish in his *The Philosophy of Sleep* (1834) was clearly influenced by nightmare experiences as described in the Gothic novel with which he grew up, and to which he refers:

> If [...] we have been engaged in the perusal of such works as 'The Monk', 'The Mysteries of Udolpho', or 'Satan's Invisible World Discovered', and if an attack of night-mare should supervene, it will be exaggerated into sevenfold horror by the spectral phantoms with which our minds have been thereby filled.[7]

Elsewhere he refers to Hoffmann, De Quincey and Polydori (sic),[8] using the term 'daymare' to describe the waking nightmare that was to form the basis of Kafka's work.

Writing of the 'modern novel' in 1800, Sade argued that it was necessary to 'call hell to the rescue [...] and to find in the world of nightmare images adequate to 'the history of man in this Iron Age of ours'.[9] More than adequate nightmare images were subsequently found by Goya, who did indeed 'call hell to the rescue' when he produced his terrible *Black Paintings* at the end of the Gothic period proper, in the early 1820s. Fiedler, quoting Sade, commented that 'The key words are "nightmare" and "hell", revealing how consciously [...] some gothic writers turned to the night side of life, the irrational world of sleep, for themes and symbols appropriate to the terrors bred by the Age of Reason,'[10] and there is a further point, also admirably made by Fiedler:

---

6   See Caesar Careña, *Tractatus de Officio Sanctissimae Inquisitionis* (Cremona: Belpier, 1641).
7   Robert Macnish, *The Philosophy of Sleep*, 2nd edn (Glasgow: W. R. M'Phun, 1834), 137.
8   Macnish, 94, 95, 155.
9   I quote the paraphrase by Leslie A. Fiedler from his *Love and Death in the American Novel* (Normal, IL: Dalkey Archive, 1997), 136 as being more to my point than a literal translation.
10 Fiedler, 136. The concept of the 'night-side' of life entered the English language in 1848 with Catherine Crowe's *The Night-Side of Nature*, which was inspired by Gotthilf Heinrich von Schubert's *Ansichten von der Nachtseite der Naturwissenschaft* of 1808.

Implicit in the gothic novel from the beginning is a final way of redeeming it that is precisely opposite in its implications to the device of the explained supernatural, a way of proving not that its terror is less true than it seems but more true. There *is* a place in men's lives where pictures [...] bleed, ghosts gibber and shriek, maidens run forever through mysterious landscapes from nameless foes; that place is, of course, the world of dreams and [...] the repressed guilts and fears that motivate them. This world the dogmatic optimism and shallow psychology of the Age of Reason had denied; and yet this world it is the final, perhaps the essential, purpose of the gothic romance to assert. [11]

Fiedler rightly saw symbolic fiction, in which character, setting and incident are true 'not in their own right, but as they symbolize in outward terms an inward reality'[12] as coming to a climax in Kafka.

Such fiction originated in the period of literary High Gothic, which saw the appearance, in 1814, of Gotthilf Heinrich von Schubert's *Die Symbolik des Traumes*, in which it was argued that the dreamer is confronted by certain qualities or actions in the guise of persons and of ideas in the form of pictorial images; that dreams take metaphors literally, work by means of association of ideas, and tend to invert their meaning; and that in 'Halbschlummer' (Freud's 'hypnagogic state') the two different, alternative languages of waking and sleep are liable to intermingle. For good measure, there is much talk of the 'shadow-side of the self', thus anticipating one of Jung's most important ideas as well as a number of Freud's. Schubert regarded the symbolic language of dreams as superior in expressivity to the language of waking.[13] And then there was Arthur Schopenhauer's astutely provocative romantic question in 1818: 'We have dreams; may not our whole life be a dream? Or, more exactly: is there any sure way of distinguishing between dreams and reality, between phantasms and real objects?'[14] Schopenhauer (1788-1860), most genial and literary of philosophers, is the philosopher of Gothic[15] as Goya (1746-1828) is its illustrator. The two come together as background to *Das Schloß*. On a linguistic level, Kafka's starting-point for his third and final novel was Schopenhauer's remark about 'a man walking round a castle, looking in vain for an entrance',[16] which belongs together with one of Goya's *Black Paintings*, the 'Fantastic Vision' ('Al aquilarre') of *c.* 1820 that features a totally inaccessible Gothic edifice. Schopenhauer's suspicion that life itself may be a kind of dream was shared by one of Kafka's favourite writers, the Viennese playwright Franz Grillparzer, and, as *Through the Looking-Glass* shows, by Lewis Carroll (see 5.5.2).

The alternative, virtual reality of the dream is as basic to Gothic as it is to Kafka's work. Fiedler's statement that 'The flight of the gothic heroine into a dark region of

---

[11]   Fiedler, 140.
[12]   Fiedler, 141.
[13]   See Blackall, 148ff. That is why Hoffmann regarded artistic activity as a superior form of dream.
[14]   Schopenhauer, *The World as Will and Idea*, tr. R. B. Haldane & J. Kemp (London: Kegan Paul, Trench, Trübner & Co., n.d.), I, 20.
[15]   And, of course, of Kafka (see T. J. Reed, 'Kafka und Schopenhauer. Philosophisches Denken und dichterisches Bild,' *Euphorion*, 1965, 160-72).
[16]   *Arthur Schopenhauer's sämmtliche Werke in sechs Bänden*, ed. Eduard Grisebach (Leipzig: Reclam, n.d.), I, 150.

make-believe [...] along the shadowy corridors of the haunted castle, which is to say, through a world of ancestral and infantile fears projected in dreams'[17] puts the reader in mind of *Der Proceß* and *Das Schloß,* but also of *Der Verschollene,* in which Karl Rossmann plays the part of Gothic heroine against a theatrical backdrop and later, as liftboy, plays the gallant in a no less theatrical way ('Aufzug', lift, also means act [of a play]). The dreamlike nature of Kafka's work, especially the novels, is fundamental both in itself and as a link with Gothic and fairytale. All three symbolical forms use the same universal symbolism.

4.3. Kafka, Dream and Nightmare

Even in early Gothic the emphasis came increasingly to be on psychological forces:

> [In the early nineteenth century,] psychological rather than supernatural forces became the prime movers in worlds where individuals could be sure neither of others nor of themselves [...] Gothic subjects were alienated, divided from themselves [...] Nature, wild and untameable, was as much within as without.[18]

There is not a page in Kafka's novels that does not illustrate the primal Gothic conflict, which is 'internal, between one's own selves'.[19] Gothic, re-emerging (for much of it had been present in the sixteenth century, notably in Webster) from the shadows of the mind as the darker side of Romanticism, became part of an 'internalized world of guilt, anxiety [and] despair', its ultimate concern 'the uncertain bounds of imaginative freedom and human knowledge'.[20] Kafka is not exactly a Romantic, but his work is in the tradition of what in German is called *schwarze Romantik* (Gothic Romanticism), and marks the final phase of the internalization of Gothic forms that began back in the Romantic period. His world being akin to the inner worlds of Hoffmann, Maturin, Brockden Brown, Dana and Poe, it is true to say that 'The focus [in Kafka] on disturbed psychological states, on social alienation and inner turmoil, relates to the horrors glimpsed by [the Gothic] Romantics'.[21] The most important aspect of the Gothic inner world is the dream.

In his classic study of *The Fantastic,*[22] Todorov observed that '[Kafka's] entire world obeys an oneiric logic, if not indeed a nightmare one'. Kafka's novels are not 'about' a dream or dreams in the literal sense, although Karl Rossmann comes to Pollunder's country house 'as in a dream', the alternative ending of *Der Proceß* was entitled 'Ein Traum', and *Das Schloß* includes a notable account of a dream. All three

---

17 Fiedler, 128.
18 Botting, 12.
19 Scarborough, 76.
20 Botting, 10.
21 Botting, 160.
22 Tzvetan Todorov, *The Fantastic* (Ithaca, N.Y.: Cornell University Press, 1975), 173.

novels are, however, literary dreams, the dream in question being, like those in so many nineteenth-century novels, a dream of authority[23] reflecting and challenging the position of the Victorian *pater familias*, the type of which Kafka *père* was a bizarre Bohemian variant. The dreamer is, of course, Kafka himself, there being, in this respect, a parallel with Bunyan, whose *Pilgrim's Progress*, 'delivered under the Similitude of a Dream', begins 'As I walked through the wilderness of this world, I lighted on a certain place [...] and I laid me down in that place to sleep: and as I slept, I dreamed a dream.' One would not expect Kafka, writing well over two hundred years later, to be as plain. Nor is he.

The dream of authority, with Kafka, is a dream about paternal-patriarchal control and the experience of losing control over self when faced with such a challenge. When Josef K. goes to call on the artist Titorelli, he sees, in a tinsmith's workshop, a 'great sheet of tin' hanging on the wall that is reminiscent of the 'sheet of tin' in Freud's description of 'The dream of a young man inhibited by his father-complex',[24] a fact which tends to confirm that Kafka knew *The Interpretation of Dreams.*[25] Habitually writing in a condition akin to dream, he was invariably writing about himself and, metafictionally, about his writing. Like dreams in the nineteenth-century Gothic novel, his novels are 'sites of a struggle to gain authority over the self through language'.[26] It was because they ultimately failed to generate any such authority, leaving their author as uncertain as ever, afraid that he had caught himself in a snare of his own making, that Kafka, ever his own severest critic, professed to see them as failures.

In *Der Proceß* and *Das Schloß*, K. - like Rossmann before him - loses control of himself, and is thereby reduced to insignificance: 'you are nothing', he is told in a throwaway remark that reveals one of the themes of *Der Proceß*, and indeed of *Das Schloß*, to be the same as that of *Die Nachtwachen des Bonaventura* (1804): the experience of nothingness, of what the French Existentialists used to call *le néant*. Like Young's *Night Thoughts*, which was similarly divided into Nights, *Die Nachtwachen des Bonaventura* is based on the very hours for which Kafka lived and died, the night-hours of creation. The idea of the poet as night-watchman or measurer of time is peculiarly applicable to Kafka, who, like Hoffmann and Maturin, wrote mostly at night, his dreamlike inner life transposed in a stream of semi-consciousness into never-ending paragraphs in which time is visibly transformed into space, the domain of the poetic land-surveyor.

---

23 See Ronald R. Thomas, *Dreams of Authority: Freud and the Fictions of the Unconscious* (Ithaca & London: Cornell University Press, 1990), 1.
24 *The Interpretation of Dreams,* 365.
25 Calvin S. Hall and Richard E. Lind, *Dreams, Life and Literature* (Chapel Hill: The University of North Carolina Press, 1970), 9. Hall and Lind refer to *The Interpretation of Dreams* as 'a work with which Kafka was familiar'.
26 Cf. Hall and Lind, 80.

The protagonist in each of Kafka's novels is, in Henry James's terminology, his 'centre of consciousness'. The other figures are projections of this focus character, their symbolical identity with him or with one another (when they happen to symbolize the same thing) mostly represented, as in dreams, by means of contiguity. These figures merge, overlap and give way to new ones, but all are projections of the 'dreamer'-protagonist, for dreams are wholly egoistical, dramas in which all the actors are parts of the dreamer.[27] The dreamer in question is Franz Kafka, and, through him, Josef K. *Der Proceß*, that 'Pilgrim's Progress of the sub-conscious',[28] is the account of a dreamlike process going on in Kafka's mind and projected by him into Josef K.'s mind, and the same is true of *Das Schloß* and even of *Der Verschollene*, although this was written before Kafka's literary dream-method was fully established. As in *The Necromancer* and Shelley's dreamlike Gothic *Zastrozzi* (see 4.5 below), inner impulses are consistently dramatized as external figures; as in Ann Radcliffe's *The Romance of the Forest*, Kafka's narrative, in each of his novels, is a 'drama of the interior',[29] the interiority of the narrative subject becoming all-important as the outward trappings of Gothic are turned inward. The Inquisition becomes a symbol of the conscience; the Gothic Castle becomes 'one's own castle', the citadel-cum-prison-cell of the self, for Kafka is concerned, like the more cerebral of the early Gothic novelists, to explore the dark and often frightening interior regions in which we dwell. If, therefore, the Gothic novel involves a mode or code for the representation of fragmented subjectivity,[30] Kafka is the Gothic novelist *par excellence* in the sense that his three novels represent the deepest and most single-minded exploration yet of subjectivity and some of its murky recesses. In showing that subjectivity is the only certainty, his trilogy of self-exploration becomes more (and therefore by definition less) Gothic than Gothic. The way in which Gothic motifs are, in Kafka, transformed and displaced, often to the point where the 'Gothic' element is swallowed up by the post-Gothic narrrative, is part of the process of displacement underlying the creative process that makes it so dreamlike.

The characters within the dream-fiction are therefore real and unreal in much the same way as the characters in dreams and fairytales. What counts is not just the methodology and iconography of dreams, but their nature, for

> every dream represents the fulfilment in the imagination of some desire [...] that has [...] been repressed in the waking state [because it is] unacceptable to the subject's consciousness [...] This repressed desire can [...] be allowed to obtain imaginary gratification [in the dream] only when it

---

27   See *The Interpretation of Dreams*, 322, and J. A. Hadfield, *Dreams and Nightmares* (Harmondsworth: Pelican, 1954), 146.
28   Quoted from the blurb of the Penguin edition.
29   Miles, 142.
30   Eve Kosofsky Sedgwick, *The Coherence of Gothic Conventions* (New York: Arno Press, 1980), 11f.

is not recognizable by the subject, so that it appears in another form by becoming distorted, perverted and disguised.[31]

So dreamlike is *Der Verschollene* that this description applies to it in an exemplary way. The first chapter, like the first part of a dream, reveals the problem and recalls the cause that gave rise to it. The replications of the key event, involving Klara, Theresa and Brunelda, are therefore increasingly 'distorted, perverted and disguised' to the point where they are almost - but not quite - unrecognizable, the masking being necessary because Karl also enjoyed the experience more than he is willing to admit, hence all the references to the Devil, notorious for his licentiousness, with whom Karl eventually identifies.

If works such as *Das Urteil*, *Die Verwandlung*, *Der Proceß* and *Das Schloß*, among others, are in effect transcripts of linked day-dreams, and in that sense virtual dreams, they can be compared with a work described by its author as 'the legend of some hideous dream that can return no more', Thomas De Quincey's *Confessions of an English Opium-Eater*, which remains important not least for its thematic and formal affinities with the Gothic novel that forms one of the central reference points in De Quincey's work. If De Quincey's *Confessions*, like so much Gothic fiction, strives to 'speak the unspeakable language of the dream',[32] Kafka's work as a whole is the most consequential attempt ever made since De Quincey to describe the author's dreamlike inner world in order to define himself. There are, of course, major differences between the two writers, one of whom was writing under the influence of opium and the other merely in a regular state of exhaustion, and De Quincey also emphasized that his self-accusation did not amount to a confession of guilt; in this it differs from Kafka's self-accusations, all of them premised on the unshakeable conviction of his guilt. De Quincey claimed to be writing to help others; Kafka was writing to help himself.

Like the Gothic novel, Kafka's novels stand comparison not merely with the dream as such, but with the combination of dream and anxiety attack known as nightmare, a phenomenon common in Gothic fiction and one which occupies an important place in the mythology of the Gothic imagination.[33] In the course of the preceding discussion reference was made to Ernest Jones's standard work on nightmare, the American edition of which was entitled *Nightmare, Witches and Devils*. This title reflects Jones's concern with 'the part that Nightmare experiences have played in the production of certain false ideas', the ideas in question - incubus, vampire, werewolf, devil and witch - having much in common. The only one that is not directly relevant to Kafka's novels is the werewolf, and even that is not far away: one thinks of the victim of the torture-machine, who identifies with the wolf in *Little Red Riding Hood*

---

[31] Jones, 42.

[32] Thomas, 100.

[33] Thus Philip W. Martin, in *The Handbook to Gothic Literature*, ed. Marie Mulvey-Roberts, 164.

in saying 'Throw that whip away or I will eat you up', of the northern cannibal hordes (cf. the men-hyenas of folklore and the identification of the Devil with the hyena[34]) in *The Great Wall of China* with 'their gaping mouths, their jaws furnished with great pointed teeth, their half-shut eyes that already seem to be seeking out the victim that their jaws will rend and devour', and of the jackals (an animal that features in numerous folktales) in *Schakale und Araber.* Vampirism and cannibalism are related, and Kafka's 'cannibal' also corresponds (at one extreme of meaning) to the werewolf, so that, as we shall see in the following chapters, all these extraordinary figures of nightmare, or references to them, feature in the novels and related shorter works. This is appropriate, for not only is it 'generally recognized that the Nightmare has exercised a greater influence on waking phantasy than any other dream,'[35] but the nightmare is the expression of Kafka's deepest anxieties. I am thinking, particularly, of the anxiety associated with the 'repressed wish for a particular sexual experience'. In the dream such things are disguised, often heavily so, and with good reason, for 'The mere dimly realized possibility of becoming against his will overmastered by a form of desire that the whole strength of the rest of his mind is endeavouring to resist is often sufficient to induce in a given person a state of panic-stricken terror.'[36] This particular nightmare form of anxiety was clearly experienced by Kafka and displaced by him on to the naive protagonist of his first novel.

4.4. Kafka and the Dream-Work

If Janouch is to be believed, Kafka remarked to him that 'Dreams reveal the reality that the conscious mind is unable to conceive'. (J 30). Borne out by his work as it is, there is no reason to doubt this particular comment. Kafka distinguished between 'the human world' and the dream-world, calling himself 'a citizen of this other [dream]world', an appropriate term, given that the dream discloses consciousness of the 'other' or shadow. In his work the boundary between 'dream' and 'reality' is continually eroded: for him dreams are the 'tangible reality'[37] they were for Schopenhauer, hence his remark to Janouch, echoing Dostoevsky's 'What other people call fantastic, I hold to be the inmost essence of truth,'[38] that true reality is always unrealistic. He rejected materiality, which he equated with evil, defining it, with Schopenhauer, as 'das Böse in der geistigen Welt' ('the evil in a world essentially spiritual'). His work has such a strongly oneiric character because much of it was based on actual or virtual dreams and was produced under dreamlike conditions.

---

34   See Stith Thompson, *Motif-Index*, D313.4 & 5, G303.3.3.2.9.
35   Jones, 73.
36   Jones, 43.
37   *The World as Will and Idea*, I, § 5.
38   Quoted from Jackson, *Fantasy*, 135.

Like Maturin, he wrote mostly by night, when a darker self seized control of the pen[39] as he wrote in the state of exhaustion in which the mind, on the edge of sleep, is in the eidetic mode described by Mary Shelley in the Author's Introduction to the 1831 edition of *Frankenstein* ('I did not sleep, nor could I be said to think. My imagination [...] possessed and guided me, sifting the successive images that arose in my mind with a vividness far beyond the usual bound of reverie'), and dream logic and expression prevail. Mary Shelley described *Frankenstein* as 'a transcript of the grim terrors of my waking dream'. While oneiric states of mind are common in the Gothic novel[40] with its 'artificial hallucinations',[41] few, if any, novels before Kafka's had been so precisely dreamlike, so wholly the product of a process analogous to the 'dream-work' described by Freud in *The Interpretation of Dreams.* What makes this applicable to the present context is a paper published in 1909[42] by the Freudian Herbert Silberer which showed that in a state of fatigue and drowsiness - the state in which Kafka habitually wrote - the mind tends to slip into dream-mode, with a given thought being replaced by an 'auto-symbolic' image. Day-dreams, it has since been shown, work in a similar way. Kafka rightly called such virtual dreams 'Halbschlaffantasien' (dreamlike fantasies experienced on the threshold of sleep). They correspond to what Freud called 'hypnagogic hallucinations', the content of which is identical with dream-images and, often, with the iconography of fairytales.

The settings of Kafka's novels, like those of the typical Gothic romance, are remote from the realism and reality that are the stock-in-trade of the mainstream novel. Like dream-Gothic, they possess the verisimilitude, the mocking, deceptive appearance of 'reality' of the dream; they consist, that is, of *Gaukelbilder* (phantasms), figments of the imagination mixed with just enough of material actuality to sustain the misleading notion that this is their subject matter. The dream does the same: there too the ghosts of actuality flit across the surface of an overall fiction that obeys its own laws and logic because its aim is to put a gloss or spin on something that has happened in the external world. The plots of Gothic novels have been said to 'correspond suggestively to certain aspects of the dream process', uncanny dream experience in particular being often central to Gothic.[43] For all the residue of realism in their settings, the events that take place in *Der Verschollene* are as strangely unrealistic as they are realistically strange, and the same is even truer of *Der Proceß* and *Das Schloß*, the obsessive, seemingly inconsequential plots of which are a form of

---

[39] Julian Cowley, in his Introduction to Charles Maturin, *Fatal Revenge* (Far Thrupp: Alan Sutton, 1994). v.
[40] See Thomas, 71-81 ('Recovering Nightmares: Nineteenth-Century Gothic').
[41] Marshall Brown, 'A Philosophical View of the Gothic Novel', *Studies in Romanticism*, 26 (1987), 275.
[42] 'Bericht über eine Methode, gewisse symbolische Halluzinations-Erscheinungen hervorzurufen und zu betrachten', *Jahrbuch psychoanalytisch-psychopathologischer Forschungen*, 1 (1909), 344f, 503ff.
[43] Thomas, 6, 69.

phantasmagoria in the proper meaning of that term as a shifting series of phantasms or imaginary figures as seen in a dream or fevered (or drug-induced) condition or as called up by a febrile imagination. In effect they are a form of daymare or waking dream, experienced and recorded on the edge of sleep.

The uncanny, nightmarish effect of Kafka's work amounts to corroboration of Freud's thesis that uncanniness in fiction comes from unreal events being presented as real: 'The narration of events and visions from a night-world in the ordinary, accustomed prose of waking life produces exactly that sense of dissolving reason which makes reality a dream and the dream a reality, in essence the quality of uncanniness.'[44] This is the threshold not only of the uncanny, but also of the fantastic, for, as Dostoevsky said, 'The fantastic must be so close to the real that you are practically obliged to believe in it'.[45] Reading *Die Verwandlung*, it is virtually impossible not to believe in what has happened, so persuasive is the detail.

While Kafka's novels, unlike many Gothic novels, contain few accounts of dreams in the literal sense, as opposed to often over-determined narrations based on nocturnal day-dreams and dreamlike states of consciousness, they are, by common consent, uncommonly dreamlike. The hieroglyphic, pictorial language of his works being the 'primordial language' (Freud) or 'symbolic language' (Fromm) in which dreams are visualized, its central feature the regressive translation of thoughts into images, his creative method is tantamount to the 'dream-work' by means of which dreams are visualized and expressed:

> Kafka's people, the people of his stories [...] do not live; they imitate the living. They are human abstractions and abstractions of human qualities exactly as dream people are. We could never believe in Kafka's people if we did not take them as dream people and accept Kafka's world as a dream world.[46]

This is ironical, for in addition to being a dreamer, Kafka was a markedly visual person who detested abstractions; but however 'abstract' his work may ultimately be in the sense of having a model only in the hallucinatory virtual reality of the mind, the all-important expression is highly concrete, the narrative being visualized as a dream-like chain of images. Particularly important is the visualization and literal enactment of metaphors, which is also the basic mechanism of what Freud calls the 'dream-work', as well as being a feature both of *Pragerdeutsch* and of the language of the Hebrew Prophets as seen in the parables of the Old Testament which Kafka knew so well.[47] In his dream work, which is the product of 'dream-work' in the technical, Freudian sense, words and metaphors are given back their original concrete meanings in a technique that is best called counter-metaphor. Other forms of verbal

---

44 Selma Fraiberg, 'Kafka and the Dream', *Partisan Review*, 23 (1956), 54.
45 Quoted from Jackson, *Fantasy*, 27.
46 Fraiberg, 66.
47 He possessed Hermann Gunkel, *Das Märchen im alten Testament* (1921).

displacement (including displacement along a chain of associations, condensation, inversion, secondary revision, and so on) are relevant as some of the ways in which he disguises his meaning. The crux of the matter is that his work, long since recognized as 'the closest approximation to dreams that has ever been achieved in fiction',[48] needs finally to be approached as such.

Of the three novels it is *Der Proceß* that is most clearly a dreamlike process taking place within the protagonist's mind:

> An outstanding example of a work of art written in symbolic language is Kafka's *The Trial*. As in so many dreams, events are presented, each of which is in itself concrete and realistic; yet the whole is impossible and fantastic. The novel, in order to be understood, must be read as if we [were] listen[ing] to a dream - a long complicated dream in which external events happen in space and time, being representations of thoughts and feelings within the dreamer, in this case the novel's hero, K.[49]

Der Proceß can therefore be compared to *Die Elixiere des Teufels*, an 'early psychological novel or [...] dream sequence in which Hoffmann attempts to portray the hero's psychological state by assigning external forms to his inward experience'.[50] The same method had been more tentatively employed in *Der Verschollene*, and was to be used again, in its most developed form, in *Das Schloß*. In addition, certain key chapters and passages in all three novels are so over-determined, so densely and ambiguously symbolical, that they are more obviously dreamlike than others and in that sense can be regarded as dreams-within-a-dream. A case in point is the crucial last chapter of *Der Verschollene*, a dream in the classical Freudian sense of wish-fulfilment, in which all Karl Rossmann's problems appear to be miraculously solved after Kafka has spent the preceding chapters showing them to be insoluble. Many individual words in the novels are also overdetermined in the sense of being laden with ambiguity.

Similarly, while much of the symbolism of *Der Proceß* is recurrent to the point of obsession, this being added confirmation of the oneiric character of the whole process in question, the fifth and last chapters are so intensely and concentratedly dreamlike that they too are best regarded as dreams-within-a-dream. In Chapter 5 Josef K. experiences a typical punishment-dream in the Freudian sense as in his mind's eye he sees himself, in the dual guise of Franz and Willem, being punished for the way in which he has behaved since his supposed awakening at the beginning of the novel, and particularly for his libidinous behaviour vis-à-vis Frl B. and the washerwoman who also embodies a reference to the unlikely story of his innocence (*das kannst du der Wäscherin erzählen* means 'tell that to the marines'). It is for this that he is imagining himself being punished. All three figures involved in the static and

---

48   *TLS*, 14 August 1959.
49   Erich Fromm, *The Forgotten Language* (London: Victor Gollancz, 1952), 213.
50   Horst S. Daemmrich, '*The Devil's Elixirs*: Precursor of the Modern Psychological Novel', *Papers on Language and Literature*, 6 (1970), 374.

therefore doubly nightmarish sado-masochistic scene represent Josef K. himself. The man-with-the-lash's leather garb is the sign of his function: 'ledern' is a synonym for 'prügeln' (to beat). The ultimate punishment dream is that in which the dreamer dreams that he is being put to death, which is precisely what happens in the last chapter of *Der Proceß* (discussed in 7.2.3).

Some passages in *Das Schloß*, for instance the cottage bath-tub scene and the distribution of files, are also over-determined, but more important than these is K.'s actual dream in Chapter 18, which is preceded by a description of the hypnagogic or near-sleep state to which he has been reduced by exhaustion. From this he slips into a remarkable dream that prefigures Bürgel's following revelations. The reverse time-sequence in this dream, which illustrates Silberer's thesis concerning the auto-symbolism of fatigued thoughts, is a good example of the inversion by which cause follows effect. First comes the vision of a victory celebration, then the dream of victory, then the dream of the fight which resulted in victory. With its characteristic reverse-sequence stages and strange logic it is in its way a perfect dream. K.'s twilight train of thoughts begins with the idea that he has achieved something of which no one can deprive him. The 'achievement' is simply the disappearance of the consciousness that he has been finding so irksome, for he is dog-tired. He has, in that sense, won a victory, and therefore sees himself, with the natural logic of dreams, as celebrating a real victory. Since this celebration needs explaining, he then sees himself winning a victory, sees himself defeating a 'secretary, naked, like the statue of a Greek god', who begins to squeal like a girl being tickled. Suddenly the secretary-cum-Greek-god disappears and K. is left alone; ready for battle, he turns round looking for his opponent, but there is no one there. This is both the most significant incident in the dream and its outcome: K.'s only real opponent is himself, compare the animal in *Der Bau* whose imaginary opponent is itself. The point is clear, and the dream ends as logically as it began. All that remains of the victory celebration (for no real victory has been won, just the real opponent indicated) is the champagne glass which K. stamps to pieces. He cuts himself in the process, and naturally wakes up.

Kafka turned to the 'auto-symbolism' of dream-language as a means of expression because of his distrust of language and dislike of the black holes of allegory that encourage slippage ('When it comes to the expression of extra-sensory reality, language can only ever employ symbolism, never anything even remotely like allegory'[51]). His doubts about language, like Hofmannsthal's, centre on what would now be called the distance between signifier and signified. For him it is the sine qua non of poetic or creative language that it should quietly point beyond itself (his term, *andeuten*, means to suggest or hint at), eschewing facile and misleading comparisons. What Freud said of the symbolism of dreams, that 'things employed as symbols do not

---

[51] *Betrachtungen*, No. 57.

thereby cease to be themselves',[52] is fundamentally true of Kafka's symbols, hence his distrust of allegory. There are, he knew, no exact equivalences; everything is itself, not the equivalent of something else. It follows that anything that could be completely said would not be worth saying, and that the perfectly finished novel would be nothing but an artistic construct, hence the Romantic cult of the 'fragment'. This is one of the reasons why his own novels remain incomplete, their meaning residing less in any narrative (narratorial) teleology than deep within their fragmented, fractal structures. Full of meanings, they have no meaning as such: they *are* their own meaning. Like some Gothic novelists (e.g. the author of *Die Nachtwachen des Bonaventura*, or Dostoevsky in *The Double*, which is subtitled 'A Poem of St Petersburg' [by the same token *Der Proceß* might be called 'A Poem of Prague']), Kafka subverts the novel by treating it as though it were a poem, and therefore subject to the 'alternative' logic of that genre. His novels amount to a subversion of the Gothic novel, which he transforms into an aesthetically refined form of symbolical autobiography in metaphoric disguise. Shelley had done something similar a century earlier, but by mistake as it were, and if he was subsequently embarrassed by *Zastrozzi* in particular, he would surely have been even more embarrassed if he had understood what he had written.

4.5. Kafka and Shelley's *Zastrozzi*

A particularly revealing intertextuality in the present context is that between Shelley's *Zastrozzi* and Kafka's novels. *Zastrozzi* is more interesting than is generally allowed: unbelievably bad though it may be in conventional literary terms, it comes into its own when considered side by side with Kafka's work. It is fundamentally different from the average Gothic potboiler, of which it is ostensibly a travesty, in that it has been shown to come straight out of the unconscious and to reveal a mind in conflict with itself seeking to extricate itself from that conflict by a flight from reality.[53] That this also applies to Kafka, who was no less creatively neurotic, hardly needs arguing, for the figures in *Der Proceß* resemble those in *Zastrozzi* in embodying the contradictory forces at work within the author's psyche. Shelley was writing for himself in the sense that his Gothic novelette is a kind of 'daydream in which unconscious conflicts are worked out in disguise',[54] which is precisely what *Der Proceß* also is. Both works are dream-fantasies in which all the characters are projections of the author/narrator and his protagonist, although *Der Proceß* does not

---

52 Freud, *Introductory Lectures on Psycho-Analysis,* 2nd edn [9th imp.] (London: George Allen & Unwin, 1952), 93.
53 Freud, *Introductory Lectures,* 7, 9.
54 Eustace Chesser, *Shelley & Zastrozzi: self-revelation of a neurotic* (London: Gregg/Archive, 1965), 7. My discussion is generally indebted to this little-known, wholly convincing book.

70

have such an obviously Satanic hero-villain. The 'dark, cave-like depths of the unconscious',[55] which appear both in the form of the cave (borrowed from Brockden Brown's *Edgar Huntly*) in which Verezzi is incarcerated by Zastrozzi, and in the form of Kafka's 'Bau', are basic to Gothic as such, for

> Beneath the haunted castle lies the dungeon deep: the womb from whose darkness the ego first emerged, the tomb to which it knows it must return at last. Beneath the crumbling shell of paternal authority lies the maternal blackness, imagined by the gothic writer as a prison, a torture chamber [...] The upper and lower levels of the ruined castle [...] represent the contradictory fears at the heart of gothic terror: the dread of the super-ego, whose splendid battlements have been battered but not quite cast down - and of the id, whose buried darkness abounds in dark visions no stormer of the castle had even touched.[56]

In Kafka the Gothic vault has been internalized and the unconscious appears in more varied spatial contexts (attic, corridor, lumber-room, torture-chamber, engine-room, penal colony, bedroom, burrow), but the basic meanings have hardly changed. Kafka's burrower trapped in its burrow - the writer trapped forever in the work he wanted destroyed because it fell short of his impossible ideal - is a classic case of the hapless, helpless prisoner immured in a Gothic vault.

Kafka's Karl Rossmann can be compared with Shelley's Verezzi. The latter, as a self-projection of Shelley, may be deemed to be seventeen; Karl Rossmann is sixteen. Both of them, that is to say, are self-projections of their respective Peter Pan-like authors at a similar age. Karl, like Verezzi, lives in what is in some ways still the 'magical' world of childhood. Both are taken in by a mother-figure (Claudine, Grete Mitzelbach) to whom they turn in their distress. Eustace Chesser's argument that, in psychological terms, the authority of the father has been introjected and has become a tyrannical inward monitor, applies to Kafka as well as to Shelley. One need look no further than the autocratic figure of his father to find the cause of Kafka's often exaggerated self-criticism, and it is entirely possible that his sense of guilt, too, derives in part from a desire for experience beyond his reach. Kafka needed the emotional stability of a permanent relationship, but this was beyond his reach in two ways: because of his creative lifestyle, and because of the feelings of guilt that he associated with any physical relationship as such. Shelley, though twice married, was, if Chesser is right, scarcely more fitted for marriage than Kafka.

If *Zastrozzi* is an incarnation of Shelley's revolt against his father, Georg Bendemann, Karl R. and Josef K. are incarnations of the Kafka condemned by his father, from whose authoritarianism and censure of his son comes Kafka's over-developed, over-sensitive super ego, the 'gatekeeper' of conscience that gave him such trouble. Like Shelley, Kafka projects himself and his divided mind into all his characters: in the novels there are many figures representing the protagonist's and

---

55 Chesser, 24.
56 Fiedler, 132.

author's conscience, often in conflict with other figures representing their self-respect or, more often, the pride which sits with the protagonist's 'diabolical' licentiousness. The women figures, who are also self-projections in exactly the way in which Matilda, in *Zastrozzi*, is a projection of Shelley, mostly represent Kafka's sensual nature in the guise of the 'licentiousness' of which he was accused by his father; a much smaller number either represent an aspect of his calm, rational mother, or are in some other way the opposite of the phallic females of the novels. In *Das Schloß*, as in *Zastrozzi*, there are opposing female self-projections, Frieda (cf. Matilda) and the 'girl from the Castle', the hoyden and the madonna, the latter equivalent to Shelley's Julia. The difference between Frieda and the 'girl from the Castle' is much the same as that between Matilda and Julia. In each case the latter figure is a phantom of the mind, an ideal: Julia's 'mild heavenly countenance' is as it were replicated in the 'girl from the castle', who is more an iconic *Mater dolorosa* than a flesh-and-blood female figure. Although Kafka's novels and stories are internalized by means of slow, involuted paragraphs reminiscent of *St Irvyne*, it is *Zastrozzi* that they resemble in being profoundly autobiographical and wholly dreamlike.

5. FAIRYTALE

5.1. Introductory

The Gothic novel being, for all its real and supposed part-German origins, essentially an Anglo-American (and, to a lesser extent, Anglo-French) phenomenon, I have so far argued that what we see in Kafka is in effect a development of Gothic that continues and goes beyond the internalization of English-language Gothic of the Romantic period. His relation to his own German-language tradition is less different than it may at first sight seem. The difference has to do with the development of German 'Gothic', for in German literature too a process of internalization takes place as the centre of literary and philosophical interest shifts, at the turn of the eighteenth century, from the material world to the world within, but 'Gothic' (I use the English term because German has no blanket term for the genre,[1] the subdivisions of which are unimportant in the present context) is, in German Romanticism, sublimated into *Märchen* or fairytale.[2]

Kafka was 'especially fond of the *Märchen* and folk tales of all countries',[3] several collections of which were found in his library, others almost certainly having been given away. Found there were Ludwig Bechstein's *Ausgewählte Märchen* (1. Sammlung), the Grimms' *Kinder- und Haus-Märchen* (Vol. 2: Die Märchen der Weltliteratur) and other collections of tales from the Near East and Far East (China). As we have seen, his interest extended to folktale in the Old Testament. His library did not contain - or no longer contained - Grimm's German fairytales and Andersen's tales, from both of which he borrowed motifs, but he wrote to Felice about Andersen's tales, and in a late letter referred to 'Grimms Märchen (vollständige Ausgabe 3 Bände, Georg Müller Verlag)' as 'ein schöner Besitz' (a nice book to own).[4]

He almost certainly acquired his love of fairytale from the French governess (Mlle Bailly) who joined the family when he was five, and who taught him French. What more likely than that the tales of Perrault, d'Aulnoy and others were used to help him to a knowledge of French, and that in the process he acquired the lifelong love of the genre that was to leave a profound mark on his work? The young Franz will very

---

[1]   German uses either *Schauerroman* or, increasingly, the English term Gothic novel.
[2]   Cf. Blackall, 64.
[3]   Franz Kafka, *Short Stories*, ed. Pasley, 12.
[4]   Franz Kafka, *Briefe an die Eltern aus den Jahren 1922-1924*, ed. J. Cermák & M. Svatos (Frankfurt a. M.: S. Fischer, 1990), 31. The reference is to Jakob Grimm, *Kinder-Märchen*, ed. Paul Ernst (München: Georg Müller, 1910).

likely have been struck by the fact that Perrault called his *Tales of Mother Goose (Contes de ma Mère l'Oye)* 'old wives' tales told by governesses [...] to little children', for one of the traditional functions of the governess was to tell fairy stories. It was because the atmosphere in the Kafka family household was implicitly so baneful ('kinderauszehrend': Br 347) that fairytales appealed so much to the young Kafka: the typical ogre household was all too familiar to him. His imaginative concern with 'cannibalism' may well go back to his early reading of French (Perrault) and German (Grimm) fairytales. In his lonely childhood he must have been fascinated by fairytale not only because he identified with the child lost in the forest, but also, and increasingly, because there the ogre gets his come-uppance. On the other hand, stories such as *Das Urteil* and *Die Verwandlung*, in which the father-ogre, far from being outwitted (as he would have been in fairytale), is responsible for his son's death, prove Kafka's point that there are no fairytales nowadays. He retained a vivid memory of the fairytales that were such a light in the lonely darkness of his childhood.

His first German teacher, Ferdinand Deml, an enthusiast who regarded the fairytale as a talismanic guard against 'any perversion in thought or writing',[5] taught such tales as part of the course, and Božena Němcová, whose *Babička* was used as the text for Czech lessons in the Altstädter Gymnasium, is also famous for her collections of Czech fairytales (1845-47), which Kafka must have known, given his admiration of her best-known novel and her letters; even *Babička*, the impact of which on Kafka Brod seems to have misunderstood - the parallel with *Das Schloß* is misleading - Kafka probably read as a fairytale. Later, in adolescence, Kafka is said, on the doubtful evidence of a single unguarded phrase, to have undergone a 'Teutonic folklore phase'.[6] Be this as it may, fairytale was later used to define his doomed relationship with Felice Bauer: 'I cannot believe that any character in any fairytale ever fought longer and more desperately for a woman than I did for you' (BF 730). His words, dating from 1916, show again the automatic way in which he identified with fairytale figures and situations, confirming the truth of Brod's statement that he was accustomed to think in fairytale terms. When Kafka said of Prague that 'Prag läßt nicht los. Dieses Mütterchen hat Krallen' (Prague will not let go of me. This old woman [witch] has [her] claws [into me]), he was again using the language of fairytale. On the most specific, verbal level this may have been an echo of his early knowledge of Paul Delarue's 1885 version of the tale of Little Red Riding Hood, entitled 'The Story of Grandmother' ('Conte de la mère grand'), which includes the words 'Oh, granny, what long nails you have!' In nineteenth-century German one of the meanings of 'Krallen' is 'long fingernails'. In this version of the tale Little Red Riding Hood escapes. Kafka, by comparison, failed to escape from the grip of Prague.

---

5   Ernst Pawel, *The Nightmare of Reason. A Life of Franz Kafka* (London: Harv ill Press, 1984). 74.
6   Pawel, 91.

The reference to 'long nails (claws)' does not feature in the Grimms' 'Rotkäppchen', although there the wolf does have 'big hands', 'the better to grab you with', and every illustrated edition of Grimm shows the wolf's claws; the witch in 'Hansel and Gretel' has 'scrawny hands'. In writing of Prague as an old woman (witch) with long finger nails (claws), Kafka is demonizing the city which had its claws into him to the extent that he was never able to escape its influence; it is a strange fact that he, the most individual and original of writers, was so much the product of his background. His remark about Prague is applicable to the early impression left on him by fairytales, and particularly by the nightmarish French peasant Mother Goose tales. Before his death he wrote to Max Brod that he was wandering round in circles 'wie ein Kind in den Wäldern des Mannesalters' (like a child in the forests of adulthood), a metaphor which shows him still identifying with the child-outcasts of the Grimms' fairytales. On different occasions he said he would like to write autobiography and fairytale: 'I would love to write fairytales (why do I hate that word so much?)' (T 323f.). In fact he wrote both: they are combined in all his major works, regardless of their ostensible genre, which are fairytale-like not least in having many meanings beneath a crystal-clear surface. The way in which he takes the figurative literally suggests that in a sense he never left the mental universe of childhood, but whether he ever wholly escaped from the imaginative bounds of childhood, or was, to his literary advantage, held there as a result of being dominated by his ogre-father, is less important than the fact that it was in the fairytale tradition that he found a way of escaping from what could so easily have become a private and arbitrary mode of narration into an alternative one that was not merely public, but deep as dream and time-hallowed to boot.

The fairytale is in some ways a mysterious genre as regards its origin and significance. It appears to go back, in its original oral form, to an ancient Shamanistic past when cannibalism, if not still practised, at least lived on in the folk memory,[7] and metamorphism and the like were still believed in. That there is overlap between myth and fairytale is shown by the fact that Greek *mythos* means 'tale'; *mythos graos* means 'old wives tale' and therefore 'fairytale'; repetition of function by various characters is a feature of both genres. The fact that cannibalism and metamorphism loomed large in the witchcraft trials of the late middle ages and early modern period, and that there are parallels between the worlds of fairytale and medieval witchcraft, is misleading in that the fairytale is much older than the late medieval witch-hunt, although they embody similar folk beliefs.

The earliest proto-fairytale, 'The Doomed Prince', is found in ancient Egypt in 1350 BC. Elements of fairytale proper go back at least as far as Plato, who wrote in

---

7   Recent archaeological finds have shown it to have been far more widespread than was previously thought.

his *Gorgias* of 'old wives tales' being told to amuse and/or chasten children, and there is every reason to suppose that the main types of fairytale go back at least to classical antiquity, surviving by oral transmission until the middle ages, when they began to enter the literary canon. In historical terms the fairytale goes back, like Gothic, via the sixteenth century (Gianfrancesco Straparola, *Le piacevoli notti*, 1550-53: *The Nights of Straparola*, tr. W. G. Waters, 1894; *The Most Delectable Nights of Straparola*, anon. tr., [Paris,] 1906) to classical antiquity, and proceeded via Giambattista Basile (*Lo cunto de li cunti*, 5 vols, 1634-6: *The Pentamerone*, tr. J. E. Taylor, 1848; tr. Richard Burton, 1893), Charles Perrault (*Contes de ma Mère d'Oye*, 1697: *Mother Goose Tales,* tr. Robert Samber, 1729), Mme d'Aulnoy (*Tales of the Fairies*, 1707) to the era of Johann Karl August Musäus (*Volksmärchen der Deutschen*, 5 vols, 1782-7), the now little-known *Kindermärchen aus mündlichen Erzählungen gesammelt* (1787), and, eventually, in 1812, to the first volume of the Grimm brothers' *Kinder- und Haus-Märchen*. Wieland's remark, in the Preface to his collection *Dschinnistan* (1786), that 'It is all right for popular fairytales, popularly told, to be transmitted orally, but they ought not to be printed,' does not apply to Musäus's tales, which were no more 'popularly told' than were the French rococo fairytales from which, stylistically speaking, they derived.

Musäus's collection was followed, in 1789-92, by another collection, *Neue Volksmärchen der Deutschen* (5 vols), by Benedikte Naubert, one of the German early Gothic/historical novelists. Here already is one of a number of early links in the modern period between Gothic and fairytale. M. G. Lewis obtained 'the Legend of the Bleeding Nun, Lindenberg Castle and the proposed abduction of Agnes, together with the episode in which Raymond appears',[8] all of which appear in *The Monk*, from Musäus's tale 'Die Entführung',[9] and was also evidently impressed by the tale 'Die weiße Frau' in Naubert's collection.[10] However, the idea that Musäus was 'personally known to and often discussed German literature with Lewis when "the Monk" was residing in [Weimar]'[11] is apocryphal and fanciful. At the time of Musäus's death in 1787 Lewis was 12; he did not go to Weimar until 1792. That he knew not only Musäus's *Volksmärchen der Deutschen* but also Naubert's *Neue Volksmärchen der Deutschen* is shown by his letter of 2 October 1807 to Walter Scott: 'Besides Musäus's five volumes (in which by the bye [sic] I found the same tradition employed under the name of "Die Entführung" which furnished me with the Bleeding Nun) I have read five more volumes entitled "Neue Volksmärchen der Deutschen"'.[12] Presumably he

---

8   Eino Railo, *The Haunted Castle* (London: Routledge, 1927), 345.
9   *Volksmärchen der Deutschen*, V, 247-276.
10 Benedikte Naubert, *Neue Volksmärchen der Deutschen*, 4 vols (Göttingen: Wallstein Verlag, 2001), III, 89-130.
11 M. Summers, *The Gothic Quest* (New York: Russell & Russell, 1964), 223.
12 Quoted from Karl S. Guthke, *Englische Vorromantik und deutscher Sturm und Drang* (Göttingen: Vandenhoeck & Ruprecht, 1958), 177.

got to know both sets of *Volksmärchen* while he was in Weimar in 1792, the year in which Naubert's collection completed publication, unless, of course, he first came across Musäus's collection in English shortly before setting out for Germany. Be this as it may, in 1806 Lewis published, under his own name, a typically Gothic 'free translation' (*Feudal Tyrants*, 4 vols) of Naubert's *Elisabeth, Erbin von Toggenburg* (1789), and the fourth volume of his *Romantic Tales* (1808) opened with 'My Uncle's Garret Window',[13] a 'pantomimic' or popular tale of the kind later written by Hans Christian Andersen. Montague Summers, noting this, failed to refer to Andersen's novel *Ahasverus* (1848), which features that stock figure of the Gothic novel, the Wandering Jew, with whom Kafka identified so strongly. Cajetan Tschink, another supposedly 'Gothic'[14] novelist of the time (author of *Geschichte eines Geistersehers* (1790-93: *The Victim of Magical Delusion*, tr. Peter Will, 1795), published a volume of tales of wonder, *Wundergeschichten samt dem Schlüssel zu ihrer Erklärung*, in 1792, in the explained supernatural convention that lasted until G. P. R. James's *Ehrenstein* of 1847, the year that saw a minor Gothic revival.

Musäus's and Naubert's collections were followed by a work which, if not better known nowadays, certainly has, in literary as opposed to literary-historical terms, stronger credentials: Ludwig Tieck's three-volume collection of *Volksmärchen* (1797). When Tieck uses the term *Volksmärchen,* he means *Märchen* à la Musäus, the literary redaction of an oral tale. There are, however, important differences between Musäus and Tieck as regards literary treatment. Unlike Tieck's *Volksmärchen*, which are twice-told tales in the sense of having been subjected to two separate literary treatments (typically, by d'Aulnoy and then by Tieck), Musäus's tales come straight from the melting-pot of Germano-Slav oral tradition. By the time Carlyle came to translate three of the tales in the 1820s, Musäus had been criticized both for 'adulterating' the folktale by his knowing, literary treatment of it, and for the perceived incongruity of his subject and style, although, as Carlyle did not fail to note, 'Lovers of unadulterated primeval poetry may censure Musäus; but they join with the public at large in reading him.'[15]

Musäus, like the Grimms after him, took down his tales from oral storytellers. What distinguishes his tales from theirs is what happens to the oral version once it has been written down verbatim, that is, the amount of editing, 'improvement', rewriting and stylization, to say nothing of ironization (in the case of Musäus) and moral sanitization (in the case of Wilhelm Grimm), to which it is subjected. Carlyle was of the opinion that the popularity of Musäus's tales owed less to his material than to his

---

13 It was reprinted in *The Romancist and Novelist's Library*, ed. William Hazlitt, N.S., Vol. I (London: John Clements, 1841), to which the reader is referred.
14 As its title implies, *Geschichte eines Geistersehers* is not a Gothic novel but a ghost-seer novel. On the difference, see Michael Hadley, *The Undiscovered Genre* (Berne: Peter Lang, 1978), passim.
15 Thomas Carlyle, *German Romance*, 2 vols (London: Chapman and Hall, 1898), I, 14.

quirky way of treating it, meaning the way in which he subjected his texts to the whimsicality of his fancy, subverting their primitive poetry into drollery. It was, however, for better or worse, in Musäus's *Volksmärchen der Deutschen* that the German Romantics discovered the fairytale, and Tieck, for one, followed Musäus in treating it as amusement pure and simple. His *Volksmärchen* have more in common with Mme d'Aulnoy's elaborate rococo fairytales than with Perrault's plain, unadorned ones: he uses the fairytale rather as the rococo writers in France and Germany had done, 'as amusement for sophisticated, grown-up children in the literary salon',[16] much the same audience as that for which Oscar Wilde was to write his fairytales a century later and Margaret Atwood and Angela Carter their Gothic fairytales a further century later. Playing with received forms was a feature of Tieck's early work. His horror-novel *Abdallah* (1795) is indebted not only to Karl Grosse's *Der Genius*, but also to Jean-Paul Bignon's *Les Avantures d'Abdalla, fils d'Hanif* (1712-14), and thence to the *Arabian Nights* (*Les mille et une nuits*, tr. into Fr. Antoine Galland, 12 vols, 1704-17; this edn tr. into German, 6 vols, 1781-85), one of the many links between Gothic and fairytale.

Musäus's collection was in effect superseded by the fairytale as we know it today in the form of the Grimms' *Kinder- und Haus-Märchen* (3 vols, 1812-22) and then of Hans Christian Andersen's rather more literary collections, five of which appeared in English in 1846 (his collected works in German, published between 1853 and 1872, amounted to 50 volumes).[17] In England it was the appearance, in 1823, of *German Popular Stories* (translations from the *Kinder- und Haus-Märchen* by Edgar Taylor)[18] that marked the arrival of the Grimms' fairytales. Prior to that, Italian, French and English tales had been known from collections such as *Fairy Stories* (*c.* 1750), Joseph Ritson's *Fairy Tales Selected from the Best Authors* (2 vols, 1788), and Benjamin Tabart's *Tabart's Collection of Popular Stories* (4 vols, 1804-9). It was following its rediscovery at this time that the fairytale began to be taken seriously, academic study of it being a by-product of German Romanticism.

5.2. Fairytale and Gothic

The German Romantics, growing up before the Grimms' collection had begun to appear, read the collections of Musäus and Naubert along with the horror stories of the time, and naturally put the two together in their minds, for they knew very well that there can be malign 'wonders' as well as benign ones. The Bluebeard tales, for

---

[16] Roger Paulin, *Ludwig Tieck: A Literary Biography* (Oxford: Oxford University Press, 1985), 61.

[17] Mention should also be made of A. L. Grimm's *Kindermährchen* of 1809, scorned but consulted by J. and W. Grimm, and the *Kindermärchen* of (Wilhelm Salice-) Contessa, Hoffmann and Fouqué (2 vols, 1816-7).

[18] By 1889 the collection acquired an introduction by Ruskin.

instance, are more 'Gothic' than most Gothic novels of the literary kind, and the *Kunstmärchen* as written by Tieck and Hoffmann in particular overlaps with Gothic, the 'ruined castle' of local legend, say, being as much a property of the Tieckian *Märchen* as it is of the Gothic novel and tale. Tieck's *Der blonde Eckbert* is as much fairytale as Gothic tale in the sense that it combines and transcends both forms, and Hoffmann's *Märchen* involve more than a little of what was later called the *Greuelmärchen,* which is by definition close to Gothic. Indeed, some of the Grimms' *Nursery and Household Tales* are in effect Gothic tales, and Musäus's *Volksmärchen der Deutschen* came into the domain of the Gothic novel when it was translated into English, supposedly by William Beckford,[19] as *Popular Tales of the Germans* (2 vols) in 1791.

What makes this little known translation so interesting in the present context is the fact that it was greeted by a reviewer in the *European Magazine* (19 [1791], 350-2) as 'a very singular display of the most risible absurdities of the Gothic Romance'. In other words, even informed readers of the time found it impossible to tell the fairytale from the Gothic tale. Anthologies such as *Popular Tales of the Northern Nation*s (3 vols, 1823) made no distinction between them. Given the common origin, features and formulae of the two genres, this is hardly surprising. Edith Birkhead wrote of the novel *Babylonica* by the Greek second-century neoplatonist Iamblikhos as anticipating the Gothic novel, and added that a contemporaneous Latin novel, Apuleius's *The Golden Ass*, included incidents as 'horrid' as any of those devised by the writers of Gothic romance. That fairytale and Gothic have a common origin is shown by the fact that *The Golden Ass* contains models for the fairytale as well as for Gothic, and by the narrative stocks-in-trade common to both.

The 'innate desire for the marvellous', to which Clara Reeve referred when she wrote in the Preface to the second edition (*The Old English Baron*, 1778) of *The Champion of Virtue* (1777) that a work of fiction needed 'a sufficient degree of the marvellous, to excite the attention', was met at the time above all by such works as D'Aulnoy's collection of wonder tales.[20] Birkhead was surely right to suppose that Ann Radcliffe

> adopted some of the familiar figures of old story [...] Montoni, in *The Mysteries of Udolpho* [...] may well [be] descended from the wicked uncle of the folk tale *[The Babes in the Wood].* The cruel stepmother is disguised as a haughty, scheming marchioness in *[A] Sicilian Romance.* The ogre drops his club, assumes a veneer of polite refinement and relies on the more gentlemanlike method of the dagger and stiletto for gaining his ends. The banditti and robbers who infest the countryside in Gothic fiction are time-honoured figures.[21]

---

19 Recent research suggests that the translator was not Beckford but, as Walter Scott knew, Thomas Beddoes (1760-1808), the father of the Gothic poet.

20 Edith Birkhead, *The Tale of Terror* (London: Constable, 1921),12.

21 Birkhead, 12-13. See also W. Gaunt, *Bandits in a Landscape. A Study of Romantic Painting from Caravaggio to Delacroix* (London: The Studio, 1937).

Being (in literate hands) no less moral a form, Gothic à la Radcliffe needed stereotypes just as much as fairytale needed them. Given the 'strong connections' that have been shown to exist[22] between Mme d'Aulnoy's *The Earl of Douglas. An English Story* (*Histoire d'Hypolite, Comte de Duglas*, 1690; the English translation originally appeared in 1708; there was an edition in 1774) and Ann Radcliffe's *A Sicilian Romance*, it is likely that most of the fairytale elements in Ann Radcliffe's novels also go back to Mme d'Aulnoy, a 'Select Collection of only the Best, most Instructive and Entertaining' of whose fairytales appeared in English, under the title of *Queen Mab*, in 1770, at exactly the right time to catch the imagination of the future Gothic novelist. Queen Mab is, of course, a reminder of the link between dream and fairytale.

Ann Radcliffe herself drew attention to the parallel between her best-known novel and fairytale when, in Chapter 5 of *The Mysteries of Udolpho*, she made Annette say 'I can almost believe in giants again, for this is just like one of their castles.' Which giant's castle she had in mind, is not known (it may have been that in 'The History of Jack and the Giants' featuring Blunderboar's 'inchanted Castle, situated in the midst of a loansome wood'), but Montoni is clearly both the wicked ogre and the wicked uncle of folktale, a monster of ill-tempered pride with a thought for nothing save his own self-aggrandizement; he and his wife (the cruel aunt or wicked stepmother of fairytale) deserve one another. Frederick Garber has developed the general parallel in an exemplary way:

> Perhaps the closest generic analogy appears in the fairytale [...] Both genres present beings in human form (the wicked witch and the abbess, the ogre and the villainous count) who [...] wield demonic powers and cause the innocent to suffer for a while. [...] Furthermore, Mrs Radcliffe's evil characters bring other demonic elements into play, [...] most particularly the underworld of caverns and dungeons in which so much of the evil takes place. For over a century, students of folklore and fairytales have emphasized how these have roots in the mythic, subconscious strata of our lives, the levels we would now call archetypal. [...] Her heroines are always running down long corridors towards doors that appear to recede as they do in nightmares, producing the same terrific shudder.[23]

The Mysteries of Udolpho contains a number of explicit references to giants and fairies, the last chapter, which includes several of them, amounting to the cosy 'they both lived happily ever after' formula of fairytale. Indeed, the novel ends, like Perrault's and d'Aulnoy's tales (albeit not in verse), with an explicit moral ('though the vicious can sometimes pour affliction upon the good, their power is transient and their punishment certain; [...] innocence, though oppressed by injustice, shall, supported by patience, finally triumph over misfortune!'). Nothing shows more clearly the indebtedness of the early Gothic novel to the fairytale convention. Radcliffe is rightly credited with being the most successsful of the early Gothic novelists, but her novels

---

22 Alison Milbank, in the excellent Introduction to her edition of Ann Radclife, *A Sicilian Romance* (Oxford: Oxford University Press, 1993, 203.
23 Ann Radcliffe, *The Italian*, ed. Frederick Garber (Oxford & New York: Oxford University Press,1968, repr. 1987), xi.

are not simply 'Gothic'; they could equally well be described as fairytales for grown-ups.

There are important parallels between these two non-realistic conventions with their linked kinds of fantasy, which are combined in Kafka and, more knowingly still, in the late twentieth-century Gothic fairytale.[24] Gothic is no less formulaic than fairytale, fairytale scarcely less sinisterly ambivalent than Gothic, and the dramatis personae and 'machinery' of the two forms have much in common; in each case transgression is the motor of the plot.[25] Both forms involve an autotelic world of high artifice and share not only a symbolical approach to story-telling, but a string of common themes and motifs, including the incarceration and actual or threatened murder of the innocent and the punishment of evil-doers; the empty silent castle (with the table maybe set for one); the forbidden door/chamber; the chamber of horrors; transgressive desire; and cannibalism, which, paradoxically, looms far larger in the fairytale or tale of wonder than in the tale of terror. Shared stereotypical stock figures include, among others, the Devil (commoner in the fairytale than in the Gothic novel, to which he migrated), the father/ogre, the wicked stepmother or witch, the innocent victim, the wanderer, and banditti. They share locations too: the accursed (enchanted) castle or house in the forest, the robbers' lair in the forest, imprisoning space (vault, cage, etc.), and so on. Such parallels show that Gothic drew some of its motifs from fairytale and from the chapbook literature which comes, in part, from the same sources, but the close relationship between Gothic and fairytale goes deeper than motifs and character types, extending to the structure or pattern of 'functions' which they also have in common, a subject to which I return in Chapter 10.

Like Gothic, pantomime and opera, fairytale focusses on situation rather than character, and therefore features stock types and situations. Being concerned with symbolical forms and figures rather than material ones, neither genre is concerned with character development, or indeed with rounded characters, whose activities would be unpredictable, but, rather, with the punishment of evildoers, who are seen as incorrigible, and with the reward of the incorruptible. The stock stereotypes therefore most often embody the clash between good and evil that informs both these varieties of cautionary tale, although the fairytale, which rewards altruism and punishes selfishness, as often as not in a barbaric way, is a more moral form than Gothic: far from being a simple source of delight that came as a relief after the terrors of the moral tale and the horrors of the tale of terror, the fairytale, older than both, combines something of each.

---

24   Lucie Armitt's recent note on this (in *The Handbook to Gothic Literature*, ed. Marie Mulvey-Roberts, 268-9) arguably missed an opportunity to go beyond its immediate subject.
25   Maria Tatar, *The Hard Facts of the Grimms' Fairy Tales* (Princeton, NJ: Princeton University Press, 1987), 56.

The aims of these two stylized, anti-mimetic genres go beyond the Horatian one of conveying delight and instruction, although the element of beguilement remains strong. When children delight in the fairytale, and adult readers in both forms of tale, they are responding to an imaginatively spun tale based on universal types and situations. The situations in question combine the satisfying spectacle of evildoers getting their come-uppance with the *frisson* that accompanies the realization that is the beginning of wisdom - that life is an uncertain, risky affair - but undercuts it with the knowledge that these particular dangers, uncertainties and insecurities at least are paper ones which end with the end of the tale. Readers of all ages enjoy being frightened within safe limits. Tales of both types are intended not only to give pleasure in this sense, but to have a chastening effect. Whether foregrounded or not, a subversive effect is usually also present, what is subverted being the childish idea that the great are also the good, to say nothing of the idea that life is a straightforward matter of cause and effect, material values and rewards, and so on. Instead, Gothic tale and fairytale alike introduce the autonomous realm of the imagination, which is a law unto itself and shows that the rich and poor are punished and rewarded not according to their status, but according to their deserts. Equally subversive of any short-sighted materiality or unquestioning acceptance of things as they seem is the power of imagination which in each case holds the reader in thrall. Like the fairytale, the Gothic tale is a kind of tale of wonder, what they have in common being wonder at the way in which a secure position in life may suddenly give way to an insecure one, often as a result of the evil in human nature.

The degree of kinship between Gothic and fairytale becomes particularly clear in relation to the Grimms' fairytales, which are not only marked by a high incidence of violence, cruelty and transgressive sex, but are at the same time, thanks to Wilhelm Grimm, unblushingly moralistic. Many of these tales are grim indeed: compared with Gothic, they get away with murder, and with incest too. It is the German fairytales collected by the Grimm brothers that are the bloodiest, the closest to Gothic, and the most used or referenced by Kafka, who commented that 'There are no fairytales without bloodshed', adding: 'Every fairytale comes from the depths of the folk and its sense of insecurity.' Gothic and fairytale are related kinds of fantasy, the genre that is practically indistinguishable from fairytale, having inherited from it the basic plot (the hero leaves home, meets helpers and opponents, goes through trials, etc.).[26] The most basic, pre-literary form of fantasy is conscious or semi-conscious daydreaming, the state in which Kafka habitually wrote. It has been said that 'If fantasy is a literature which resolves anxiety through the medicament of story [...] then Kafka is not a writer

---

[26] See Maria Nikolajeva, 'Fantasy Literature and Fairy Tales', in *The Oxford Companion to Fairy Tales*, ed. Zipes, 150-4.

of fantasy',[27] a view that overlooks the obvious similarities that his novels share with fairytale and fantasy:

> Most fantasy novels have many similarities to fairy tales. They have inherited the fairy-tale system of characters, set out by Vladimir Propp and his followers: hero, princess, helper, giver, antagonist. The essential difference between fairy-tale hero and the fantasy protagonist is that then latter often lacks heroic features[...]and can sometimes fail.[28]

Some of the key concepts used to define fantasy tales - crosshatch, portal, threshold[29] - also apply par excellence to Kafka's works. The Parable of the Door-Keeper is a classical portal-text. On the other hand, that his writing failed to 'resolve anxiety' is proved by *Der Bau*, which shows that describing and defining anxiety, far from resolving it, in fact magnifies it by putting it in sharper focus.

In aesthetic terms both Gothic and fairytale mark a reaction against the limitations of the Age of Reason, among them the low-mimetic mode in literature. This may seem questionable, given the limited, formulaic nature of both conventions, but the limitations in question are those of the human condition, not the human imagination. The development of the fairytale and Gothic tale from the late eighteenth century onwards involves a process of internalization as physical horrors are augmented and, increasingly, supplanted by psychological ones. In their symbolism fairytale and Gothic alike parallel the nightmare, which is similarly limited in its recurrent figurations and situations, presumably because human beings' basic fears are few in number, but the chief external link between Gothic and fairytale, and between both these forms and Kafka's writings, is the dream as such, which, like the fairytale, clings to the visible, around which it draws a veil of enigma. It is no chance that Queen Mab was credited with delivering man's brain of dreams.

It was at one time thought[30] that fairytales were re-narrated dream-sequences, the products of psycho-sexual problems. Although this is no longer believed to be the case, both Freud and Jung commented on the connexion between dreams and fairytales, and more recently Lüthi has written of the folk fairytale's 'dreamlike vision'. Not only does the fairytale resemble the dream in embodying universal archetypes;[31] both work in much the same way. Bruno Bettelheim's statement that 'In a fairy tale internal processes are externalized and become comprehensible as represented by the figures of the story and its events',[32] which applies equally well to dreams, corresponds to Erich Fromm's description of *Der Proceß* as a dreamlike narrative in

---

27 *The Encyclopedia of Fantasy*, ed. J. Clute & J. Grant (London: Orbit, 1997), 528.

28 Nikolajeva, 151.

29 See *The Encyclopedia of Fantasy*, 237, 776, 945.

30 By Géza Róheim, see *The Gates of the Dream* (New York: New York International University Press, 1952).

31 C. G. Jung, 'The Phenomenology of the Spirit in Fairytales', in his *The Archetypes of the Spirit in Fairytales* (Vol. 9 of *The Collected Works of C. G. Jung* (Princeton, N.J.: Princeton University Press, 1968).

32 Bruno Bettelheim, *The Uses of Enchantment* (New York: Vintage Books, 1989), 25.

which 'external events happen in space and time, being representations of thoughts and feelings within the dreamer'.[33] Known for overinterpreting fairytales, Fromm makes good sense in general terms when he writes of Kafka.

All three of Kafka's novels have in full measure the literary fairytale's 'alogical, dreamlike character'.[34] The difference is that while fairytales too 'translate psychic realities into concrete images, characters, and events', they differ from dreams, and from Kafka's work, in that 'rather than giving us personalized wishes and fears, they offer collective truths, realities that transcend individual experience and that have stood the test of time'.[35] In artistic terms the undifferentiated raw material of the dream - if that is what it is - contrasts with the artistically arranged narrative of the fairytale, so that, however dreamlike in their pictorial imagery and extensive use of displacement, Kafka's tales resemble the fairytale rather than the dream in being artistically so highly developed. The fairytale, like the dream, to which it is closely related, and like Kafka's novels, has its roots in the subconscious that Kafka, writing as and when he did, was able to tap.

5.3. Kinds of *Märchen*

There are many kinds of fairytale, of which the Gothic tale for children is but one, just as there are several different kinds of Gothic novel, of which the fairytale for adults is one. Basically the fairytale or *Märchen* is either a kind of folktale, a naive peasant tale of magic, wonder and cruelty, or a literary simulation of such a tale. Unlike the folk fairytale, which is an orally transmitted tale and as such a peasant form, the written fairytale is a bourgeois form.

The distinction between the *Volksmärchen* (folktale, folk fairytale) and the *Buchmärchen* (written fairytale) or *Kunstmärchen* (literary fairytale: the prefix denotes not 'art' but 'artfulness' or 'artificiality'), long regarded as fundamental, can now be seen to be merely a matter of different points on a spectrum or continuum extending all the way from the oral fairytale to the *Metamärchen*. In any case the word *Volksmärchen* does not only denote the popular (fairy)tale of oral tradition; it was also used by Tieck to denote his literary adaptations of such tales. The *Buchmärchen* is the popular literary fairytale à la Andersen, as opposed to the *Kunstmärchen* or artful literary fairytale as produced by the German Romantics, but also by George Macdonald, Lewis Carroll, and Hugo von Hofmannsthal, among others. The traditional post-Romantic distinction between *Volksmärchen* and *Kunstmärchen* is exemplified in the difference between the original version of some

---

33   Erich Fromm, *The Forgotten Language* (London: Victor Gollancz, 1952), 213.
34   Marianne Thalmann, *The Romantic Fairy Tale* (Ann Arbor: University of Michigan Press, 1964), 11.
35   Tatar, *The Hard Facts of the Grimms' Fairy Tales*, xv-xvi.

of their *Kinder- und Haus-Märchen*, which the Grimm brothers gave to Clemens Brentano in 1810, and Brentano's own fairytales, that 'sophisticatedly expand folk legend into narrative structures of great complexity and irony and beauty'.[36] The Grimms' first versions were still *Volksmärchen*, but Wilhelm Grimm's final versions, which had been stylized and expurgated to the point where, far from 'unadulterated', they had become a vehicle for inculcating German Protestant middle-class moral values, were on the way to being *Buchmärchen*. There is a clear difference between what the Grimms set out to do in the first edition of their tales, and what Wilhelm Grimm actually did in subsequent editions. Their original intention was to preserve the oral folk tales in an unadulterated form, but in practice their literary, moral and national values led them to edit the tales without admitting, and maybe without fully realizing, the extent to which they were changing them. Their very literacy and good intentions were against them, for in wishing to preserve these products of old German culture in a 'pure' form, they were inevitably influenced by their notion of what constituted that culture.

The German Romantics themselves did not distinguish between the *Volksmärchen* and the *Kunstmärchen*; for the good reason that the latter term did not exist at the time. The modern term *Kunstmärchen* denotes a purely literary form, the *Märchen* made up by the author on the basis of the morphology of the folktale, a form cultivated especially, but not exclusively, by the German Romantics and those influenced by them: a purely imaginative tale, then, fairytale-like in often carrying a good deal of allegory and therefore of morality, although this is sometimes absent, as in the case of *Alice in Wonderland*. However, if the Romantic *Kunstmärchen* had no intrinsic moral purpose, the *Volksmärchen* self-evidently did; this is why Perrault gave his *Contes du temps passé* the subtitle *Avec des Moralitez*, and why the Grimms thought of their collection as an *Erziehungsbuch*. In calling Grimm's fairytales *Household Stories* and Andersen's *Stories for the Household*, the Victorians were not only emphasizing that such tales were addressed to adults as well as children; they were also signalling their relevance to the moral economy of the household.

All *Märchen* are imaginative, and therefore 'not true', to those who measure truth by the yard; indeed, the *Volksmärchen*, though imaginatively and morally true, is frequently a tall story in terms of the impossible or marvellous or supernatural events it takes in its stride. The word *Ammenmärchen*, which in Wieland's day meant nursery tale, now simply means an unlikely story, whereas the *Lügenmärchen* is the preposterously tall story (cf. Poe's 'The 1002nd Tale'), one of the earliest collections of such stories being Lucian's mendaciously titled *Vera Historia*[37] (translated by Wieland as part of *Lukians sämtliche Werke*, 1788-9) which contains some early

---

36 Blackall, 174.
37 *Lucian's Wonderland*, tr. St. J. Basil Wynne Willson (Edinburgh & London: William Blackwood, 1899).

versions of stories which are also found in the *Arabian Nights*. Raspe incorporated incidents borrowed from Lucian, together with others found elsewhere, in his *Baron Münchhausen's Narrative of his Marvellous Travels and Campaigns in Russia* (1785). Because there is a considerable difference between what was believed in the eighteenth and early nineteenth centuries, and what is believed today, a characteristic of the fairytale as told or read today is that it is unbelievable; in both English and German the term itself - fairytale, *Märchen* - has come to mean a cock-and-bull story, although the word, like the word 'dream', often has what is assumed to be a positive connotation in terms of wish-fulfilment. In modern terminology, 'fairytales' are more specifically *Zaubermärchen* (wonder tales),[38] a term more particularly applicable to the tales of Contessa. While many *Volksmärchen* and some *Kunstmärchen,* for example Tieck's *Der blonde Eckbert* and *Der Runenberg*, include horrific events, the tale of horror as such is, in more modern terminology, a *Greuelmärchen*. By inverting the classical fairytale and playing with its motifs Kafka created what has been called the 'Antimärchen' (anti-fairytale), but the term, simplistic in relation to Kafka, is better used to mean a fairytale without the customary happy ending. The 'fractured fairytale'[39] is a traditional fairytale re-arranged to generate new plots with new meanings, while the fairytale parody, which overlaps with it, mocks individual tales and/or the genre as a whole. The 'Gothic fairytale' is a sub-genre of female Gothic.The terms 'Halbmärchen' and 'Metamärchen'[40] have been used recently to designate texts that are respectively part-fairytale and metafictions in the guise of fairytale. The idea of *Metamärchen*, though not the name, can be traced back to Basile's 'Lo cunto de li cunti'. As a category used to reevaluate and (re-)define the (Romantic) *Kunstmärchen,* it has not gone unchallenged.[41] We return to it, and to the *Märchenroman* (fairytale novel), in Chapter 10.

5.4. Kafka and the *Volksmärchen*

> On the surface [Kafka's stories] seem to be fairy-tales, or dream-sequences, or extended jokes; what occurs appears fantastic, and remote from our everyday world; yet [...] what we recognize at one level as a game of fantasy declares itself at a deeper level to be intensely serious and intensely real.[42]

Kafka's novels subvert their form by being in so many ways fairytale-like, and even as they do so, they subvert the fairytale by the reversal of fairytale motifs and the denial

---

[38] See Jack Zipes, in *The Classic Fairy Tales*, ed. Tatar (New York & London: Norton, 1999), 334-6.

[39] See *The Oxford Companion to Fairy Tales*, ed. Zipes, 172f.

[40] See B. W. Rosen, in *Folklore Forum*, 18 (1985), 15-31

[41] See E. L. Montonyohl, 'A Response to B. W. Rosen's "Metamärchen",' *Folklore Forum,* 18(1986), 218-220.

[42] *Franz Kafka, Short Stories*, ed. Pasley, 31-2.

of fairytale magic. Fairytale motifs form the building blocks of the novels, but when it comes to articulating them, the novels play with the motifs in question, thus doing what Ludwig Tieck had done a century earlier and what the Devil, in Thomas Mann's *Doktor Faustus*, was to say was all that remained to be done by the twentieth century, playing with old forms in a travesty of the aesthetic *Spieltrieb* (play-impulse).The more closely one studies Kafka's novels, the more important their fairytale situations, motifs)and style come to seem, but while all the motifs which he borrows from the folk fairytale add considerably to the ambiguities of his work and its impact on the reader, what makes it fairytale-like is less individual motifs than the functional relationship in which these stand to one another,[43] although this inevitably departs from the ordered sequence of plot segments identified by Propp.

The folk fairytale depicts a self-contained, archetypal world of universal validity, an 'otherworld' in the sense of an alternative version of reality with its own symbolic formations and chains of motifs tied together in a logical plot sequence that moves toward a preconceived goal in accordance with the laws of its internal structure,[44] which are also the laws of imaginative necessity. In most of this it is as it were a model for Kafka's novels, to which Friedrich Schlegel's statement that the essence of the *Märchen* is infinite association and meaning applies in an exemplary way. Although none of his works is a *Märchen* as such, in the German context it is in many ways to the *Märchen* tradition that Kafka's work is most closely related. To his novels and major tales applies Max Lüthi's statement that 'A folktale can be interpreted, but any single interpretation will impoverish it and will miss what is essential'.[45]

Like dreams, fairytales are concerned with inner realities which they translate into vivid concrete images conveying figurative meanings, often by means of that literalization of metaphor which is central to Kafka's technique:

> In fairy tales, the hero escapes the tiresome clichés of reality by entering a world where the figurative or metaphorical dimension of language takes on literal meaning [...] In taking the figurative literally, fairy tales once again display the degree to which they are situated in the mental universe of childhood. There, as in fairy tales, the literal dimension of language reigns supreme.[46]

Not the least significant of the senses in which fairytales are tales of wonder is that they depend on the magic that is inherent in language, particularly when metaphors are taken literally and symbols generated by such literalized metaphors. It is the fact that the literalization of metaphor which is central to Kafka's literary method is the stock-in-trade of fairytale that makes the parallel so important.

---

[43] Mayer & Tismar, 141.

[44] Hans Biedermann, *The Wordsworth Dictionary of Symbolism*, tr. James Hulbert (Ware: Wordsworth, 1996), 124.

[45] Max Lüthi, *The European Folktale: Form and Nature* (Bloomington: Indiana University Press, 1986), 94.

[46] Tatar, *The Hard Facts of the Grimms' Fairy Tales*, 80.

Given that reversal or displacement is Kafka's favourite technique, it is not surprising that the sudden change or reversal of situation (seduction, arrest, non-appointment or disappointment, transformation, etc.), that is typical alike of fairytale and Gothic, applies to all three of his novels. The basic model, folk fairytale, is characterized by the sudden intrusion of the extraordinary into the domain of the ordinary, of the other into the hitherto uniform, of the otherworld of the unconscious into the conscious world: 'The folktale [...] depicts a world that unfolds before us as the antitype of the uncertain, confusing, unclear, and threatening world of reality'.[47] Kafka's work, lacking the reassurance and metaphysical consolation of the folk fairytale, reverses it in this respect as it reveals the threatening, destructive Other within the protagonist. Although they wear the guise of the godless, bureaucratic modern world, events in Kafka's work have something of the force of the bewildering signs and challenges issuing from the threatening 'otherworld' of legend. In the K.-novels in particular, but also in some of the best known shorter pieces, we see the same merging of world and shadow-world, in which the Other is found to be ominously omnipresent in what passes for the 'real' world, as in fairytale. By 'otherworld' I mean simply an invasive, intrusive, hostile, destructive 'Other' or sense of Otherness. Court and Castle, Burrow and Penal Colony variously embody this alien dimension, but so too, as the major punitive fantasies show, do even the most mundane locations. Equivalent to the figures of fairytale who belong to a higher or lower world are the figures in all three novels who, as the supernatural yields to psychology, represent the higher and lower self. The burden (of guilt or self-knowledge; the feeling of worthlessness, or whatever) that Kafka's protagonists have to carry is tantamount to the curse or enchantment of fairytale, except that it is not lifted.

The typical fairytale involves a problem or difficulty and its resolution, a struggle leading to victory, or a task or imperative (to make good in one sense or another) and its mostly successful completion, in other words, the wresting of order from chaos. The fairytale idea of a goal which the hero either reaches or fails to reach (the prototype and origin of the Gothic 'Quest') informs all three of Kafka's novels, but especially *Der Proceß* and *Das Schloß*. As a rule the folktale depicts 'the surmounting of obstacles, the harmonious solution of all problems, and the restoration of the natural order', for 'The folktale's true happiness comes from mastering the art of life',[48] whereas all three of Kafka's novels involve the 'impossible task' of folklore (often assigned by the Devil, which in a symbolical sense is the case here too. In each novel the task - to restore lost innocence; to prove the innocence of one who is not innocent;

[47] Lüthi, *The European Folktale*, 85.
[48] Lutz Röhrich, *Folktale and Reality* (Bloomington: Indiana University Press,1991), 209.

to prove the significance and identity of one who feels himself to be a nonentity - is a diabolically impossible one, the fact signalled by appropriate allusions to the Devil.

The Lack → Lack Liquidated pattern, which, according to Propp,[49] forms the basic structural principle of the fairytale, also informs Kafka's novels, each of which starts from a loss, but whereas in the folk fairytale being or getting lost is a temporary state, in Kafka's work it is an irremediable one. His protagonists signally fail to master the art of life. The folk fairytale depicts an ordered world, Kafka a disordered one. He uses the style, structure and motifs of the folk fairytale to deny the positive aspect or ultimate meaning of the genre. Its negative aspect, on the other hand, is present in his work, in which arrogance and greed are punished. What, after all, is *Das Schloß* if not an elaborate exemplification of the fairytale rule that 'der Vermessene geht unter' (the proud shall fall)?[50] As punitive fantasies, Kafka's novels follow the Failure → Punishment pattern of the anti-fairytale, with the protagonist as anti-hero (albeit with an heroic dimension). However one looks at them, focusing on whatever aspect, the novels are seen to be fairytales without the fairytale resolution. Even the *gerade noch* (just in time) motif is reversed, so that it is, in a Kafka text, axiomatically, just too late. There is neither grace nor grace period.

Chance no more exists in Kafka's work than it does in fairytale. There are no non-functional figures, localities or events in his novels. Everything has a function and is a product of that function. Although he does not use the, for him, inappropriately cosy formula, there are many instances of things seemingly happening 'as if by magic', although it is in reality the uncanny that this encapsulates. Examples are the way in which the country doctor finds his magic steeds, the way in which Josef K. finds his way to the courtroom, and the way in which K.'s evident helplessness magically produces the folk-fairytale figures of the 'helpers' (assistants) who might be expected to help him, but who in fact confound his efforts and compound his difficulties. In each case the 'magic' ends badly. Kafka's formulaic use of the number three and his preference for a triad of figures also parallel the fairytale, where the number three is at least vestigially of magic power.[51] Kafka uses the pattern of threes, but strips it of its magic, leaving, as it were, a vestige of a vestige: in *Der Verschollene*, three expulsions; in *Der Proceß*, three arrests; in *Das Schloß,* three jobs. The fairytale motif of being successful at the third attempt is subverted: Karl R's threefold dismissal; K's three 'appointments' - as land-surveyor, as janitor, and as stable-lad - which involve a clear downward progression. The three versions of Amalia's story (as viewed by Amalia, Olga, and their father) parallel the three tales told (with plots invented) by

---

[49] See also Max Lüthi, *The Fairytale as Art Form* (Bloomington: Indiana University Press, 1987), 54.
[50] Max Lüthi, *Märchen*, 9. Aufl. (Stuttgart: Metzler, 1996), 31.
[51] See Lüthi, *The European Folktale,* 67.

the Queen in 'Sneewittchen'. Such vestiges serve to subvert superstition in the form of number-magic.

For Kafka's protagonists, as for the characters of the folk fairytale, time is a function of psychological (moral) experience. While all three unfinished novels were to have ended in the protagonist's death - one of the main types of fairytale is the unfinished tale - they lack temporal depth in any other sense; temporality is replaced by morality and mortality, with death the result not of time, but of sin. Like the heroes of the folk fairytale, the protagonists in Kafka's novels act in accordance with laws and forces they do not understand, but with the characteristic difference that while in the *Volksmärchen* everything tends to turn out for the best, with Kafka the opposite is the case. Like the folk-fairytale hero, Kafka's protagonists are isolated figures. They are, as we have seen, mostly hero and antihero in one, although the man-from-the-country is the simple antihero who fails in his task. The ambiguity of Kafka's protagonist as hero and anti-hero, victim and villain, is in line not only with the depiction of the fairytale hero, but also with Lüthi's statement that the unity of the protagonist is split, so that 'only a single one of his components may be evident and may take effect in any one scene, and yet in the end all these components form one integral whole'.[52] This is exactly applicable to Kafka's protagonist. More generally, the parallel between Kafka's figures and those of fairytale has also been well described by Lüthi:

> The stories of Franz Kafka [...] have been characterized as out-and-out anti-fairy tales. And yet they have much in common with fairy tales. Their figures, like those of the fairy tale, are not primarily individuals, personalities, characters, but simply figures: doers and receivers of the action. They are no more masters of their destiny than are the figures in the fairy tale. They move through a world which they do not understand, but in which they are nonetheless involved. [53]

Lüthi does not distinguish between primary and secondary figures in Kafka, and what he says applies to both. The fact that with Kafka the secondary figures are all projections of the protagonist does not necessarily constitute a major difference from fairytale. For Jung, for instance, the various figures in folk fairytales are aspects of one and the same personality. With the single exception of the protagonist, the figures in Kafka's stories resemble the flat, anonymous figures of the folk fairytale rather than the psychologically differentiated characters of the literary fairytale. Since there is little characterization as such, there is little sign of emotional interaction or human warmth. Like the folk fairytale, Kafka's novels avoid portraying feeling, even the protagonist's feelings being translated into actions as his internal world is transposed on to the level of external event. Kafka's figures too are 'sleepwalkers'[54] who glide

---

52 Lüthi, *The European Folktale*, 44.
53 Max Lüthi, *Once upon a Time. On the Nature of Fairy Tales* (New York: Frederick Ungar, 1970), 145.
54 Cf. Janouch, 62.

through the narrative as through a dream; in a revealing alternative ending to *Der Proceß* Josef K. only wakes up when he finds himself standing in his own grave. They are passive and strangely patient; even the motif of waiting, which is so important in Kafka, is a folktale motif.[55] The reader is struck by their passivity and lack of surprise at the often untoward turn of events: things simply happen to them, as they happen to the child, it being assumed that this is the way things are; there is the same childlike acceptance of the complexity of life with its unexpected perils, the same lack of reactive emotion, the same acceptance of evil. Even Josef K., for all his huffing and puffing, goes along with events as they happen, although it is Karl Rossmann who is closest to the naive hero of fairytale.

Despite being named, the subsidiary figures in Kafka's novels are of a kind with the generalized figures of fairytale. In each case their *raison d'être* derives from their relationship to the protagonist, whose taskmaster, helper, evil spirit, and so on, they are. The emphasis is on the protagonist and whether he will win through. Like the secondary characters of folktale, the subsidiary figures in Kafka's novels are important only as foils, but with the difference, if it is a difference, that they are projections of the protagonist, so that Kafka can be seen as internalizing the fairytale just as he in effect internalized Gothic. It goes without saying that neither the characters of folktale nor the figures of Kafka's work know of the interrelationships of which they are part. Kafka's secondary figures do not know how they relate to the protagonist, and neither does he. Because they all represent an impulse that is, for a limited time, dominant in the protagonist's mind, there can, by definition, be little or no interaction between them; on the contrary, each must of necessity, in accordance with his (or occasionally her) symbolical nature, give way to the next. It is the same with episode or event: only one is foregrounded at any given time, and for the same reason: that the protagonist's mind can only be moved, and his attention held, by one motivating idea at a time.

The fact that fairytale events are based not on rational cause and effect, but on a more primitive (alternative, imaginative, poetic, symbolic) logic of their own, again underlines the fairytale-like nature of these novels with their symbolical logic, space and time. *Märchen* and Kafkaesque novel alike are, in terms of their inner logic, a law unto themselves, for these novels possess, to a high degree, the logical consistency and inner necessity that is characteristic of fairytale style. Like dreams, the fairytale combines a crystal-clear narrative technique with a fantastic or mysterious content. Kafka's work has the same mixture of lucidity and mystery, of reality and unreality. His tales have the same kind of praeternatural simplicity and visuality, together with the same memorably concrete yet symbolical portrayal of objects; their symbols, like those of the folk fairytale,[56] simultaneously conceal and reveal their meaning. There is

---

55   See Stith Thompson, *Motif-Index*, VI, 843.
56   Lüthi, *The European Folktale*, 95.

the same *Flächenhaftigkeit* or apparent lack of depth as in the fairytale. In both cases the surface elaboration serves to distract attention from the profoundly challenging and often disturbing depths of the tale. The complexity of Kafka's work, then, like that of the dream and fairytale, lies concealed beneath the surface of the narrative, for few readers will realize the ambiguous depths of so many of the words that together comprise the limpid surface of the work in question.

Like the fairytale, Kafka's texts with their unitary hero-view perspective are one-dimensional, single-stranded[57] and episodic. The narration of the novels involves a strange combination of circularity and linearity: the initial challange is replicated, but with the replications leading, cumulatively, to an outcome, though this is admittedly negative. Without standing in total isolation from the other episodes, to which they mostly make some minimal reference, the episodes are thus, like the scenes in epic theatre, more or less self-contained. The novels have the narrative single-mindedness and narrowness of focus of the folk fairytale, the plurality of episodes strung on a single narrative line, hence their hero-view perspective. But if they thus have precisely the singlestrandedness and episodic structure that Lüthi sees as 'the foundation and the precondition of the abstract style [of the European folktale]',[58] they differ from this in including much more descriptive detail. Indeed, while the novels have, with the exception of the protagonist, the flat, one-dimensional figures of the folktale, they replace its abstract style with the concrete 'fulness that bewilders' of the *Arabian Nights*, the mass of detail that challenges the reader's ability to maintain perspective. Presumably Kafka knew the *Arabian Nights (Tausendundeine Nacht),* new German translations of which (tr. Cary & Karwall, 10 vols, 1906-11; tr. Greve, 12 vols, 1907-08) at a time when, given his love of the genre, they were likely to attract his attention. With this fundamental difference, Kafka's works resemble the European folk fairytale in that every single detail is relevant and significant. The mixture of abstraction and realism, together with the deployment of folk-fairytale motifs and residual formulaic elements in these novels, bring them close to *Märchen..* They are essentially concrete in the sense that they consist of and depend upon concrete detail, but insofar as this detail is imaginary and symbolic and touches the concrete materiality of the external world only occasionally and as it were coincidentally, they are abstract. While illustrating Kafka's belief that truth consists of concrete particulars, they thus also possess the abstract stylization of the folk fairytale and the inner logic that goes with it it.

When Kafka describes objects in such detail, it is because, being symbolical, they illuminate the process that is underway in the protagonist's mind. The emphasis is continually on the protagonist. Nothing ever happens in his absence, nor could it do

---

57 On the 'einsträngig geführte Handlung', see Lüthi, *Märchen,* 29.
58 Lüthi, *The European Folktale,* 34.

so. Every location in *Der Proceß* resembles every other in being a reification of the same sense of existential unease and distress. As in the folk fairytale, only what impinges on the protagonist and his path through life is in focus, but then the focus is sharp and exact.[59] Whereas his depiction of external reality is as depthless as that of the folktale, Kafka's delineation of the protagonist's inner world has great verbal and conceptual depth. The concept of the 'straight and narrow path' is as important in the folktale as it is with Kafka.

5.5. Kafka and the *Kunstmärchen*

Like the nineteenth-century *Kunstmärchen*, Kafka's works need to be read intertextually with the *Volksmärchen*. In using the folk fairytale as a 'Stoffreservoir'[60] or reservoir of motifs, Kafka was not only doing what nineteenth-century writers of *Kunstmärchen* did; he was also both giving his work the historical depth it would otherwise have lacked, and at the same time establishing his own literary stance. His tales, which go beyond the fairytale in much the same way as they go beyond Gothic - by internalizing and thus intensifying it, and by subverting cliché in the process - are parables or, better, *exempla*, cases in point, the case in point being, in the first instance, the case of Franz Kafka, who is not in business to write anything as crude as a *moralité* or didactic piece. We have already seen that Kafka's fairytale-like works involve many echoes of the folk-fairytale, their purpose being, typically, to deny the hope that was a fundamental feature of this, while at the same time, indirectly, expressing a nostalgia for it. In incorporating so many fairytale motifs into his works, Kafka is drawing attention to their fictionality, rightly dismissing them as so many 'fairy stories', for they are more fictionalized autobiography than fiction pure and simple, and fictionalization spells falsification.

Kafka reacts to folk fairytales in much the same way as Romantic writers of *Kunstmärchen* do, but he goes further than they do in internalizing and deconstructing them, so that his subversive use of fairytale is in some ways comparable to Oscar Wilde's. Both men's fairytales revolve around the problems of the isolated protagonist, but Wilde, in whose work - unlike Kafka's - there is a conflict between aestheticism and morality, was a moralist in a way in which Kafka was not. Whereas Wilde was making moral judgments, Kafka was showing the impossibility of such judgments in an age of moral relativism. Wilde's aim was didactic, Kafka's was not. Although they differ from fairytales in being not moral tales but tales turning on the problematical nature of moral values and judgments, Kafka's tales nonetheless share fundamental

---

59 Lüthi, *Märchen*, 30.
60 See H. H. Ewers' important epilogue to his anthology of German *Kunstmärchen* from Wieland to Hofmannsthal, *Zauberei im Herbste* (Stuttgart: Reclams UB, 1987).

themes (justice/injustice, human folly, etc.) with the classical fairytale. From the exotic background of Wilde's fairytales, which comes from the *Arabian Nights*, it is a far cry to Kafka, whose tales resemble the *Arabian Nights* only in possessing the mass of detail that puts the reader in constant danger of losing control over the text. Both admired Hans Andersen, many of whose fairytales do not have a happy ending; their own tales mostly end in death.

Because he used the *Volksmärchen* as a reservoir of motifs, as the Romantics had done, Kafka's novels and major tales have not a little in common with the Romantic *Märchen* as described by T. J. Reed:

> the same distance or even escape from reality shows in Romantic creative work. Its typical form is the Märchen, which in the hands of the Romantics becomes a strange mixture of the primitive and the sophisticated. The fairy-tale world is at once a release, the willing return of modern intellect to the non- or pre-rational, *das Wunderbare*; and also the source of motifs and arabesques through which deeper meanings can be cryptically implied. In other words, primitive Märchen will accommodate cerebral allegory. It is a mixture of extremes.[61]

Much of this is applicable to Kafka, whose work involves escape from an oppressive outer world into an inner world that was more real and meant more to him. It too combines the primitive (in the form of the childlike) and the sophisticated, doing so in both a personal and a literary historical sense. In echoing the fairytale as he did, Kafka too was willingly returning to the non-rational, for he, the most cerebral (if least allegorical) of men, paradoxically mistrusted the rational. The difference is that he went further than the Romantics in undermining his own position.

The fact that he was 'averse to the clichés of literary Romanticism',[62] as he was averse to all cliché whatsoever, does not mean that he would have denied his own literary roots in Romanticism, for the truth is that he is himself a late Romantic, albeit of the classical kind. No one but a Romantic could have written *Der Bau*, and the inset stories in the novels (the story of Karl's seduction, of Amalia's refusal to let herself be seduced, and, in between, the story of the man-from-the-country's futile attempt to penetrate the Law) are all reminiscent of the nineteenth-century literary fairytale, with which, notwithstanding the fact that in detail they owe much more to the folk fairytale, the novels should be compared in general terms.

5.5.1. Kafka, Hoffmann and Tieck

The literary fairytale, which combines traditional folk-motifs with increasingly sophisticated narrative techniques,[63] is known, like Kafka's novels, for its 'alogical',

---

61 In *Germany. A Companion to German Studies,* ed. M. Pasley, 2nd edn (London: Methuen, 1972), 523.
62 *Franz Kafka: Short Stories*, ed. Pasley 11.
63 See *Tales of the Dead, The Ghost Stories of the Villa Diodati,* ed. Terry Hale (Chislehurst: The Gothic Society, 1992), 10.

dreamlike character. Challenging the reality of reality as it is normally conceived, and expressing an alternative, poetical view of it, the Romantic *Kunstmärchen* describes life as a kind of dream, the Romantic mind supposedly making 'no absolute distinction between the spontaneous surrender to imaginative, perhaps subconscious, impulses[,] and the deliberate [...] feigning of the dream-technique of narrative'.[64] What Tymms wrote of Tieck - that 'his success with the *Märchen*-genre depends on the more or less successful translation of the dream into literary form' - applies to Kafka too, who knew that the dream from its roots in the unconscious reveals the reality that reason is unable to conceive or with which it is unable to cope. We have seen that Kafka's novels are close alike to dreams and to fairytales, which were at one time taken for dreams which 'take shape in waking'. This is just what Kafka's texts are. It was Novalis who said that a fairytale is 'like a vision in a dream - incoherent [...] a fantasy', referring to it, presciently, as 'chaos' (as opposed to classical harmony and logic). I say 'presciently' because twentieth-century chaos theory finally caught up with his insight and showed 'chaos' to be an alternative, marginal, unstable form of order. While Kafka is not known to have read Novalis, the fairytale of the 'Mädchen aus dem Schloß' and her two children, Hans and Frieda, who reappear at other ages later in the novel, is reminiscent of the *Märchen* in *Heinrich von Ofterdingen*. The *Kunstmärchen*, known for the artful simplicity of its style and for its circular, fractal logic, works, as Kafka's novels also work, via the subversion of the everyday as it is subjected to a higher, imaginative vision. Unlike the *Volksmärchen*, it has neither moral purpose nor a predisposition to happy endings, and therefore employs symbolism rather than allegory. Its yardstick is poetry, its logic its own. It is the *Kunstmärchen* as written by Hoffmann, Tieck and Lewis Carroll that is most revealing from the point of view of intertextuality with Kafka.

No one but a Romantic would have left his main works unfinished, as Kafka did with his novels and Hoffmann with *Meister Floh* and *Kater Murr*. There is a strange symmetry between the creative lives of Kafka, most of whose work was written between 1912 and 1924, and Hoffmann, whose work was mostly published just a century earlier, in 1814-1822. The intellectual and literary kinship between these two legal gentlemen, who possessed similar kinds of imagination, wrote into the early hours, and died in their forties, is shown by the parallels between *Die Verwandlung* (about a man following his transformation into an *Ungeziefer*) and *Meister Floh* (Master Flea is, in German terminology, an *Ungeziefer*), and between *Forschungen eines Hundes (Investigations of a Dog)* and *Kater Murr*, that delightfully sophisticated and sophistical autobiography of a cat, and between the *Bericht für eine Akademie* and the *Nachricht von einem gebildeten jungen Mann*.[65] The difference, in the latter case,

---

64   Ralph Tymms, *German Romantic Literature* (London: Methuen, 1955), 4.
65   On the last pair, see Patrick Bridgwater, *The Learned Ape* (Durham: University of Durham, 1978), 11-15, 18-24.

is that Kafka's guilt complex led him to identify with an unclean animal, while Hoffmann 'identified' in quite different terms with his favourite cat. In terms of his attitude towards reality, and of his fairytale world being 'overrun by demons', Kafka's work parallels Hoffmann's. It was in Hoffmann's use of *Märchen*, and therefore in the internalization, poeticization and subversion of reality in his work that he was most interested. By comparison with Hoffmann, who made such positive, structural use of the fairytale, to which he was historically that much closer, Kafka's use of it is a matter of individual motifs rather than of overall, quasi-musical structure.

Hoffmann, who wrote in *Der Sandmann* that 'nothing is more singular and more fantastic than real life [...] all a writer can [...] do is present it as "in a glass darkly"' (compare Kafka's statement that 'true reality is always unrealistic'), grounded his fantasies in 'reality' in a way that pointed forward to Kafka, who was evidently interested in the combination and interplay of reality and fantasy in Hoffmann and the Russian Hoffmannists, and more especially in the way in which each constantly throws the other into doubt. Kafka shares with Hoffmann a predilection for precipitate openings: with Josef K.'s sudden arrest, compare the way in which, in *Der goldene Topf*, the student Anselmus runs full-tilt into the old witch's basket of apples, from which all else follows. The fantastic and the banal feed off one another: Josef K.'s arrest is all the more telling for taking place when he is lying in bed in a common-or-garden boarding-house thinking of his breakfast. Like Hoffmann, Kafka makes creative use of doubt, challenging his readers to do as much with the doubt that he deliberately implants in their minds, for *Der Proceß* and *Das Schloß* can, like Hoffmann's *Die Elixiere des Teufels*, be read in a variety of ways, none of them completely excluding the others.[66] The most serious doubt is, of course, that which surrounds the concept of reality, for Kafka, like Hoffmann before him, shows how 'unreality' quietly seeps out from between the lines of the most mundane supposed 'reality', so that at any moment the material foreground of life, the very stuff of Josef K.'s *Bankmenschentum*, simply ceases to be real, ceding its 'reality' to the inner world. What price commercial travellerdom once one has turned into a giant bug? As a result our conception of the reality of things, and through it our hold on reality, is undermined. Novalis, another notable *Märchendichter*, belongs here too, for, as Blackall has said, the famous symbol of the blue flower in *Heinrich von Ofterdingen* 'hovers over the whole novel as something the true meaning of which is never established but always being sought - like Kafka's Castle'.[67]

If a deconstructive reading shows conflicting forces dissipating the seeming definiteness of a text's structure and meanings into an indefinite array of incompatible

---

[66] Cf. Blackall, 230.
[67] Blackall, 120.

and undecidable possibilities,[68] such a reading of Kafka's novels is unnecessary since his method of narrative construction with its polysemy and semantic depth is itself deconstructive in this sense. The job of deconstruction is done in advance of publication, leaving the reader to wrestle with the predetermined possibilities of meaning, and with the no less predetermined absence of meaning. Hoffmann produced *Kunstmärchen* which played with and subverted existing *Volksmärchen* in much the same way as Kafka was to do a century later; the distinction between the *Kunstmärchen* as written by Hoffmann and the *Metamärchen* as written by Kafka in *Der Bau* is one of degree rather than kind. Many now classical *Kunstmärchen* are in part about themselves. Kafka's *Nachtstücke* (as his tales are) go beyond Hoffmann's *Halbschlaffantasien* (as his tales surely are), but the real difference between their work has to do with differences in their philosophies of life and historical positions. Hoffmann was writing in a late Romantic, and in that sense late fairytale world, Kafka in a post-fairytale one. Kafka goes further than Hoffmann in subverting and deconstructing the existing stock of fairytales. Hoffmann was writing at a time 'when hope still helped', although it was fast becoming the preserve of the naive. Kafka, by contrast, is the poet of a world which is beyond hope and therefore beyond *Märchen*, a world in which fairytale motifs merely underline how much has been lost.

Given that he knew Hoffmann's and Arnim's work, it is likely that Kafka also knew some of Tieck's, especially since he shares with Tieck both a narratorial playfulness and a stylistic lucidity that sets off to perfection the nightmare complications of, say, *Der Proceß*, to say nothing of a concern with similar states of mind, foremost among them that most disruptive of states, anxiety. Marianne Thalmann's claim that her *The Romantic Fairy Tale* has a bearing on Kafka's stories and novels is true above all in relation to her analysis of Tieck's fairytales.[69] Tieck uses the *Märchen* as Kafka uses the novel, to investigate and elaborate his own problems; like Tieck, Kafka uses his *Märchen*-like work to 'populate [the] tremendous emptiness' of his inner world. Though nothing was more important to Kafka than the truth he believed human beings to engender by their truthfulness, his heroes, like those of Tieck's fairytales, search not merely for the truth about themselves, but for the secret of life, which in the case of Kafka appears in the guise of the inscrutable, infinitely challenging 'Law' outside which the Man-from-the-Country stands nonplussed and afraid. If Tieck concentrates on the inner life of 'the person whose symbols, perceptions, memories, and reactions have many different levels', this is exactly what Kafka also does, albeit with the qualification that the person in question is always himself. He it is who, in the guise of Josef K./K., follows Tieck's hero in

---

68   The definition is basically that given by M. H .Abrams in *A Glossary of Literary Terms,* 7th edn (Orlando, FL: Harcourt Brace, 1999), 55.

69   Marianne Thalmann, *The Romantic Fairy Tale* (Ann Arbor: University of Michigan Press, 1964), vi, 34-56 and passim. My following discussion is indebted to these pages.

wandering through dark streets in search of the unknown. Like Tieck's *Märchen*, Kafka's Gothic fairytale-novels begin with a critical moment in the hero's life which sets the narrative flux in motion. Equivalent to the lack of chapters in Tieck's fairytales are the near-endless paragraphs of these novels. If Tieck's *Liebeszauber* and *Der Pokal* are 'plotted in two large narrative curves', Kafka's novels too are circular in structure, their end in their beginning, the circle a vicious one from which there is no escape and therefore in narrative terms no ending. Like *Liebeszauber*, *Der Proceß* opens ominously and has an ending that is as horrible as it is grotesque, while the motif, in Tieck's 'Die Elfen', of daring to cross the bridge, is called to mind when K., in the opening paragraph of *Das Schloß*, finds himself on the wooden bridge leading from the main road to the village. He crosses it without a thought, in the mistaken belief that it is bringing him nearer to his goal; arguably he would have done better to turn back. Kafka's work is abstract in the same sense as Tieck's fairytales, in embodying an invisible inner world; otherwise the one is, like the other, wholly concrete, as indeed are Lewis Carroll's literary fairytales, which Kafka's novels resemble in that the episodes of which they consist, like those in *Alice in Wonderland*, read like the interchangeable, seemingly nonsensical, non-sequential episodes of a dream.

5.5.2. Kafka and Lewis Carroll

One of the most basic features of Kafka's work is the way in which, as in *Alice in Wonderland* and *Through the Looking Glass*, reason is replaced by the seemingly irrational. I say 'seemingly' because Lewis Carroll constructed his looking-glass world in a scientific way, on strictly rational, reverse-logic lines. Kafka's world, by contrast, has its own dream-logic which immediately shows the world of simple logic and single meanings to have been left behind. While Alice's world is a topsy-turvy, upside-down, reverse-image one with, it may be thought, no real metaphysical or moral implications, Josef K.'s world has profound and profoundly sinister implications, this being shown by the looking-glass logic which responds to Josef K.'s statement that he is innocent with the unanswerable 'That's what the guilty always say'. In *Das Schloß* there are similar long-distance exchanges regarding K.'s status and activities as 'land-surveyor'. In *Alice in Wonderland* the words 'Sentence first - verdict afterwards' are a joke, but in *Der Proceß* Josef K. realizes, right from the beginning, that there is nothing funny about his arrest and implication in a case which can only end in a guilty verdict, and Kafka's penal colony is even closer to Wonderland, for there guilt is seen even more starkly to be beyond doubt. In the first (1962) film version of *Der Proceß*, the parallel with *Alice in Wonderland*, 'implicit throughout,

[was] made explicit in a brief sequence where a court guard emulates the White Rabbit'.[70]

Lewis Carroll, unlike Kafka, writes obvious fantasy. Alice's is a dream-world with, like German fairytale in particular, a Gothic edge. K.'s is a nightmare world. Alice stays wide awake, capable of saying 'You are all a pack of cards', while K., by contrast, is sucked into a world he can neither understand nor control, for he completely lacks Alice's calmness and perspective. The figures associated with the Court in *Der Proceß* are nonetheless, like the figures in the trial at the end of the proceedings in the quasi-Gothic dream world of Wonderland, 'nothing but a pack of cards'. Like the supposed judges in *Der Proceß*, the figures in Alice's trial have no meaning or authority beyond that conferred on them by the protagonist, whose projections they are. As such they are real only so long as the dream lasts. The ultimate judge comes to life when Josef K. feels compelled to judge himself; his trials are as peculiar to him as Alice's adventures are to her. The truth is that Josef K./K., in both novels, is as much reduced to confusion about his identity as Alice is about hers, and with good reason, for if Kafka had not been radically uncertain of his own identity and its constituent imperatives, he would in all probability not have been writing in the first place.

There is, too, a world of difference between the trial in *Alice in Wonderland* and that in *Der Proceß*. *Alice in Wonderland* is a literary fairytale in the form of a dream, and while it follows that the figures in it would, if the dream were real, be projections of the dreamer, Alice, they do not relate to her in the way in which the figures in *Der Proceß* relate to Josef K. In other words, they do not represent particular aspects either of Alice herself or of her creator. One of the most extraordinary and characteristic things about Kafka's novel is the contrast between the extreme psychological depth of the protagonist and the total lack of such depth of all the subsidiary figures. This contrast parallels that between Alice (who is real) and the playing-cards-come-to-life (who are real only within the confines of Alice's dream). The difference is that, in the case of *Alice in Wonderland,* the playing-card figures are projections of Alice only insofar as they inhabit her dream. *Alice in Wonderland* is not just an artificial fairytale; it is also an artificial dream in which only the beginning and ending are dreamlike, whereas *Der Proceß*, which is also an artificial (but undeclared) dream, is in every respect wholly dreamlike - if ever there was a dream that 'took shape in waking', it is this. Alice's trial, on the other hand, in which she is a witness, not the accused, comes as her final adventure and ends with her waking up. The trial is not serious; the Queen's words 'Off with her head' need not and indeed cannot be taken seriously, at least not by adults. On the contrary, the trial is the logical outcome of a nonsense rhyme and is itself so much nonsense, a crazy version of a real trial with

---

70 Clute and Grant, *The Encyclopedia of Fantasy*, 963.

every now and then a lucid moment; like Kafka's work after it, it is precise to the point of unreality. It ends when, following the return of the supposedly stolen tarts, Alice says 'You're nothing but a pack of cards'. The cards fly at her, and she wakes up. *Der Proceß* is very different. For a start, despite the English title, there is no trial as such. Instead, the whole novel is a trial of sorts, premised on the assumption of Josef K.'s guilt, so that in novel and fairytale alike we have 'Sentence first - verdict afterwards'. In the last chapter Josef K. condemns himself to death, and although it seems that he survives to feature again in *Das Schloß*, as Alice does in *Through the Looking Glass*, he has first to experience the ultimate in self-punishment dreams in the form of a humiliating imaginary death. The whole novel is a precisely dream-like process going on in Kafka's mind and, by extension, in Josef K.'s mind. The figures associated with the Court in *Der Proceß* are in a figurative sense like the figures in the trial at the end of *Alice in Wonderland*, who have no meaning or authority beyond that conferred on them by the protagonist, whose projections they are. The real difference between these two dream-fictions is that *Alice in Wonderland*, unlike *Der Proceß*, is a fairytale written for children which is given the form of a dream to explain the marvellous, otherwise incredible events that take place in it. It is the product of Lewis Carroll's fancy, not of an overwrought mind in dream-mode; all the figures it produces are projections of itself. *Der Proceß*, on the other hand, is about Kafka in a way in which *Alice in Wonderland*, however much it may happen to tell us about him, is not about Lewis Carroll.

Alice in Wonderland and *Der Proceß* are both examples of the fantastic, the literary kind to which Gothic and fairytale belong, that has been said to exist 'in the hinterland between "real" and "imaginary"', shifting the relations between them through its indeterminacy'.[71] Such works question the nature of reality. What is 'real'? Are dreams real? Is fairytale real? It being through language that the concept of reality is both posited and challenged, Rosemary Jackson went on to say, 'From Carroll, through Kafka [...] there is a progressive dissolution of any predictable or reliable relation between signifier and signified'.[72] One thinks, here, of Kafka's highly apposite diary entry for 27 December 1911: 'How inadequate metaphor is. The original feeling is separated from its metaphorical description by an unwarranted assumption [as to the identity of the two]' (The German, which I have had to interpret in order to translate, reads 'Wie wenig kräftig ist das obere Bild. Zwischen tatsächliches Gefühl und vergleichende Beschreibung ist wie ein Brett eine zusammenhanglose Voraussetzung eingelegt'). Just as Alice enters 'a realm of non-signification, of non-sense'[73] in which things slip away from words, so too does Gregor Samsa, from whom language similarly slips away as his alienation sets in and his words become

---

71 Jackson, *Fantasy*, 35.
72 Jackson, *Fantasy*, 40.
73 Jackson, *Fantasy*, 140.

unintelligible to others. 'A semantic emptiness, present in Carroll [...] and much horror fiction', Jackson wrote, 'provides the centre of Kafka's work.' In this respect too *Alice in Wonderland* and *Der Proceß* are similar yet different. 'When I use a word', Humpty Dumpty says in a rather scornful tone, 'it means just what I choose it to mean'. While this does not exactly apply to Kafka, many of his words do carry multiple meanings, and therefore an often overdetermined ambiguity, that paradoxically has the effect of leading the reader towards that same semantic emptiness.

There is a world of difference between the underground world of *Alice in Wonderland* and that of *Der Bau*. Alice enters her appointed wonderland when, falling asleep, she dreams of entering a rabbit-hole and falling down a kind of shaft, at the bottom of which she finds a wonderland peopled by a pack of real, fabled and fanciful animals and of playing cards come to life. Her adventures mostly involve repeated changes of size and being exposed to the reverse logic of her dream companions. At the end she wakes up, full-size, none the worse for her experience. How different is Kafka's *Der Bau* (discussed in terms of fairytale and Gothic in 9.5), which is about the burrow his animal-narrator (the writer as Giant Mole) has spent his life constructing and in which he then finds himself imprisoned, fearfully awaiting the moment when his 'animal adversary' (himself as Other, as his own Death) will break into what was intended to be an impregnable underground fortress and kill him. Notwithstanding its claustrophobic opening, Carroll's tale is harmless, at worst whimsical. Not so Kafka's anti-fairytale, written on his death-bed, which combines many meanings, some of them highly personal, others having manifold ramifications in folktale, all of them spelling the death of the terrified burrower and variously identifying the burrower with Kafka as man and artist, the burrow with his work, life and dying body. The story, which is unfinished, was to have ended with the burrower's death. In the nature of things *Der Bau* is more nightmare than dream, more Gothic tale than fairytale. Its meaning goes way beyond Gothic in terms both of psychology and of subjectivity, but the basic image and locus is that staple of Gothic, the underground vault in which the terrified victim is left to rot.

6. *DER VERSCHOLLENE*
6.1. Fairytale Motifs

Pasley has rightly commented on the 'quality of child-like innocence'[1] informing *Der Verschollene*. The 'naive' way in which the adult world is there presented in a pre-adult perspective is important, for it is the perspective of the fairytale, regardless of its target readership. Of the novels it is the first that is closest to *Märchen* in the sense of containing the greatest number of fairytale motifs and what Vladimir Propp called 'functions', that is, plot segments or component parts of the model tale. Of Propp's thirty-one functions *Der Verschollene* has half; to qualify as a fully-fledged *Märchen* it would have had to have all the functions, in the right order, but half the functions is a remarkable figure for a modern novel. The regular sequence of plot segments which Propp thought had to be observed probably represents a formulaic ossification resulting from the fairytale's long history.

Der Verschollene embodies the constantly frustrated quest for a lost paradise that underlies all three novels and is seen at its most fairytale-like in the Parable of the Doorkeeper in *Der Proceß*. It is strikingly fairytale-like in story-line and structure. The structure of the novel is that of the classical fairytale, consisting of exposition (the crisis, outlined in the opening lines, of which Onkel Jakob gives the Captain an exposé), repeated peripeteiai (shown literally as the ups and down of Karl's experience, symbolized in his job of lift-boy), and lysis.[2] The opening chapter, which sets the scene for the novel and establishes its major symbols, amounts to the fairytale formula: Once upon a time there was a young man named Karl Rossmann who was given the boot by his parents for allowing himself to be seduced by the kitchenmaid. The ending of the novel, for its part, both corresponds to those of the most primitive stories, which simply peter out, and emphasizes the circular pattern of the novel, and with it the 'weary sorrrowful circle' of existence, for the final journey replicates the initial one.

The structural replication and symbolical re-enactments of the novel can be compared with the reprises of the folk fairytale:

> One and the same stylistic impulse permeates the entire folktale. From this impulse all episodes arise; it keeps on forming the same characters, so that they all resemble one another, while at the same time each stands alone [...] The subsequent scene [...] resembles the [preceding one] so

---

[1] In *Der Heizer*, ed. Pasley, 9.
[2] See Marie Louise von Franz, III/3.

closely [...] because it originates from the same source. In relation to each other, the two scenes are isolated, but [...] they are [...] formed and sustained by one and the same center.[3]

The structural replication in *Der Verschollene* parallels the formulaic repetition of the folktale, though without running to verbal repetition. The stylistic impulse that keeps on forming the same figures (as we have seen, in the novel they are not 'characters') is clearly active in the naming of those figures. What Lüthi has written of the phenomenon of repetition and the relationship of the parts to the whole in the folk fairytale is, on the face of it, strikingly applicable to the scenes or episodes in *Der Verschollene*, but there is a crucial difference between fairytale and novel in that in the novel the replication is necessitated by the idea of original sin, which it illustrates, whereas in the fairytale this is not the case.

The paradise lost motif, common to myth and fairytale, involves both of Karl's symbolical forebears, Adam and Lucifer. Banishment by the father is a common fairytale motif, as is the idea of failure or transgression leading to punishment. Karl's banishment is clearly a punishment for breaking an unwritten and unvoiced commandment. Whether Kafka knew, at the time of writing the novel, that banishment was also one of the punishments for heresy (see 7.2.2) is not clear. Like fairytale, the novel teems with implicit interdictions (not to enter Johanna's room, not to enter Klara's room, not to enter Brunelda's room, not to wait until a deadline has just passed (cf. tale type AT425G) before receiving Onkel Jakob's letter, not to desert his post as liftboy, not to play a drinking song on his trumpet, and so on), the number of which serves to underline the enormity of the initial fateful transgression (dreams cannot and folk fairytales normally do not employ adverbs of degree, for which repetition stands in). Like the fairytale hero, Karl Rossmann is, following his banishment, no longer embedded in a family structure. His parents, though instigators of the plot, lack all reality; even the father, whom we assume to be the prime mover in Karl's expulsion since all those who replicate his action are father-figures, is no more than a cipher or trigger of the action, much less real than the Captain, Onkel Jakob, and the Head Porter, all three of whom substitute for him, although Karl's real *Schädiger* (evil genius) is his own id or shadow.

If the story of Karl's seduction by Johanna Brummer (the 'false bride' of fairytale) is also as it were a looking-glass or reverse-gender version of 'La belle et la bête', the 'discovery of the rich uncle [...] (who subsequently rejects [Karl], like Cinderella, for failing to return by midnight) is a pure fairy-tale motif'.[4] Karl, as seduced rather than seducer, is appropriately seen as a reverse-gender Cinderella, this then being acted out in his pursuit by Klara (another fairytale motif, though out of sequence), which necessarily also involves gender-reversal since it symbolizes his original pursuit and

---

3   Lüthi, *The European Folktale*, 50f.
4   *Der Heizer*, ed. Pasley, 11.

entrapment by Johanna. A male Cinderella (type AT511A)[5] is, however, not simply a further instance of subversion, for German male Cinderellas outnumbered female ones prior to the eighteenth century, and Kafka may well also have known of the male Cinderella of Turkish folktale, if the fact that he possessed *Der Zauberspiegel. Türkische Märchen* (1924) indicates a prior interest in the subject. He could also have come across it elsewhere, for male Cinderellas feature, in the guise of the 'unpromising hero', in the folktales of many countries. That point made, it is more likely that this is simply another example of his subversion (reversal) of fairytale motifs. In terms of the novel, Klara is an avatar of Johanna; in fairytale terms she is the 'beautiful daughter of the task-setting demon' - her father - who was responsible for Karl's failure to return by midnight. As in tales of the 'Amor and Psyche' type (AT425G), the deadline set (in our case, unbeknown to the protagonist) is just missed; typically, the novel lacks the second part, in which this is made good.

If the discovery of the rich uncle is 'sheer fairytale' in the sense of being too good to be true, precisely the sort of thing that, according to Kafka, does not happen in real life, at least not nowadays (in the text the words 'the signs and wonders that still happen in America if nowhere else', which may go back to Kafka's original conception of the novel, are meant ironically), the expulsion of Karl is as final and fatal as such negative outcomes always are. The 'Head Porter' at the Hotel Occidental, instead of preventing Karl from entering, ironically does all he can to prevent him from leaving, a Gothic reversal of the usual fairytale and mythological motif. In *Der Verschollene* a spin is put on the violation-of-a-prohibition motif that is basic to fairytale in that Karl twice breaks a prohibition of which he had not been specifically aware; the third occasion is different ('Being absent from duty without leave spells dismissal') and, reversing fairytale convention, fatal.

The forbidden door/chamber is another major fairytale motif (cf. the Bluebeard complex of tales by Perrault, Tieck, Grimm and Bechstein, among others; Kafka certainly knew Becbstein's 'Märchen vom Ritter Blaubart'), notably in the form of the motif of desired knowledge hidden behind a locked door. In the Grimms' 'Der Froschkönig' it has the same Freudian connotation as in *Der Verschollene*, whereas in the two K.-novels it appears, more literally, as the portal-motif of fantasy. In the present novel the 'chamber of horrors' is subverted in two ways: in that Karl was locked into the original chamber, his escape from which is re-enacted together with his expulsion, and in that it gives way to a positive 'theology of the door'. In other words, Kafka reverses fairytale/Gothic motifs regardless of whether their original meaning was positive or negative. Subversion, it seems, is all.[6]

---

5   Stith Thompson, *Motif-Index,* L.101.
6   On Kafka's 'Technik der Entstellung von Märchenzügen', see Mathias Mayer & Jens Tismar, *Kunstmärchen* (Stuttgart: Metzler, 1997), 142.

Pollunder, Robinson and Delamarche correspond to the robbers of fairytale and banditti of Gothic, the first two being identified as such by their names. The small inn, in which Karl falls in with Robinson and Delamarche is equivalent to the robbers' den (usually in a forest, here in the mist) of both traditions. Grimm's Daumerling is invited to become chief of banditti, as is (in the Gothic novel named after him) Caleb Williams. Karl Rossmann, though ostensibly more robbed than robbing, is in an analogous position. Grete Mitzelbach, who is said to have worked at the 'Golden Goose'[7] in Prague (cf. the Grimms' 'The Golden Goose' and the motif of the goose that laid the golden egg, the echoes serving to increase Karl's and the reader's unrealistic hopes), plays the symbolical part of the 'fairy godmother', but is unable to save Karl. This part of the narrative also proving to be too good to last, a mere 'fairytale', Karl's expulsion has to be re-enacted again, but not before he receives a gift appropriate to fairytale.

The biblical and folkloric motif of the giving of an apple (by Eve to Adam, a reverse-gender version of Dionysos's gift to Aphrodite) is duplicated in fairytale in the form of an ugly old woman (witch) giving a poisoned apple, which, like the philtre of Gothic, induces death-like sleep. This motif, which appears in 'Sneewittchen', reappears shortly afterwards in Hoffmann's *Der goldene Topf*, and then in an apparently harmless, heavily censored form in *Der Verschollene*, where it (appropriately, given the Freudian association of the apple with the vulva) constitutes a censored version of Johanna Brummer's 'gift' to Karl, to which the account of Therese's mother's death also alludes. Karl's three visits to Therese's room, like the three enactments of his expulsion from paradise, involve the magic number so common in folktale, but without the positive outcome normally associated with the motif, the significance of which is here reversed. The dumping of Brunelda, the biblical Scarlet Woman and 'giantess in a red dress' of Icelandic fairytale,[8] involves, as we have already seen, a reversal of the leitmotif of Musäus's 'Entführung [aus dem Serail]'. There are also many allusive fairytale details (Green as ogre and, in symbolical terms, cannibal, a point to which I return in the next section; Robinson as *Schädiger*; the dogs with their 'great bounds'; the 'old hag'; and so forth).

Searching for a prize is a classical fairytale motif. In two of Kafka's three novels the protagonist (Karl Rossmann, K.) goes out into the world like the wanderer-hero of fairytale, to seek his fortune, finding there not what he seeks, but what he deserves to find. *Der Verschollene* is a *Bildungsroman* of sorts, in which a naive young man learns the facts of life and the world. The motifs of the 'right way' and the 'wrong way' or 'false path' being as central to fairytale as they are to Kafka's work, the straight and narrow path that Karl Rossmann tries to tread corresponds to that trodden by the

---

7   Here too Kafka deconstructs his source, in this case Prague's famous Renaissance house 'Zum Goldenen Schwan'.
8   Stith Thompson, *Motif-Index*, F531.4.7.3.

fairytale hero.[9] In Kafka, as we have seen, there is no stroke of luck at the third attempt by which the fairytale hero may escape or recover, and neither does Kafka subscribe to the fairytale idea of rescue at the eleventh hour; with Kafka the eleventh hour is axiomaticaly too late. The vicious cycle of events in *Der Verschollene* is thus reminiscent alike of fairytale and nightmare. Pawel was right to argue that one gave way to the other:

> One [...] enduring aspect of [the] vision [behind *Der Verschollene*] is its fairy-tale quality [...] [Kafka initially saw] America as [...] a fairyland teeming with bad fairies [...] but still the last and only place on earth where miracles could happen [...] But in the [...] two years that Kafka took to write it, the fairy-tale turned into a nightmare and shook its author's faith in fairy-tale endings.[10]

America was to Kafka's generation an enchanted land of boundless possibility, but Karl Rossmann's experience of it is totally different, not least because his 'America' is so far from being what it seems to be. There is just enough of the real North America as described by Friedrich Gerstäcker in the mid-nineteenth century, and by Benjamin Franklin in his autobiography, a Czech translation of which Kafka possessed, to put our model unwary reader off the scent, while the Cinderella motif, for its part, makes the reader expect a fairytale ending. Since this cannot be delivered, the reiterated Fall is accompanied by a reiterated disenchantment, the effect on the reader cumulative, each disappointment, to borrrow a fairytale motif, more bitter than the one before.

Just as *Der Verschollene* as a whole takes the reader back to the German Utopian novel of *c*. 1800, only to disappoint any hopes that it too may be Utopian, so too does Kafka, in deploying fairytale motifs, trigger certain expectations in the reader which he then proceeds to dash, by reversing and subverting them, and by filling his mock-fairytale structure with an admixture of 'Gothic' motifs. It is the tension between fairytale wish fulfilment on the one hand, and Gothic reality on the other, that makes this first novel so remarkable.

6.2. Gothic Reading
6.2.1. Expulsion from Eden

Der Verschollene, mostly written between 25 September and 12 November 1912, was never completed. Until 1983 it was known as *Amerika*, the thoroughly misleading title given to it by Max Brod. It was only in 1983 that Kafka's usual name for the novel was restored. There is, of course, a world of difference between *Amerika* and *Der Verschollene*. *Amerika* implies a novel about the United States of America ('an immigrant's U.S.A', proclaimed a paperback reprint of the English translation, misrepresenting the text), about which Kafka had admittedly read a good deal. Given

---

9   Max Lüthi, *Volksmärchen und Volkssage*, 2nd edn (Berne & Munich: Francke, 1966), 15.
10   Pawel, 256f.

that he viewed the United States, in the then usual way, as a 'wonderland of boundless opportunity' (J 11), the old title implies an optimistic, realistic novel at odds not only with his other novels, but with all his literary aims and concerns, to say nothing of being at odds with the novel's structure and symbolism.

The meaning and implications of the restored title are totally different. 'Der Verschollene' means 'the man who went missing' and 'the man who went to the Devil', but it also has a stronger, legal meaning, which is the key to the novel. Kafka, who had a degree in law and worked in a quasi-legal profession, would not have used a legal term unless he was absolutely satisfied as to its meaning and implications; he went to endless trouble to get words and phrases exactly right, and evinced the greatest skill in doing so. In legal German, *jemanden für verschollen erklären* means 'to declare someone dead in law'. The implication is that the novel was to have ended in Karl's virtual death, so that an optimistic reading, always impossible if the reading was a close one, seems to be out of the question. The title confirms what Kafka once said (T 481), that Karl Rossmann, though 'schuldlos' (guiltless), was to be 'strafweise umgebracht', meaning that by way of punishment for his sinfulness he was to be brushed aside, as happens literally to Gregor Samsa's remains in *Die Verwandlung*. If this sounds Draconian, it is even more so when one realizes that the novel shows Kafka pondering his own largely imaginary sexual initiation, greatly exaggerated by poetic licence, hence his reported description of *Der Heizer* as 'the memory of a dream, of something that perhaps never took place' (J. 27), and condemning himself for his role in it. This first novel is therefore Gothic not merely in its spaces and many of its situations, but as a whole, for Karl Rossmann was to be contemptuously swept aside by patriarchy militant. The structure is not only mock-fairytale, but distinctly Gothic, and beneath the Gothic and fairytale elements lies patriarchy's ultimate model, the Old Testament. For all its motley, the novel is as much a punitive fantasy as *Der Proceß*. As such, it has much more to do with the newly created, newly transgressive world of Genesis than with the New World of America, which is a Kafkaesque literal symbol.

It is the key first chapter, centring on Karl's transgression, that immediately reveals this ostensible 'fairytale novel' to be a Gothic novel in disguise. The sword held aloft by the Statue of 'Liberty' shows that Karl, entering the 'new world', has not escaped from the patriarchal law of the old world and the violence associated with it, which also surfaces in the no less symbolical sword worn by an immigration official. The Statue of Liberty has been replaced not merely by a minatory figure in the posture of Christ in Michelangelo's *Last Judgment*, right arm held aloft ready to pronounce judgment, but by one apparently ready to put mankind (for Karl Rossmann is also an Everyman figure) to the sword. A notably eschatological opening image for a novel that has, incredibly, been seen as optimistic and realistic, it goes back to a gesture used by Kafka's father at his most forbidding and to the arms of the city of Prague and its Gothic past. It is in itself sufficient to show that Karl, far from entering a paradise, is trapped in a past that is no longer his now that he has been disinherited. The statue with the raised sword also shows that, having lost his innocence, he will be unable to regain it. Having been expelled from paradise, he will be unable to return there, the way to it being barred by the 'flaming sword' (Gen. III, 24) 'at the East of the Garden of Eden', for which the sword in the present context also stands.

Since according to the biblical and fairytale model that Kafka is following one sin is decisive, Karl's transgression constitutes a perpetual barrier to paradise. Having fallen, he can by definition only continue to fall. There is no going back to a status quo ante. That Karl is more sinned against than sinning makes no difference, for Johanna Brummer is, on one symbolical reading, a projection of his own 'monstrous' sexuality. The whole novel turns on Karl's transgression. He may be a Gothic child of misfortune, burdened with an unhappy secret, and presumptuous to boot, but above all he is, in his half-innocent way, guilty not only of revolt against the patriarchal principles personified by Onkel Jakob (ch. 2) and Oberportier Feodor (ch. 6), but, worse, of 'uncleanness'. This sense of uncleanness is the ultimate reason for the fact that there are ritual lustration scenes in two of the three novels, washing in one form or another being involved in all three. As in the following novel, the tribunal before which the protagonist is repeatedly summoned is at bottom 'the court of his own conscience',[11] but as yet Kafka's symbolical method is not sufficiently developed for this to be reified in the form of a tribunal, although he comes close to it in the Captain's cabin.

The first chapter, published independently in 1913 as 'Der Heizer', is the key to the novel in that the event related there in an inset tale - the sixteen-year-old Karl Rossmann's seduction by the family maid, Johanna Brummer, and subsequent expulsion from his childhood 'paradise' in a re-enactment of the Fall - provides the model on which the other chapters of the novel are more or less 'censored' variations that show Karl trying to come to terms with what has happened. Read thus, *Der Verschollene* centres on 'the mythic expulsion of man from Eden' and is therefore an exemplary Gothic novel, for

> the Gothic tradition replays with almost infinite variations the myths both of the temptation and fall in Eden and of the perilous experience of the post-lapsarian wilderness. The fruit consumed in Eden turns to poison, withering humanity's world into one of suffering and death rather than opening it into the bloom of divine infinity Satan had promised.[12]

'America' stands for the post-lapsarian wilderness, but also for the false paradise of fairytale and medieval ('Gothic') literary convention.

---

11   Godwin uses the term in *Caleb Williams* (III, ch. xi).
12   Stephen C. Behrendt, in his Introduction to Shelley's *Zastrozzi and St Irvyne* (Oxford & New York: Oxford University Press, 1986), xiv.

108

Karl Rossmann's first name both places him in relationship to Kafka, whose initial it echoes (in German K sounds like Kar), and indicates that he is an Everyman figure (Karl = *Kerl*, man), while his surname refers to 'riding' in the Freudian sense, that is, to the traumatic riding lesson he had from the she-devil Johanna Brummer when he lost control, cf. the phrase *ihn reitet der Teufel [die Teufelin]* (he lacks self-control, literally: he is ridden by the Devil [a She-Devil]), which is a fair description of the seduction. In a characteristic way Kafka slips in the key: 'Reiten als bloßes Vergnügen' means 'riding as sheer pleasure', the implication being, since 'bloß' also means naked, that it is sexual pleasure that is in question. The phrase 'die primitivsten Vorübungen des Reitens' (the most rudimentary [primitive] preliminaries to riding) refers to Karl's seduction. Freud was in Kafka's mind at this time and later; in July 1912 we find him discussing Freud when on holiday, and on 23 September (1912), a matter of days before beginning to draft *Der Verschollene*, he noted in his diary that he had naturally been thinking of Freud when he wrote *Das Urteil* (T 294, 668). There is no reason to think that Freud was not also in his mind as he wrote his first novel. Even Brod thought the relevance of Freud's portrayal of the subconscious could not be denied, though it needed careful handling.[13]

The latent symbolism involved in Rossmann's name can perhaps best be revealed by considering it in conjunction with the story *Ein Landarzt*, in which the horse symbolism is more fully developed. The horses there represent the 'nightmare visitor' or night-fiend (ultimately the Devil, who in folklore is given to appearing in the guise of a horse, as riding a black horse, as driving a pair of black horses, and so on),[14] who drives them (appropriate in that the story discloses a series of nightmare situations), but also those fiends in human guise, the doctor and his groom, the latter representing the doctor's id, thereby revealing his hitherto repressed attitude towards Rosa. That all these guises are disguises underlines the structural role of disguise in *Der Verschollene*. The horses appear as if by magic when the doctor needs them, but the magic is dubious, for it leaves the erstwhile country doctor reduced to an accursed-wanderer figure. There are two sides to the doctor: the quasi-sacerdotal figure and the repressed sex-fiend.

In his study of nightmare Ernest Jones considers 'The Horse and the Night-Fiend' at length,[15] and the link between riding and coitus (of which Kafka had a positively Gothic horror) was made as long ago as 1872.[16] Thence riding leads to innumerable folk beliefs to do with travel by night, these being relevant to *Ein Landarzt*, in which the sexual and folklore contexts are emphasized by the sex of the two horses and the doctor's words to them ('Hollah, Bruder, hollah, Schwester!'). 'Hollah' (more usually

---

13 M. Brod, 26.
14 Cf. the colossal demoniacal horse in Poe's *Metzengerstein*.
15 Ernest Jones, *Nightmare, Witches and Devils*, 248-272.
16 Jones, 248-53.

'Hallo'), which means 'Hello', also happens, in this less usual form, to echo the name of Frau (Mother) Holle of German folklore, the lunar goddess of witches. One of the one-time meeting-places of witches was the Hörselberg, which derived its name from the old word *horsa* (horse). Given that horse and rider are identified in folklore, which means that in a symbolical sense the doctor's name is *Roß[mann]*, the name of the maid of whose charms he becomes aware too late, Rosa, is as it were a teasing feminine form of *Roß*, hence 'Bruder' and 'Schwester', a reference to the tale and myth of 'Brüderchen und Schwesterchen' (KHM, No. 11). In fairytale/dream terms Rosa is the doctor's 'sister'. Frau Holle leads to folk beliefs to do with the idea of a storm at night, which is the background to the story, and more especially with the Night-Hunt or Wild Hunt, the chase after a (mythical) woman, here subverted in that the doctor rushes away from Rosa, only trying to head back once it is too late.

So far as Rossmann's name is concerned, then, it is the closely related sexual and diabolical connotations that need to be borne in mind, together with the fact that the name contains a hidden allusion to and identification with Kafka: in both German *(Rappe, Rabe)* and Czech *(vraník, vrána)* there is a verbal bridge between the black horse (and therefore the Devil) and Kafka's name *(kavka → vrána → vraník* and → *Krähe → Rabe → Rappe)*. Both *Der Verschollene* and *Ein Landarzt* have more hidden autobiographical significance than has hitherto been suspected.

Much the same symbolism is involved in Karl's piano-playing, which has an equally clear sexual connotation: Freud argued that musical scales are a form of step, so that the symbolism of 'mounting' applies, with every step a *gradus ad Parnassum*.[17] Mak, who links Karl's piano-playing with his riding-lessons (and their meaning) by describing it as 'amateurish' and 'very primitive', clearly represents Karl's super-ego: he is the libertine that Karl accuses himself of being, and the accomplished libertine that on a subconscious level he would like to be. In this extraordinary, heavily over-determined dream-scene we see sex, which has already damned Karl for ever and which even now he puts before conscience (Green), enthroned in all its glory in Mak's subverted Gothic chapel of a bedroom. Having once succumbed, his self-image as a Lothario, *Steiger* in the German slang of the time, hence his subsequent employment as lift-boy, in which he spends hours on end practising gallantry (or, better, chasing women *[den Frauen nachsteigen]*) in a cell-like space reminiscent of Johanna's bedrooom, is fixed. If Karl is nonetheless more hunted than hunter, his successors Josef K. and K. are seen as *Frauenjäger* (womanizers), from which it is, in German, but a short step to the idea of the *Hexenjagd* (witchhunt, see 7.2.2). In the present context man is seen, in biblical-patriarchal terms, as the victim of woman, of an act of entrapment or engulfment. Gender roles, and with them readers' expectations, are reversed. Johanna Brummer, the first in a series of phallic females in these novels, is

---

17   *The Interpretation of Dreams*, 371f.

also the first to be specifically likened to a witch. Like her grotesque avatar, Brunelda, she is a caricature of the Gothic enchantress (the false bride of fairytale), her bedroom a travesty of the enchantress's bower. The cannibalism motif which surfaces in the Muirs' translation in the words 'it was as if her eyes were devouring him' is not present in the original, but accords with its spirit.

By the 1930s, if not already by the time the novel was written, 'Brummer' meant 'young woman'. Given that Kafka hated loud noises, which he thought of as 'wüster Lärm', and thus associated with 'Wüstheit' (debauchery), the name once again alludes to Karl's transgression and punishment. The fact is that in this novel, as in the next, there is no escaping the idea of incarceration: one of the meanings of the verb *brummen* is 'to do time'. Brummer also points forward to Brunelda in two different ways: firstly, in that 'Brummer' also means a 'bad singer', and Brunelda is both bad and a singer, and secondly in that Brunelda is also a 'Brummer' in the sense of *etwas Großes, Dickes und Schwerfälliges* (something large, fat and ponderous). As if these meanings were not enough, the word 'Brummer' also refers to an insect that makes a rattling noise as it flies, notably a beetle; in this sense Brummer links with *Die Verwandlung*, and suggests, by backward association, that Gregor Samsa's beetle-form may be connected with his past licentiousness, a meaning which is supported by the 'comfort' he derives from pressing himself against (= 'covering') the picture of the woman muffled in furs in a way that corresponds to Johanna's action in pressing her 'naked belly' against Karl's. The word *decken*, which Gregor enacts, means 'to cover' and 'to serve' in the sense of a stallion serving a mare, which completes another circle of meaning (*Hengst* → Rossmann). A third link between *Der Verschollene* and *Die Verwandlung* , as well as being a link between these and *Der Proceß,* is the name of the kitchen-maid (Johanna, Anna). Again and again one is struck, in these works held together by a hidden autobiographical web, by the way in which the meanings of the names Kafka gives to his figures revolve around certain obsessive ideas. Invariably significant, these names are typically the point at which several meanings intersect and interact, the 'nodal points of numerous ideas', for, as Freud said, 'The work of condensation in dreams is seen at its clearest when it handles words and names.'[18]

The ship, as the means by which Karl's expulsion from paradise was effected, represents the reason for it. It is a floating Gothic world of infernal submarine vaults and caverns and dark rambling passages. By an invisible verbal bridge the ship is by implication a prison since in colloquial German the word *Kasten* means both ship and prison. Above all, it is the locus of patriarchal authority, represented by the Captain, against which there is no appeal, so that he is in a similar position to the Old Commandant of the Penal Colony and the domestic autocrat on whom they were both modelled, whose word was law. The symbolical parallelism is obvious enough: Karl's

---

[18] *The Interpretation of Dreams*, 340.

descent into the bowels of the ship, down endlessly recurring stairways, along gangways (corridors) with countless doors and turnings, both replicates his fall and prefigures its further recapitulations in the novel. The realm he enters, the stoker's realm, is an infernal underworld as noisy as Dante's Dis and Milton's Pandemonium. In descending to it Karl is descending to a secular Hell, although it is perhaps fanciful to link Giacomo, in whose company the reader leaves Karl in the seventh chapter after his arrival in America, with the Giacomo in the seventh circle of Hell in Dante's *Inferno*. The Stoker's realm, prison-cell, limbo (purgatory) and hell (inferno) in one, is a Gothic environment, with the stoker in his cell-like cabin very much in the power of the Captain.

The Stoker stands for the devil in Karl; both his function and the umbrella which Karl leaves in the Stoker's cabin can reasonably be interpreted in Freudian terms, hence his dismissal replicating Karl's expulsion. The ship, connected by a verbal bridge with the *Kirchenschiff* (nave) of the Cathedral that 'looms enormous in [the] dense haze' from the balcony of Karl's room in Onkel Jakob's apartment, is not only the means whereby the sudden drastic change in Karl's life is enacted; it also contains within itself much of the situational and spatial imagery of the novel. If it is as it were a secularization of *Kirchenschiff*, the skyscrapers of New York harbour are by the same token secularizations of the church towers of Gothic. It is ironic that Karl, living in a secular world, falls foul of a fossilized Old Testament theology that in the absence of God makes no more sense than do the moral codes in the penal colony of life following the death of their only begetter. Karl's continual ups and downs, shown literally, represent his recurrent Fall and re-enact its cause (Freudian symbolism of stairways, cf. Karl's employment as lift-boy, which is based on the then colloquial meaning of the word *Steiger* [rake, roué, literally mounter],[19] hence Robinson's description of the lift-boys as 'real devils'), are also, as it were, a pastiche of the preoccupation with the perpendicular that literary Gothic took over from Gothic Revival architecture.

Although Karl is being expelled and banished (a fairytale motif, the opposite of the usual Gothic motif of incarceration), the idea of imprisonment is present, both in the idea that applies to all three novels, that women are snares, the notion being as it were supported by the language, by the verbal bridge from *Fall* (Fall) to *Falle* (snare), and in the sense that the guilty conscience is a prison. The idea of incarceration is internalized: Karl is expelled into a prison of the mind, into the awareness of lost innocence, the ever-present idea of transgression, from which, disguise it as he may, he cannot escape, for the very feeling of 'Hilfsbedürftigkeit' (translated by the Muirs as yearning) was transgressive; Kafka, as often, uses the figurative word 'entsetzlich' (dreadful) literally, to mean unlawful. The ship, as a *Kasten* (glasshouse or cooler in

---

19 *The Interpretation of Dreams*, 355.

112

the military sense, so: prison) carries with it, by extension, the idea of chastisement (*kasteien*, to chastise, to practise self-denial).

Unlike those of the average, less cerebral Gothic novel, Kafka's protagonists seek not physical freedom, but freedom from guilt, from oppressive self-awareness. Karl's box (an object pregant with meaning in folklore) is much more than a symbol of the self violated by Johanna Brummer. The Stoker criticizes Karl for leaving his box 'in a stranger's hands', which clearly refers back to the seduction scene. Given the reverse-gender nature of that seduction, it is appropriate that the box, normally a female symbol, stands for Karl, while at the same time also representing both Johanna and the ship (colloquially, Koffer → Kasten), which, like the castle in Gothic, is in many ways the 'hero' of the opening chapter of the novel, a mobile Gothic locus. In Freudian terms the ship stands for the woman in the case, Johanna Brummer, but also for Karl; symbolically it represents not only transgression, of which it is a literal symbol, but punishment as well. *Kasten*, like *Bau*, means (time in) prison, and is connected, by a notable passage in Chapter 3 of *Der Proceß*, with *Der Bau:* 'He felt seasick. He had the impression that he was on a ship rolling in a heavy sea. It was as if the waters were crashing against the wooden sides of the ship, as if a roaring noise were coming from the depths.' The animal trapped in its burrow has the same feeling. Ship and burrow are linked images, both of them associated with feelings of anxiety and entrapment.

What happens after the first chapter is a series of recapitulations, disguised by varying degrees of censorship and wishful thinking, of what was related there, the most egregious wishful thinking being that informing the last chapter. In *Der Verschollene*, then, as in Grosse's *Horrid Mysteries* (1796), 'an erotic *mise-en-scène* repeats itself as a series of [...] visual tableaux'.[20] In these repeated tableaux Karl remains himself, but the other main figures are versions or variants of the ones in the master-tale (Karl's father → Onkel Jakob → Oberportier Feodor; Johanna → Klara → Brunelda). Most of the names are dream-variations on other names, the echoes indicating not so much the symbolical identity of those thus named, as Kafka's obsession with a few basic figures (Rossmann → Robinson; Karl → Klara → Kalla → Fanny ← Johanna; Karl → Ma[c]k; Green → Grete → Negro; Butterbaum → Pollunder; Bendelmayer → Mendel; Delamarche → Mitzelbach; Isbary, Feodor → Isidor; Brummer → Brunelda; Jakob → Giacomo). These inter-relationships based on the patterning or replication of certain vowels and consonants which Kafka also uses elsewhere (e.g. Samsa ↔ Kafka) amount to an exemplary illustration of the stylistic impulse that, in the folk fairytale, keeps on forming the same figures, and of the obsessive circularity of dreams. There are, it need hardly be added, many major

---

[20] Miles, 96.

differences between *Der Verschollene* on the one hand and *Horrid Mysteries*[21] and *Der Genius* on the other, foremost among them the fact that each successive episode in *Der Verschollene* goes back to the initial seduction and expulsion, which it recapitulates in a brilliantly controlled and censored form, whereas *Der Genius*, well described as 'a novel of great artifice and some power, but which also exploits shamelessly and blatantly every device known to the genre',[22] is marked by its author's moral and stylistic lack of restraint. Kafka became a past master of consistent simultaneous symbolisms; after *Der Verschollene* his method, while remaining strongly visual, is not associated with symbolical reduplication of such a relatively obvious kind.

The other notably Gothic and densely symbolical locus of the novel is Pollunder's strangely old mansion, which is larger and taller than a country house designed for one family has any need to be, with no lights except in the lower part of the house. The height and extent of the edifice are unclear. What is clear is that this chapter, to which Karl comes 'as in a dream', is heavily overdetermined. On one level the 'altes Haus' from which Karl is ritually banished in a re-enactment of his initial expulsion represents the domain of the patriarchal (in colloquial German 'altes Haus' means 'old man'), but this dark, labyrinthine house through which Karl tries to find his way is also a symbol of his own id or shadow, and therefore a reduplication of the symbolism of the belly of the ship. The dark attics of the court environment in *Der Proceß* are prefigured in this Gothic edifice.

Described as being 'like a fortress' and 'a fortress, not a mansion' (cf. the Castle and the Burrow), it has unrepaired breaches in its walls that make it resemble a ruinous Gothic castle more than anything else, Montoni's castle, say, in *the Mysteries of Udolpho*. One part of it is like the gallery of a church, and Klara's bedroom turns out to have a baldachin over the bed that turns it into an altar to sex,[23] a perversion of the chapel found in Gothic castles and houses. Displacement along a chain of associations (Nachtmahl → Abendmahl → Kirche → Kapelle → Baldachin → Bett → Johanna Brummer) underlies much of the chapter, showing that, try as he may, Karl is unable to escape his traumatic experience. The pigeon which Green is seen cutting up with such zeal stands for Karl (cf.*Küken* [chicken] in the sense of naive youngster), who is shortly to be cut up by Green in the figurative sense which is first enacted literally, and perhaps also for the cause of his predicament ('Taube' as phallic symbol: *Taubenschlag* [pigeon-loft] has the colloquial meaning of 'flies'. And 'Taube' [pigeon] carries with it the idea of being deaf *[taub]*, in this case to Onkel Jakob's warning to Karl not to neglect his study [of self]).

---

[21] I quote the English title because the novel is famous in English, virtually unknown in German.
[22] Roger Paulin, *Ludwig Tieck: A Literary Biography* (Oxford: Clarendon Press, 1985), 22.
[23] Cf. the Freudian symbolical meaning of the 'chapel': *The Interpretation of Dreams*, 366.

No wonder there is no sign of light in the upper, in symbolical terms once spiritual part of the house, the internal geography of which is confusingly inconsistent, surreal, reminiscent of Piranesi's architectural drawings in the *Carceri d'Invenzione* of *c.* 1745, although the strangely unfinished house is arguably the work not of some neo-Gothic architect, but of the Devil. This is suggested both by the symbolism of Mak's and Klara's bedroom and by the arbitrariness of Onkel Jakob's letter. The house is described as high, yet seems above all low and rambling, like the Castle of Kafka's third and last novel. The crux of the matter is, of course, that this fortress- or castle-like country house, in which the candlelight sends long eerie shadows toward the countless closed doors, is 'an American country house only in name, for it is another of Kafka's castles with a total effect [...] reminiscent of Ann Radcliffe'.[24] Karl trying to find his way through 'this huge house, the endless corridors full of doors (like those in the ship, they are reminders, via the then current word *Leibespforte* [bodily opening or orifice], cited by Freud, of the reason for Karl's banishment, Johanna Brummer), the chapel, the empty rooms, the darkness everywhere', with his candle guttering and finally going out, is pure Gothic as well as pure theatre. The stairway immediately beyond a door, by which Karl leaves, is a Gothic motif[25] as well as a pantomime one.

Karl can scarcely credit his eyes when in the first corridor they come to on their way to Klara's apartment he sees, at every twenty paces, 'a servant in rich livery holding a huge candelabrum with a shaft so thick that both the man's hands were required to grasp it', a spectacle (compare the candle as large as a mast of fairytale[26]) that would have been more at home in early exotic Gothic, in one of Vathek's palaces, say, than in this supposed American country house. Dreams are not normally as exact as that either (every twenty paces - how big is this mansion?). Nor can all this be adequately explained in terms of phallic symbolism exaggerated for comic effect, although no more is heard of the luciferous (literal, for figurative luciferian) servants after Karl's tussle with Klara, which leaves him so disenchanted that he calls her a 'cat, a wild cat', the symbolism being sustained when she bounds out of Karl's room and we find him thinking that her room is likely to be 'eine recht gefährliche Höhle' (a dangerous den/lair), as Johanna Brummer's room proved to be, and as the Burrow was to be ('Höhle' = 'Bau'). The cat simile reflects the fact that Karl is said to have been slung out by his father like a cat being put out (presumably for some feline transgression).

While Karl appears (ch. 3) to resist Klara's blandishments, he succumbs to her in the censored form of being overcome by her in a 'Rauferei' (romp) which stands for

24 R. E. Ruland, 'A View from Back Home: Kafka's *Amerika* ', *American Quarterly*, 13 (1961), 33-42.
25 See, for instance, Maturin, *Fatal Revenge* (Far Thrupp: Alan Sutton, 1994), 53.
26 Stith Thompson, *Motif-Index,* K231.3.1. F. Marion Crawford's *The Witch of Prague* (1891), features not only a character named Israel Kafka, but also (in the opening description of the Teynkirche) 'wax torches, so thick that a man might not span one of them with both his hands'.

the original *Raub* (rape). Karl's first thought on seeing her makes her symbolical identity clear: 'Die roten Lippen, die sie hat' (what red lips she has). While the wording here is somewhat reminiscent of Little Red Riding Hood's words to the wolf who is about to devour her, a closer correspondence is with Jonathan Harker's thought on first seeing the three young vampires in Castle Dracula: 'I felt in my heart a wicked, burning desire that they would kiss me with those red lips.' The fact that in each case the first sight of the lips leads to a similar thought, one explicit and the other censored, makes one wonder whether Kafka could have had the passage from *Dracula* in mind, a point to which we shall need to return, for this is the first of a number of references to vampirism in these novels.

Karl is left to find his way through the darkness by the light of a single guttering candle, so that he arrives outside Klara's and Mak's room with his suit all covered in wax (the fairytale motif of trespass betrayed by dripping wax,[27] for Karl has no business to be heading for Clara's bedroom at this time). The candle symbolism comes to a climax when he opens the door: on the bedside table a single candle is burning, but the sheets and Mak's night-shirt are so white that the candle-light reflected off them is 'almost blinding'. It is an *Irrlicht*, the visual equivalent of the 'Fehlläuten der Nachtglocke'. Shorn of its spiritual connotation, light proves all too often to be an *ignis fatui*. It is appropriate that the Czech word for *ignis fatuus*, *bludička*, also means street girl or prostitute (J 127) and thus acts (in Czech only, not in German; but Latin *ignis* meant flame or beloved object as well as fire) as an open sesame to associations between, on the one hand, the idea of woman as snare and, on the other hand, ideas (being lost, error, heresy, the labyrinth, the vicious circle) that are central to Kafka's work. One should not underestimate the significance for someone with his awareness of language of associations which, being inbuilt in the language, seem to be hallowed by it. His linguistic awareness and use of verbal association extend, like Vladimir Nabokov's after him, across several languages (in Kafka's case, German, Czech and Italian).

Patriarchal interdiction and expulsion are repeated in successive chapters, notably by Onkel Jakob, whose words 'after today's incident I have no choice but to send you forth from me' (hence Onkel Jakob's symbolical *Speditionsgeschäft* [transport business]) echo Adam being 'sent forth' from Eden after the Fall. When Karl is locked out by Onkel Jakob for failing to return by midnight, this is both a reminder of the interconnectedness of Gothic and fairytale and an *ignis fatuus* inviting the unwary reader to indulge in wishful thinking on Karl's behalf. There is, however, no Princess Charming to liberate this reverse-gender Cinderella; on the contrary, the woman in the case detains him. There are no fairytales here, just what in the next novel are dubbed echoes of earlier legends. Echoes is a peculiarly appropriate word, given the way in

---

27   Stith Thompson, *Motif-Index*, C916.1.

which Karl's name is echoed in the names of Klara and (less obviously) Mak. Mak (Mack until 1983) is not only the Prince Charming demanded by the allusion to 'Cinderella', and as such, in one definition, Karl's super-ego; he is also, necessarily, a flawed or subverted prince (cf. Czech *macek*, tom-cat, one of the Devil's disguises), and therefore a figure of fun, as well as being a figure whose name, like Klamm's name in *Das Schloß*, involves deliberate mystification of the reader (in Czech the word *mak*, literally poppy, also has the connotation of poppycock: *nerozumim tomu ani za mak*, I can't make head or tail of it).

Rossmann's position at the beginning of Chapter 4 is remarkably similar to that of Shelley's Wolfstein in his *St Irvyne* :

> Driven from his native country by an event which imposed upon him an insuperable barrier to ever again returning thither, possessing no friends, not having one single resource from which he might obtain support, where could the wretch, the exile, seek for an asylum but with those whose fortunes, expectations, and characters were desperate, and marked as darkly, by fate, as his own.[28]

Wolfstein fell in with a band of robbers inspired by Schiller. Allowing for subversion (ironization, change of register), Chapter 4 of *Der Verschollene* corresponds to the banditti-element in the Gothic novel (e.g. *Udolpho*, IV, ch. 2). Rossmann falls in with their latterday counterparts, Robinson and Delamarche. The more important figure is Robinson, whose name not only mimics Rossmann's, but, like Pollunder's, identifies him (English rob, rape; German *rauben;* Czech *rabovat*) as a 'robber', a reminder of Karl's feeling of having been robbed/raped, although he will eventually accept that he is himself the robber. It is because Robinson's name is symbolical that Kafka goes to the trouble of remarking that it is non-Irish. Robinson is 'Irish' only in the symbolical sense of being, or, better, representing one (Karl) who has erred in allowing himself to be tempted by the Devil into behaving like a madman. The reference is to Karl allowing himelf to be seduced. Kafka puns on *Irer* (Irishman), *Irrer* (madman) and *irren* (to err).

Chapter 5, which re-enacts the first three chapters, is initially close to 'fairytale' in being a matter of wish-fulfilment. The hotel which receives the weary traveller is by definition a kind of haven or harbour, and therefore retains the positive, seductive association of the harbour-image, although the, for Karl, negative (Freudian) associations of 'docking' are present in the background. The significance of Occident, which for the present can be left to speak for itself, is discussed later (in 8.2.2), in relation to Graf Westwest and Count Dracula. Above all this 'hotel' is a regressive haven, an apparent oasis in the wilderness of Karl's life. It continues and combines the symbolism of the ship, Onkel Jakob's business establishment, and Pollunder's country house; like them, and like the court in *Der Proceß* and the castle authority in *Das*

---

[28] P. B. Shelley, in the first chapter of his *St Irvyne*; see Shelley, *Zastrozzi and St Irvyne*, ed. Stephen C. Behrendt (Oxford & New York: Oxford University Press, 1986), 113.

Schloß, it is a hierarchical, heavily defended organization. In symbolical terms it represents the lost paradise Karl is still hoping to regain, a false paradise, a regressive fool's paradise in the sense of a childhood paradise implausibly regained. That is why the head cook is not only (like Therese, who 'used to be' a kitchen-maid) a sublimated version of Johanna Brummer, but a mother figure who 'stood out as an exception to the general hubbub' like Kafka's mother, whom he described as a model of reason amid the hubbub of childhood. Karl's job as liftboy shows him rehearsing the gallantry necessary to the would-be rake: his action when he 'schwang sich in den Aufzug [...] hinter ihnen' (shot into the lift after them) represents a taking literally of the very metaphor that Freud uses in relation to the word *Steiger* in the sense of rake or roué: *den Frauen nachsteigen* (to run after women; literally, to get in after them).[29] His action shows that Karl, far from regretting his part in the seduction, regrets only its unheroic nature; he has a long way to go before accepting his guilt.

In the meantime, his expulsion from paradise by patriarchal fiat, already repeated in Onkel Jakob's interdiction, is re-enacted again, in a disguised (reverse) form, when he transgresses by breaking the first commandment for lift-boys in deserting his lift, with the result that he is expelled by the patriarchal, quasi-divine Head Porter, whose name (Feodor = Theodor) indicates the 'god-given' authority that he (like Kafka's father) claims. Oberportier Feodor elaborates the Gothic and folktale motif of the forbidden door, and of the doorkeeper/gatekeeper, blowing his own trumpet (as Karl will presently do) in saying that he is in charge of all the (outside) doors in the hotel, the main door, the three central and ten side doors, not to mention innumerable little doors and doorless exits. In the first instance this mightily contrived emphasis on the door(way) shows how very large the Johanna Brummmer episode is looming in Karl's mind, but there is another point. Although Kafka's main contribution to what Martin Buber called the 'theology of the door' is made in *Der Proceß* and *Das Schloß*, it seems possible that here already he had in mind the Gnostic tradition according to which hosts of 'gate-keepers' are posted to the right and left of the entrance to the heavenly hall through which the soul must pass in its ascent to the 'Merkabah',[30] since it is from an earthly version of the 'heavenly hall' that Karl is expelled by the chief 'gate-keeper' whose authority is 'god-given'. Later in the novel there is another passage which links with the myth of the door, and more especially with the Parable of the Doorkeeper: originally Robinson had only to ask, and he was either admitted or not admitted to the holy of holies 'according to circumstances'; but having once abused this privilege, having once obeyed the 'Fehlläuten der Nachtglocke', he is forced to obey it whenever it tolls for him. And Robinson represents Karl Rossmann's id or shadow-self. It should also be remembered that, as Andrew Webber has written,

---

29 *The Interpretation of Dreams* [first published in 1900], 355.
30 Politzer, 182f.

'Gatekeeping is one of Freud's favoured metapsychological allegories. When the night-watchman sleeps, dreams play out unconscious fantasies on another, imaginary "Schauplatz".'[31] Webber makes his point with reference to Hoffmann, but it is no less relevant to Kafka, whose work, as we have seen, comprises 'Nachtstücke' in which the 'stage' metaphor is inherent, as it is in the lift symbol.

Brunelda's flat, to which Karl is taken, is the very symbol of his fallen condition. The image of Brunelda lying on the 'Kanapee' in her red dress is a mirror-image of Mak's 'Himmelsbett' and a reflection of the day-bed on which Karl was laid by Klara. In the image of the great bed with its blue silk baldachin we saw sex enthroned in all its glory; here, by contrast, we see the flesh in all its squalor and contingency. Brunelda is a grotesque Eve, an extreme version of Johanna Brummer (*Brummer* [woman] → Brunelda), with whom she is explicitly identified both as a 'bad singer' and in being large, fat and ponderous. As a nightmarish version of Johanna Brummer, whom Karl is still blaming for his downfall, her function is to fill him with nausea. Through her appearance and dress she corresponds to the 'giantess in a red dress' of Icelandic folktale and the woman arrayed in scarlet of St. John's vision. It is because Karl let himself be misled and seduced by Johanna that Brunelda's 'former husband' (dreams and fairytales tend to describe lovers as husband and wife or brother and sister) is described as a 'Kakaofabrikant' (literally, cocoa-merchant, but the word is simply a taking-literally of the phrase *jemanden durch den Kakao ziehen*, to lead someone up the garden path, the type ultimately identifiable with the Devil). German, it should be said, uses the same word for mislead and seduce. Karl has been 'whoring after a false idol' in the biblical sense, this being shown literally, as in the Bible, which in turn accounts for an apparent echo of the story of Aholah and Aholibah (Ezekiel XXIII) which precedes the Fall of Tyre, to which allusion is duly made in the 'Naturtheater von Oklahoma' scene.

It is when Brunelda in her role as Eve and avatar of Johanna Brummer is ordering Karl to make preparations for yet another re-enactment of his seduction in the form of a punitive fantasy that he makes an attempt to escape which is unsuccesful because the door of the flat is locked, as it was at the time of the original rape. This time, the re-enactment being part of a punitive fantasy, the key is missing. The missing key, charged with symbolical meaning, is nothing less than the key to his life, the emblem of his lost innocence and a sign that he is soon to go missing himself. The Gothic and fairytale forbidden door motif, which looms larger in each successive novel, reaches a climax in *Das Schloß*. In the present novel, as we have already seen (6.1.), Kafka merely toys with the 'chamber of horrors' motif, which he subverts: Karl's escape from Brunelda's flat amounts to a comic pastiche of the escape from incarceration that is so common in the Gothic novel, while the dumping of Brunelda in Unternehmen 25 is a

---

31   Andrew J.Webber, *The Doppelgänger* (Oxford: Clarendon Press, 1996), 193.

reversal of Musäus's *Entführung aus dem Serail* ([Abduction from]Il Seraglio) and at the same time the final unsuccessful attempt by Karl to get rid of the devil within himself (Brunelda ↔ Brendly).

Another extraordinary scene greets Karl in what used to be printed as the final chapter, and now appears as the penultimate fragment, when he finds hundreds of women, mounted on separate pedestals (some so high that - normal logic is reversed - they make the women look gigantic), dressed as angels in white robes and with great wings, blowing long trumpets that glitter like gold. Clearly all that glitters is not gold: the women are neither as exalted nor as angelic as they seem. Fanny explains that they blow their trumpets for two hours at a time, after which they are relieved by men dressed as devils, half of them blowing on their instruments and the other half beating drums. There is no reason to suppose that the men, for their part, are not as devilish as they seem. There is a conclusion waiting to be drawn, which Karl duly draws by identifying with the Devil shortly afterwards. Heavily disguised by wish-fulfilment, this scene appears to represent some kind of paradise regained, but what it really represents is the Fall of Tyre (Ezekiel XXVIII, 13) with its tabrets and pipes, the Fall of Babylon (Rev. XIV-XVII), the 'mother of harlots' (cf. Brunelda), and the seven angels of the apocalypse, dressed in 'pure and white linen' and sounding the seven trumps of doom. The fact that Tyre was condemned for its sacrilegious pride, while Babylon was 'drunk with the wine of her fornication', makes the allusions appropriate, given Karl's pride and 'Robinson's' drunkenness. As variants of the Paradise myth, both the Fall of Tyre and the Fall of Babylon incorporate what has been called the central Gothic event. The novel thus ends as it began, with the Fall of Man. The last chapter is simply the most heavily disguised replication of the Fall. It holds no hope at all for Karl, who identifies with the men dressed as devils, thereby acknowledging his guilt, when he chooses one of the Devil's appellations as his pseudonym.

This whole last chapter is therefore a dream, based on wish-fulfilment, with the latent meaning of the dream revealed to the reader, but withheld from the dreamer. The simple truth is that for Karl, who lost his way when he failed to defend his virginity against Johanna Brummer, there is no way back to innocence. As the German proverb says, *hin ist hin* (lost is lost). Once Karl has fallen, he can only go on falling; there is no question of being saved by some kind of miracle, not just because the age of miracles is long past, but because Karl, who has by now, in an act of self-denigration, identified with the Devil by adopting one of his appellations (Negro, the 'Black One', in German *Schwarzer*) is, as the meanings of the German word *schwarz* (shady, illicit) imply, specifically unentitled to enter any notional paradise. The misleadingly optimistic-seeming final chapter is accordingly to be read as the most heavily disguised version of his fall, the novel ending, as it must in Freudian terms, with Karl embarking on the journey to death. The immediate fate that Kafka had in mind for Karl was for him to go missing and be declared legally dead, the figurative

120

equivalent of the live burial of Gothic. It was presumably because he could not bear to give it the negative ending he knew it would have to have, that Kafka left the novel unfinished, just as it was because he was too honest to do otherwise, that he broke off the ending on an unambiguous note.

The enigmatic last fragment of the novel, entitled 'Sie fuhren zwei Tage' (They travelled for two days), ends with a reference to great mountains and mountain torrents, the chill from which numbed their faces. This is a clear echo of the sublime, on which Gothic fiction is based. A comparison with a passage from *The Mysteries of Udolpho* (II, ch. 5) is revealing. Ann Radcliffe wrote:

> From this sublime scene the travellers continued to ascend among the pines, till they entered a narrow pass of the mountains, which shut out every feature of the distant country, and, in its stead, exhibited only tremendous crags, impending over the road [...] Though the deep vallies between these mountains were, for the most part, clothed with pines, sometimes an abrupt opening presented a perspective of only barren rocks, with a cataract flashing from their summit among broken cliffs, till its waters, reaching the bottom, foamed along with unceasing fury; and sometimes pastoral scenes exhibited their 'green delights' in the narrow vales, smiles amid surrounding horror.

This mountainscape, the reader is told, is as wild as any the travellers had yet passed. There is an immediate connexion with Kafka in that this mountainscape, like his, is purely imaginary, neither writer having travelled through the country they purport to be describing.[32] Radcliffe's is a standard description of sublimity, the awe inspired by the Apennines tempered by the 'green delights' down on the human level. The broken crags foreshadow the broken battlements of Montoni's castle. The ending of *Der Verschollene* is comparable:

> On the first day they traversed a high mountain range. Masses of blue-black rock rose in sheer wedges to the railway line; even by craning their necks out of the window they could not see the summits; narrow, gloomy, jagged valleys opened out and they tried to follow with pointing fingers the direction in which these were lost to sight; broad mountain streams appeared, turning into raging torrents as they cascaded downhill in a thousand foaming wavelets, plunging under the bridges over which the train sped; they were so near that the breath of coldness rising from them numbed their faces.

What is striking about this imaginary mountainscape is, first, that it is so similar to Ann Radcliffe's, and, second, that Kafka, who normally eschews natural description, here apparently revels in it. It is not his style to be as emotional, or as obvious, as Radcliffe, so that his description is cooler and more laconic, but, although the two passages serve a different purpose, there is no mistaking the common symbolism. Radcliffe's description serves to evoke the sublime of terror, pointing ominously forward to the terrors which Montoni's castle is to hold for Emily before the eventual happy ending. Faced with the sublime in nature, Blanche's thoughts turn involuntarily

---

[32] If Kafka's reference to 'spitze Keilen' (sheer wedges) involves an allusion to the Keilberg, the highest peak of the Erzgebirge, on the Bohemian side of that range, the novel ends as it began, with a hidden reference to Kafka's and Karl's fatherland.

to the 'Great Author' of the sublime objects she is contemplating. At the end of *Der Verschollene* there is no such consoling vision. On the contrary, what was once sublime is there associated with death and the Devil. Kafka's passage, which describes an alpine landscape (and although the word *Alp* is not used, it should not be forgotten that its secondary meaning is 'nightmare') ends with a reference to the Devil (whose domain nightmare is, and from whom that chill surely emanates) who is leading Karl to damnation, for when the reader leaves him Karl is clearly going 'to the Devil'. In evoking the sublime, or once-sublime, Kafka is in effect drawing attention to the proximity of Gothic.

In his first novel, then, Kafka combines Biblical and Freudian symbolism with fairytale and Gothic motifs, and with Gothic iconography, within an overall fairytale structure, although the initial adverse situation is, of course, also a characteristic of comedy. Its central theme is Gothic enough, as is much of the detail of Chapters 1, 3 and 5 in particular, but so much displacement or disguise is involved, and so much humour is present in the detail, that, despite its ending, the novel as a whole seems rather less Gothic than its successors. The combination of Gothic and humour is as characteristic as it is original.

7. *DER PROCESS*

7.1. Fairytale Motifs

The quest for a lost paradise, or for some literal or metaphorical treasure, is one of the main types of fairytale.[1] It underlies all three of Kafka's novels, and is seen at its most fairytale-like in the summation of *Der Proceß*, the Parable of the Doorkeeper. The lost paradise in question is that of untroubled consciousness.

The way in which the folk fairytale 'expresses internal feelings through external events'[2] is reflected in Josef K.'s arrest. There are many fairytale precedents for the unsurprised way in which he accepts the presence of the 'Wächter' (watchmen) and, eventually, of his executioners. Like the hero of fairytale, Josef K. finds the right way 'as if by magic' when he goes to the Court for the first time, although the magic, if magic it is, is powerless to save him. Kafka first referred to the story of Hansel and Gretel in a letter to Oskar Pollak of 9 November 1903 ('We are all on our own like children lost in the forest'); he references it again in this novel in the form of the title of one of the pornographic books of the law, 'Die Plagen, welche Grete von ihrem Manne Hans zu erleiden hatte' ('The trouble Grete had with her husband Hans'), which subverts the famous fairytale in several obvious ways. The motif of the three drops of blood in the snow in 'Sneewittchen', also present in Wolfram's *Parzival*, to which there are many apparent references in *Der Proceß*, appears as 'dirt [...] on the melting snow' outside the building where the painter Titorelli (cf. not only Titurel, Parzival's great-grandfather, but also Titeliture, one of the names of Rumpelstiltskin) lives, a deliberate subversion of the motif, and as such a denial of whatever magic was originally inherent in it. In 'Sneewittchen' the three drops of blood in the snow prompt the queen to say 'hätt ich ein Kind so weiß wie Schnee' ('Would I had a child as white as snow'); in *Der Proceß* the sludge leads Josef K. to a depraved young 'witch' whom he inwardly wishes to the devil, and to Leni, whose webbed fingers are, apart from anything else, an example of the 'tiny flaw' of fairytale (in the text they are actually labelled a 'kleiner Fehler'); we return to them presently.

There is, in Josef K. and K., more than a little of the anti-hero ('Unheld') who in folklore 'unerringly hits upon the wrong [course of action]'.[3] The way in which the folk fairytale 'isolates people, objects, and episodes, and each character is as

---

1   See Stith Thompson, *Motif-Index*, H1250.
2   Lüthi, *The European Folktale*, 15.
3   Lüthi, *The European Folktale*, 14f.

unfamiliar to himself as the individual characters are to one another'[4] is reflected in Josef K.'s lack of self-knowledge and in the reader's relative lack of knowledge about him and his various 'helpers'. We know scarcely more of Josef K.'s background than we do of the antecedents of the typical fairytale hero. Unlike fairytales, however, Kafka's novels have no separate hero and villain; the protagonist is hero and villain in one, with the hero subverted by the villain. The isolation of fairytale characters is paralleled by the isolation of Kafka's figures, the only relationship between whom is their functional relationship to the protagonist and his inner world: the examining magistrate, Huld, Titorelli and the Priest all relate to Josef K. in the same general way, as well as in various specific ways, but there is no other connexion between them, nor could there be. There is no way in which they could meet, and no locus where they could do so, for every single location in this relentlessly Gothic novel is a reification of Josef K.'s sense of guilt, hence the unremitting sameness of Titorelli's heathscapes. As projections of Josef K., they can, by definition, exist only one after the other; as in fairytale, each new stage of Josef K.'s *Proceß* calls forth a new 'helper'. The subsidiary figures mostly vanish like the helpers of fairytale as soon as they have fulfilled their purpose. Though internalized, many of them are just this, 'helpers'; this applies, especially, to the main subsidiary figures in the second half of *Der Proceß,* each of whom offers K. something tantamount to the 'gift' of fairytale in the form of advice that is needed, but which is or seems to be wasted, like the gift offered to the anti-hero of fairytale, although they also have a cumulative effect. Josef K. is more anti-hero than hero. As Lüthi says, 'The gifts of the folktale [...] are given whenever a particular task calls for them, and they are offered - usually by total strangers - all of a sudden or as a result of an ad hoc relationship that is established quickly and rather sketchily'.[5] The relationship between Josef K. and his 'helpers' is ad hoc in this sense. It could be argued that he receives the 'gifts' he needs as he needs them; but these internalized gifts are potentialities, most of which he proceeds to waste. The formulaic 'variierte Wiederholung' (modified repetition) of phrases (Leni's 'Das ist alles Erfindung' [that's all invention] is followed by Titorelli's 'Das alles ist Erfindung' [all that's invention]) is a feature of fairytale, and the calling of the name of Josef K. in the Cathedral takes the reader back to 'Rumpelstilzchen', where the calling of the name, for which there are also Biblical precedents, is a magical motif.

The Parable of the Doorkeeper, like the story of Amalia's Secret in *Das Schloß*, is pure fairytale, based on the folk fairytale of type 465A (the quest for the unknown), as well as going back to numerous tales and myths about journeying to the otherworld. There are many instances of the forbidden-door motif in the novels, but the *locus classicus* is the Parable of the Doorkeeper, which is particularly close to Andersen, as

---

4   Lüthi, *The European Folktale,* 43.
5   Lüthi, *The European Folktale,* 57.

well as to Grimm, in that the 'forbidden chamber' of the Law, from which emanates a seemingly eternal radiance ('unverlöschlicher Glanz'), is reminiscent of the thirteenth chamber in the Grimms' 'Marienkind' ('The Woodcutter's Daughter'), which contains 'die Dreieinigkeit in Feuer und Glanz' (the Trinity in fire and splendour): the 'unverlöschlicher Glanz' is part of the motif of the forbidden room as such, powerfully underlining the taboo. Such intertextualities suggest that the Man-from-the-Country would have perished if he had had the temerity or folly to enter the chamber that was both open and forbidden to him. Forbidden rooms, which in folklore, with the ambiguity that is even commoner in Kafka's work, may have the connotation not only of Heaven, but of Hell, are liable to contain nasty surprises, as the Bluebeard tales (e.g. Grimm's 'Der Räuberbräutigam') show. The scene in the *Rumpelkammer* in *Der Proceß* involves an echo of the Bluebeard tales.

The Parable of the Doorkeeper shows that Kafka also knew and valued Andersen's work,[6] for it is based on the most famous of Andersen's early tales and the one closest to folk fairytale, 'The Tinder-Box'. The tinder-box represents the lost treasure or, in terms of the pattern of allusions in *Der Proceß*, the Grail. The gatekeeper/doorkeeper as such is a folk-fairytale stereotype, the threshold a fantasy and folktale motif, and the portal a fantasy motif of great importance. In the parable the doorkeepers, each more formidable than the one before, are clearly based on the dogs guarding successive rooms in 'The Tinder-Box', and the gleam of what might or might not be 'eternal radiance [light]' ('unverlöschlicher Glanz'), visible through the doorway to the Law, will have been suggested, in part, by the light from the three hundred lamps in the great hall in Andersen's story. While in English the radiance in question might just as well be the radiant heat of Hell as the radiant light of Heaven, in German the connotations of 'Glanz' are as positive as the epithet, although the ambiguity of the image and its meaning remains. The Man-from-the-Country is a Biblical Philistine or man-of-little-faith, but also the Am-ha'aretz of Jewish folklore, the name for an ignoramus or, to use the fairytale term, a numskull, the 'countryman in the great world' who reveals his folly at every step,[7] as in the Sicilian fairytale in which a 'numskull' comes to a river and waits for it to run dry,[8] which of course it never does. There are many such tales. Given his knowledge of Italian and love of fairytale, Kafka may well have come across the tale in question.[9] Spending one's life waiting to be allowed to enter a doorway, the door of which is all the time standing open, makes no more sense.

The ending of the novel, as interpreted in the next section, involves the fairytale motif of the evil-doer passing judgment on himself. In an alternative ending of *Der*

---

6   On Andersen, see BF 61, 722, 727.
7   Stith Thompson, *Motif-Index*, J1742 etc.
8   Stith Thompson, *Motif-Indexe*, J1967.
9   See Laura Gonzenbach, *Sicilianische Märchen*, 2 vols (Leipzig: Engelmann, 1870), No. 17.

Proceß, written in 1916, the executioner says 'You are no doubt thinking of the fairytale in which a servant was ordered to expose a child[10], but was not able to bring himself to do this, so that he apprenticed it to a shoemaker instead. That was a fairytale, but what we are talking about here is no fairytale' (T 510). Many fairytales speak of the exposed or abandoned child being rescued, to say nothing of featuring executioners and knives being whetted. The actual ending of *Der Proceß,* which comes close to late nineteenth-century Gothic in the death of the 'vampire', is far removed from fairytale.

Although the Parable of the Door-Keeper is full of fairytale motifs and is itself a literary fairytale, as a whole *Der Proceß* is less close to fairytale than the other two novels. This is because at the time Kafka's imagination was held by ideas which combined to make it the most Gothic of his novels.

7.2. Gothic Readings
7.2.1. The Internal Tribunal

Der Proceß, Kafka's second novel, written in the second half of 1914, was published posthumously in 1925. When reduced by translation to monosemy and, worse, to the naturalism Kafka eschewed, it seems to be about a forthcoming trial, and therefore to belong in a long succession of 'trial'-novels stretching back to Godwin's *Caleb Williams* (1783-84). However, while the legal 'machinery' of the novel may appear to be identifiable with the monolithic, bureaucratic machinery of Habsburg *Kakanien* in its dying years, there is no reason to think that such a reading would not be a misreading, although bureaucracy could still be one skin of the Kafkaesque onion; there is, for instance, much emphasis on empty form in *In der Strafkolonie.* Kafka was not, as a writer, interested in politics - the freedom to which he attached such importance was moral freedom, which his view of life at best curtailed and at worst precluded. Besides, consideration of his literary method and use of words and metaphors quickly takes the critical reader beyond the realm of the public and political.

The reader should from the outset be in no doubt that Josef K. is not, as Godwin's Caleb Williams is, the victim of injustice. *Der Proceß* has to do with the constitution and corruption not of society, but of the individual human being; in other words, it has to do not with things as they are, but with Kafka as he was afraid he could become, and with his projective creature, Josef K., as he is. Its moral, if it has one, is 'Judge Thyself!' *Caleb Williams* is a novel of more than one kind, but it is, above all, a political novel in the sense that its author's intention was to change society. As a

---

10 See Stith Thompson, *Motif-Index,* R130.

public novel, it works dramatically, through the confrontation of one individual with another, whereas *Der Proceß* portrays a confrontation with self, a confrontation of the higher self with the lower, a confrontation of super ego and ego, of ego and id, persona and shadow. There is, of course, much more to the novel, and to the Gothic novel, than psychology of whatever ilk, but the psychological dimension and level of meaning of neither can sensibly be ignored. *Der Proceß* can be compared with *Caleb Williams*, and with Mary Shelley's *Frankenstein*, in that in the course of it the pursued becomes the pursuer. Leaving aside their symbolical identity for the moment, K. is at first pursued by the minions of the 'Law', is 'arrested' and told to present himself for a preliminary hearing at such and such a time; but then, initially for the wrong reasons, he becomes the pursuer, increasingly determined to confront his 'judge' and force the truth out of him, as indeed he does in a final confrontation with self. However much *Der Proceß* may seem to partake of Godwin's preoccupation with injustice as it ought not to be, it is not a political novel, but a moral, metaphysical and psychological one. And, since it is also, technically, a symbolical novel, its means are very different from Godwin's. In particular it has a multiplicity of meaning, achieved through a web of metaphors taken literally and developed with legalistic precision, that gives it a brilliance that is different in kind from Godwin's brilliant psychological penetration and play of ideas. Like *Caleb Williams*, it was given alternative endings; but while the two endings of Godwin's novel are totally different, the three alternative endings of *Der Proceß* all boil down to the same thing.

Whereas the emphasis in *Caleb Williams* is on psychological motivation, with the decisive events of the novel, those which trigger psychological change, taking place in public, in *Der Proceß* everything takes place in the mind. If both are 'psychological novels', they are so in quite different senses. Godwin writes as a social philosopher, Kafka as meta-physician and moral physician, and it is Kafka who arguably wields the 'metaphysical dissecting knife', of which Godwin speaks, to the greater *metaphysical* effect. Godwin believed, passionately, and, it is to be feared, mistakenly, in the perfectibility of Man and hence of human society. For Kafka on the other hand, no less of an idealist than Godwin, and no less concerned with uncovering the wellsprings of human conduct, the individual, let alone that fearfully miscellaneous monster, Society, is far from perfectible, being trapped in a time-warp world of predetermined universal guilt that is theological in origin and psychological in effect. *Der Proceß* can be read in more ways than one, although the number of readings appropriately contingent on Kafka's method, mind-set and preoccupations is limited; but it is neither detective story, nor adventure story, nor Jacobin novel, nor political allegory. For two novels equally concerned with freedom and justice, *Caleb Williams* and *Der Proceß* could in the end hardly be more different. We therefore pass from *Der Proceß* as it is not, to *Der Proceß* as it is.

Like virtually all Kafka's work, *Der Proceß* is the expression of what he called his 'dreamlike inner life'. This is what it explores. Any understanding of the novel must begin with the meanings of the word 'Proceß' and take into account the implications of Kafka's spelling of it. The word 'Prozeß' (as the title was spelt until 1990, when Kafka's original spelling of 'Proceß' was reinstated) means not only 'trial', but '(mental) process' and 'course (of a disease)'. All three meanings are relevant, the second being fundamental, and the reader also needs to know that when he began writing *Der Proceß* Kafka had already had two spells in different sanatoria, although his pulmonary tuberculosis as such was not diagnosed until September 1917. My readings concentrate on other issues, but we need to remember that ill-health, both real and imaginary, was (in English, but not in German) a 'trial' for Kafka for much of his life.

We shall have cause to return to his spelling of the word presently, but first let us consider the famous opening sentence: 'Someone must have been taking Josef K.'s name in vain, for, without having done anything wrong, he was arrested one morning.' That ominous, enigmatic opening of *Der Proceß* is dramatically Gothic in that it marks the sudden end of the protagonist's hitherto secure, unquestioning and to that extent unproblematical, though in this case at least boorish and mindlessly materialistic existence, and the beginning of a new, haunted, perpetually challenged and ultimately impossible one. The supposed anonymous denunciation, here purely imaginary, is as it were an internalization of the procedure described in *The Mysteries of Udolpho* (III, ch. 8), which involved a letter of accusation being placed in the letter-box for *Denunzie secrete* in the Doge's palace: 'As, on these occasions, the accuser is not confronted with the accused, a man may falsely impeach his enemy, and accomplish an unjust revenge, without fear of imprisonment or detection' - a method rightly described as a 'diabolical means of ruining a person'.

Josef K. is *not* guilty of any transgression of the civil law, which is simply not in question, or of any particular violation of any symbolical law, or even of any single reprehensible act. In a general way this opening connects with the *Brief an den Vater*, in which Kafka wrote, of his father, that 'you don't charge me with anything downright improper or wicked', for the words 'etwas [...] Böses' (anything [...] wicked) are used in both cases. This autobiographical dimension was underlined when he went on to write, also in the *Brief an den Vater*, of 'this terrible trial that is pending between us [Franz and Ottla] and you [...] a trial in which you keep on claiming to be the judge'(BV 164). We shall return to this in our second reading. The Court is simply a metaphor, elaborated in Kafka's usual deadpan, often hilarious way, in this case for the workings of the Conscience, for *Der Proceß*, like all his punishment fantasies, is less about guilt as such than about a sense of guilt.

Josef K.'s famous awakening is a symbolical one: he awakens to a sense of unease, his conscience slowly filling with a sense first of uneasiness and then of guilt about

128

the thoughtless, materialistic and, in Kafka's terms, corrupt way in which he has been conducting his life. He has allowed himself to become over-attached ('verhaftet' in German, literally 'arrested'), hence the opening of the novel, in which 'verhaftet' is taken literally but meant figuratively, so that *Verhaftung* stands for *Verhaftetsein* in the sense of over-attachment (to the world, the flesh and the Devil), in other words, to what Kafka, in aphorism 54, calls 'das Böse in der geistigen Welt' (the evil in an essentially spiritual world). Initially Josef K. sees himself as the victim of arbitrary power, as indeed he is on the next reading, though not on this one, and even then not in the most obvious sense. In the course of the novel, which takes up exactly one year of his life, he slowly comes to see himself as a villain. He should know; his own judgment is the only relevant one, and ultimately the only one available to him. If there are no fairytales, there are no miracles and therefore no (accessible) God, let alone a god in a machine.

To speak of *Der Proceß* as lasting a year, and *Das Schloß* a week, is, however, largely beside the point, which is that in the revealed subconscious which is their domain, there is no more teleology than there is in dreams: in each case the protagonist has simply had all he can take of the dreadful cyclic disorder that has taken over his life. The whole of *Der Proceß* is about the gradual awakening of conscience, the dawning of the idea of transgression against the law of Josef K.'s own existence as a more than animal being, and in that sense moral guilt, but also about existential guilt, for he is guilty not only in the moral terms which he eventually defines in the last chapter of the novel, but also in existential terms. Whether this is described in Christian terms as 'original sin', or in Schopenhauerian-Buddhist terms, as the guilt inherent in an existence that comes about as a result of the sexual self-indulgence of others, makes little difference. Kafka came under the spell of Schopenhauer's mixture of profundity and lucidity, but it was the Fall of Man by which he was still obsessed at this time. Josef K.'s 'sinfulness' is tantamount to original sin as defined in the aphorism series *Er* : 'Original sin, that age-old wrong done by Man, consists in the complaint [...] that he has been treated unjustly, that he is the victim of original sin.' In brief, Josef K. is guilty of being who and what he is, and of acting against his own first unconscious, then conscious judgment of how he should have been conducting his life.

Having indicated that Josef K. is guilty, albeit not guilty as charged, it is time to turn our attention to the Court that appears to claim the right to try him, as Kafka's father is said to have claimed the right to try his son. The Court represents, in the first instance, what Kant, in the *Critique of Practical Reason*, called the 'internal tribunal' of conscience. Kant used an elaborate legal metaphor to describe the workings of conscience, by which he means the knowledge people have about what they have done, in a way which, when applied to it, amounts to a key to *Der Proceß* :

The consciousness of an internal *tribunal* in man (before which 'his thoughts accuse or excuse one another') is Conscience.

Every man has a conscience, and finds himself observed by an inward judge which threatens and keeps him in awe (reverence combined with fear); and this power which watches over the laws within him is not something which he himself (arbitrarily) *makes*, but it is incorporated in his being. It follows him like his shadow, when he thinks to escape. He may [...] stupefy himself with pleasures and distractions, but he cannot avoid now and then coming to himself or awaking, and then he at once perceives its awful voice. In his utmost depravity he may, indeed, pay no attention to it, but he cannot avoid *hearing* it.

Now this [...] moral capacity, called *conscience*, has this peculiarity in it, that although its business is a business of man with himself, yet he finds himself compelled by his reason to transact it as if at the command of *another person*. For the transaction here is the conduct of a *trial (causa)* before a tribunal. But that he who is *accused* by his conscience should be conceived as *one and the same person* with the judge is an absurd conception of a judicial court; for then the complainant would always lose his case. Therefore in all duties the conscience of the man must regard *another* than himself as the judge of his actions, if it is to avoid self-contradiction [...] this other may be an actual or a merely ideal person which reason frames to itself. [11]

In a footnote Kant explains a man's dual identity as his own accuser before the metaphorical bar of moral judgment and as his own judge by referring to the distinction between *homo noumenon* and the rationally endowed *homo sensibilis;* the fact that in ancient Greek the Devil's name (διάβολος) means 'an Accuser',[12] serves to emphasize the fact that Kafka's own conscience regularly gave him the devil of a time, and that in the course of the novel Josef K., like his predecessor Karl Rossmann, is to go to the Devil. Josef K. is thus identifiable with the Devil both as a 'teuflischer Mensch' and as his own accuser.

Schopenhauer, in his discussion of 'Kant's Doctrine of Conscience' in *The Basis of Morality*, argued that

if this tribunal, as portrayed by Kant, really existed in our breasts, it would be astonishing if a single person could be found to be, I do not say, so bad, but so stupid, as to act against his conscience. For such a supernatural assize, of an entirely special kind, set up in our consciousness, such a secret court - like another Fehmgericht - held in the dark recesses of our innermost being, would inspire everybody with a terror and fear of the gods strong enough to [...] keep him from grasping at short transient advantages, in face of the dreadful threats of superhuman powers, speaking in tones so near and so clear.[13]

Yet Josef K. seems to be just such a stupid person, for Kant's account of the workings of conscience, and, if I am not mistaken, Schopenhauer's analysis of it, provided Kafka with an elaborate model for the 'court' in *Der Proceß*,[14] a model which links with Gothic in that Kant refers to this internal tribunal or 'supernatural assize', as Schopenhauer calls it, as a 'disguised *Vehmgericht* that takes place in the mysterious darkness inside us'. The *Vehmgericht*, let us remember, was an open-air court or tribunal, held in Germany, and especially in Westphalia, from the fourteenth to

---

[11] I. Kant, *Critique of Practical Reason and other works on the Theory of Ethics,* tr. Thomas Kingsmill Abbott, 3rd edn, (London: Longmans, Green , 1883), 321ff.

[12] Shelley, 'Essay on the Devil and Devils', 268.

[13] Schopenhauer, *The Basis of Morality*, 109.

[14] It is discussed at greater length in Patrick Bridgwater, *Kafka and Nietzsche,* 2nd edn (Bonn: Bouvier, 1987*),* 67-78.

sixteenth centuries, for the suppression of crime, notably heresy and witchcraft, at which the death-sentence, the only sentence available to the court, was carried out immediately after an admission of guilt. It featured notably in Goethe's *Götz von Berlichingen* [1773], Benedikte Naubert's *Hermann von Unna* (1788, one of the first of the German *Schauerromane* to be translated into English [*Herman of Unna: A Series of Adventures of the Fifteenth Century [...]*, London: Robinson, 3 vols, 1794], the text being preceded by a prefatory 'Essay on the Secret Tribunal and its Judges, formerly existing in Westphalia', said to be by one Baron Bock), and in Chapter 20 of Scott's *Anne of Geierstein* (1829), and is as much a Gothic institution and feature of Gothic as the Spanish Inquisition itself.[15] This is shown by the way in which it features in German Gothic novels such as J. B. Durach's *Die Adelritter, ein Gräuelgemälde aus den Zeiten der Vehmgerichte* (1793) and Veit Weber's *Die Heilige Vehme* (Vol. 6 of his *Sagen der Vorzeit,* 1796).There is also an early Gothic anonymous chapbook, *The Secret Tribunal: or, The Court of Winceslaus. A Mysterious Tale,* published in London in 1803,[16] when the future metaphysician of Gothic, Arthur Schopenhauer,[17] was incarcerated in Thomas Lancaster's academy in Wimbledon.[18] The prisoner who appears before this Secret Tribunal is told, in Scott's novel, that 'you would be safer if you were suspended by the hair over the abyss of Schaffhausen, or if you lay below an axe which a thread of silk alone kept back from the fall'. The way in which the *Vehmgericht* in effect becomes a metaphor for conscience is an excellent example of Kafka's internalization of Gothic forms.

Der Proceß portrays the awakening of conscience and the process through and as a result of which this internal judge or super-ego comes to pass judgment, that is, the way in which Josef K. comes to condemn himself for his egoistical, licentious way of living, which is, of course, a caricature of Kafka's 'dissolute' way of living as seen by his father; a fragment speaks of Josef K.'s (sic) father reproaching him for his 'dissolute behaviour' (diary, 29 July 1914), a charge which is reflected in Chapter 5 in the reference to Franz's marriage plans, which reflect Kafka's own. There is also a further charge and form of guilt, to which we come in the next section. Much of the novel illustrates the conflict within Josef K.'s mind between his conscience (first personified in the first guard or watchman, Franz, who is seen sitting by the open window because he is a *Beisitzer*, a member of the court) and his pride (personified in the second watchman, Willem, whose Dutch name derives from the phrase *den dicken Wilhelm machen*, to boast). The term 'Behörde' to denote the authority served by these 'Wächter' is used in its basic sense, that is, as the noun from the verb *behören* (to listen to, intercept, monitor), and therefore symbolizes the super-ego, the inner

---

15 The Star Chamber and the Chambre Ardente were similar institions.
16 Andrew Block, *The English Novel, 1740-1850. A Catalogue* (London: Dawsons, 1967), 211.
17 His main work appeared in German in 1819.
18 See Patrick Bridgwater, *Arthur Schopenhauer's English Schooling* (London: Routledge, 1988).

monitor or moral censor (or gatekeeper in Freud's suggestive terminology), to the first unclear promptings of which Josef K. is loath to listen.

In accordance with the Kantian model and metaphor the attics associated with the court represent Josef K.'s head/mind, in which the whole process (*der ganze Rummel* → 'Rumpelkammer') is taking place, the corridors *(Gänge → Gedankengänge)* representing his thoughts and the progress of his case, the 'Gang seiner Angelegenheit'. Kafka, as usual, simply takes literally the meanings he finds embedded in the language in the form of metaphors which he undoes and embeds within the text (*Haus = Mensch:* house = human being (man); *Dach/Dachboden [cf. Schädeldach] = Kopf:* attic = head, mind).[19] Every court-official and judge is accordingly a projection of K. himself, whose whole way of life, he slowly begins to realize, has been a mindlessly selfish one, vulgar and meaningless. Josef K. is shown as literally working in a bank because he is a *Bankmensch*, a person (in the German of the time, modern *Gewohnheitstier*) governed by habit rather than thought. The elaborate legal metaphor or fiction of K.'s impending 'trial' is continued in the second chapter, when he is seen going off to 'court' to attend a preliminary hearing of his case, but it is the figurative meaning of the phrase *mit sich selbst ins Gericht gehen* (to take oneself to task) that explains the 'court', for Josef K. is his own accuser and therefore the devil in question. Kafka simply takes the phrase literally and shows Josef K. going off on his own to the court which represents (the reader is, as usual, left to work out Kafka's meaning, for part of the metaphor is suppressed) K.'s first unconscious and eventually conscious sense of guilt. His first examination by an examining magistrate is accordingly a self-examination, the first of several; it cannot be otherwise. The examining magistrate, who is found sitting behind an appropriately small table, for this is the lowest court, is described as a fat, wheezing little man who every now and then gesticulates as though he were caricaturing someone. This magistrate is in fact a caricature of Josef K., who is insignificant, proud ('dick', cf. Willem) and out of his element in the domain of the conscience he hasn't used for years.

The washerwoman to whom Josef K. feels momentarily attracted is both a projection of his own libido and a personification of the phrase *das kannst du der Wäscherin erzählen* (tell that to the marines), the reference being to the unlikely story (fairytale) of his innocence. Another projection of his libido is the red-bearded (diabolical, lecherous) student Berthold (Josef K. is, of course, the only real student - of the court and its proceedings - in the novel), of whom the 'Gerichtsdiener' (Josef

---

[19] Freud drew attention to this meaning, via the phrase *einem eins aufs Dachl geben* (to hit someone on the head), in his *Introductory Lectures on Psycho-Analysis* (London: George Allen & Unwin, 1922), 134, where he also noted that 'In German, an old acquaintance is often addressed as "old house"*(altes Haus).* The latter term is equivalent to 'old man', which includes 'my old man' (father).

K.'s super-ego) says that what he needs is a good thrashing, which is precisely what he gets in a symbolical sense in Chapter 5. This key chapter, the turning-point of the novel and a classic example of the uncanny;[20] is a punishment dream pointing forward to another, intensified such dream in the form of the final chapter of the novel. A particularly interesting symbol of libido is Leni, who embodies what Kafka called *die geplatzte Sexualität der Frauen* (the sexuality with which women are bursting; *platzen* means to burst or smash); he takes his own phrase literally when he has Leni throw a plate at the wall in order to attract Josef K.'s attention. Leni's 'körperlicher Fehler' (physical defect), her webbed hand, Josef K. calls 'eine hübsche Kralle' (a fine claw [to translate it as paw would be to miss the vampiric point, to which we return in 8.2.2.]), which identifies her as one of the sirens - the classical personalization of woman as snare - who recur throughout Kafka's work and whose claws are featured in one of the less known stories, 'Das Schweigen der Sirenen'.[21] The voice of the siren that features in K's attack of 'sea-sickness' in the empty courtroom points forward to Leni, who is also identifiable with Josef K., standing for his habit of following the line of least resistance in his thoughts, which tend to revolve around women and the sensuality Kafka associates with them, so that she also represents Josef K.'s libido. When he remarks to the Priest (ch. 9) that the Court consists almost entirely of 'Frauenjäger' Josef K. is , on one level, referrring to his own skirt-chasing or petticoat-hunting proclivities, but his words have another meaning, to which we will come presently, for Kafka avoids the usual 'Schürzenjäger' in favour of a word which has a more literal meaning and, with it, a more ominous implication.

While he is in the Cathedral, waiting, without realizing it, for the Priest to appear, that is, waiting as it were for his own thoughts to pass from the aesthetic to the spiritual, Josef K. wanders off to a side-chapel in which he sees one of the many remarkable pictures in the novel. Since *Der Proceß* is the exposition of a mental process, dreamlike in its 'regressive translation of thoughts into images', it is natural that pictures, concentrated pictorializations, should occur at important stages in the process it describes. The present 'Entombment of Christ' is necessarily symbolical. The foreground-figure of the great knight in armour at the extreme left of the picture is a mirror-image of Josef K., who in his subconscious mind's eye visualizes himself, self-importantly, as a knight in armour because even at this late stage he is still deluding himself, still thinking evasively, still picturing himself as fighting the good fight against a corrupt legal system. The knight prefigures the man-from-the-country in the soon to be related Parable of the Doorkeeper in that he too stands idly by. K.'s idea that the knight is perhaps appointed 'Wache zu stehen' (to stand guard) seems an inept notion since the fact that his sword is stuck in the ground suggests that he is not

---

20 Prawer, *Caligari's Children.*, 136.
21 Cf. the 1917 diary-entry in which he wrote 'immer wiederschlugen [...] die Krallenhände der Sirene in meine Brust' (again and again the clawed hands of the siren struck at my chest: T 528).

'wach' (on guard) at all, although he should be, as should Josef K., for whom he stands. 'Wache' is synomymous with 'Wächter', so the knight also points back to the beginning of K.'s 'Proceß' and forward to the Parable of the Doorkeeper. The process which this conspicuously slothful knight is watching is the entombment of Christ (by Joseph of Arimathea). The Gothic connotations of entombment have already been discussed. The prime function of this picture is to foreshadow Josef K.'s death: he is foreseeing his own entombment (inhumation).

The Parable of the Doorkeeper turns on the man-from-the-country's lack of faith: if he had believed in the Law, he would not have insisted on seeing it with his own eyes. Applied to Josef K.'s case, which it is intended to illustrate, the Parable of the Doorkeeper means that if K. had believed in his own innocence, he would not have felt it necessary to prove it. Following the dramatic dialogue with the Priest, who represents his higher self (Kant's 'homo noumenon'), Josef K. (Kant's 'homo sensibilis') finally has no choice but to condemn himself to death because he is incapable of living in any other way and is implicitly unwilling to face the 'demon of insanity' faced by Stanton in *Melmoth the Wanderer*.[22] The most significant event anywhere in Kafka's novels is the closing of the door in the Parable of the Doorkeeper. *Der Proceß* opens with the symbolical closure of Josef K.'s hitherto untroubled existence, and the pattern, once established, continues throughout the novel, as it did in the previous novel and will do in the next one, each closure a foreclosure, a putting away of what has been. What counts, now, is not the weekly visit to Elsa by which Josef K. used to define himself, but the subjection to death that is the real meaning of his physicality. Although in many ways Kafka-like, K. is the very opposite of Kafka in lacking his obstinate belief in the presence of 'something indestructible' in himself: the novel is what it was intended to be, a proof *ex negativo* of Kafka's need to cling to that fundamental belief in the face of every adversity. Josef K. is totally unable to accept Kant's three regulative ideals or necessary, unprovable beliefs (God, freedom, and immortality), to which the Priest refers in the words 'there is no need to accept everything as true; some things simply have to be accepted as necessary.' Josef K., unable to accept the idea of such necessary fictions, calls them by that other word for a fiction, a lie. His attitude towards religion, or superstition, as he would call it, is very much that of Shelley in his essay on the Devil. Since the Gothic novel tests the limits of these beliefs by means of their perversion,[23] Kafka can again be said to be operating within the Gothic convention.

It is ultimately because he cannot live with himself, that Josef K. condemns himself, but he does so in what might be called a conventionally Gothic way, condemning himself for his excess. The words of his confession, 'Ich wollte immer

---

[22] C. R. Maturin, *Melmoth the Wanderer*, 3 vols (London: Richard Bentley & Son., 1892), I, 88.
[23] See Marshall Brown, 'A Philosophical View of the Gothic Novel', *Studies in Romanticism*, 26 (1987), 275-301.

mit zwanzig Händen in die Welt hineinfahren, und überdies zu einem nicht zu billigenden Zweck ' ('I always wanted to grab as much of the world as possible, and for no very laudable reason, either') may be compared with the confession made by Schedoni, in Ann Radcliffe's *The Italian* (III, ch. 7) to his confessor: 'I have been through life [...] the slave of my passions, and they have led me into horrible excesses'. As Marshall Brown has said,

> Typically [romantic gothic novels] devote far more space to the thoughts and feelings of the victim and (often) of the persecuting demon than to the mechanisms of punishment and torment. What would be left of a man, these novels ask, if all human society were stripped away, all customary perceptions, all the expected regularity of cause and effect? They ask, in other words, what man is in himself, when deprived of all the external supports that channel ordinary experience. What resources, if any, does the mind retain in isolation? What is the nature of pure consciousness?[24]

If Josef K. could have answered, he would have said that 'pure consciousness' in this sense is hell. Within a generation hell will be declared to be the others, but at this stage it is one's self. Brown's meticulous analysis is peculiarly relevant to Kafka's K.-novels, where victim and persecuting demon are one and the same. As the victim of the demon of self, Josef K. exists in the limbo of which Brown proceeds to say that 'The greatest intensity of despair comes where the victim is released into a limbo, uprooted and driven out into a world seemingly beyond space and time.'[25] K. lives in just such a limbo, beyond space (for there is only the prison of the mind) and time (there is no real change, for the more things change, the more they are the same), which is symbolized in the *Rumpelkammer* (lumber room; figuratively, limbo. Both limbo and lumber have the connotation of prison) a further Gothic locus, compare Ann Radcliffe's *The Romance of the Forest* with its static (timeless) scene like a child's nightmare come true. He therefore comes to know 'all the impotent agony of an incarcerated mind', 'the agony of consciousness'[26] of a Melmoth.

The whole paraphernalia of the Court and its Cathedral adjunct is full of Gothic elements in both a literary and a non-literary sense. Botting's reading of the novel ('In *The Trial* [...] individual guilt is inscribed throughout social and legal systems as a mysterious, arbitrary and impenetrable condition'[27]), accurately though it describes how things appear to Josef K. in the guilty determination to prove his innocence that in fact proves his guilt, reveals no awareness of what is going on beneath the surface of the text. While seeming to be about an institution of power in the form of the Law and all its hierarchical ramifications, implicit in the Kantian model, in reality *Der Proceß*, like that model, is in the first instance about self-control. Until the last chapter Josef K. lacks self-control, and in that sense can be said to be *des Teufels* (literally, to

---

24 Brown, 280.
25 Brown, 285.
26 Maturin, *Melmoth*, I, 87f.
27 Botting, 160.

be possessed by the Devil [in the form of arrogance, lechery and selfishness]), and then in the last chapter he sees himself finally losing all control as his life is terminated by two stooges acting for the Devil as Accuser, that is, for Josef K. as his own Accuser-Devil. As the reification of the sense of guilt that he drags around with him like the proverbial block, the Court and its labyrinthine workings are, in accordance with Kant's paradigm, to be found wherever K. goes. The metaphor, which was clearly in Kafka's mind (hence Block), is more than a literalization of the verb *verschleppen:* it continues the legal metaphor (*jemanden vor den Richter schleppen* means to haul someone up before a judge) and at the same time points back to the ultimate origin of Josef K.'s condition in the form of the Fall suffered by his precursor, for *(ver)schleppen* also means much the same as *spedieren,* which takes the reader back via Onkel Jakob's 'Speditionsgeschäft' to Karl Rossmann's expulsion from a state if not of innocence, then certainly of ignorance.

The whole Gothic rigmarole of the so-called Court, that farrago of fantasy and logic worthy of Wonderland, is, as Block rightly says, 'beyond reason'. It shows that, in Emily Dickinson's words,

One need not be a Chamber - to be haunted -
One need not be a House -
The brain has corridors - surpassing
Material Place - [28]

There is, however, more to the Court than the human brain's ability to torment itself. The Court and the Law it claims to serve are presented as a diabolical patriarchal system, hence the figures of the bearded patriarchs in the front row of the courtroom, because Kafka's own sense of guilt, which is what is being explored here, took the specific form of a sense of guilt vis-à-vis his father, who prided himself on being a 'vereidigter Sachverständiger bei Gericht' (sworn expert witness), and on his supposedly 'orthodox' Jewish faith, in which he was in reality, as his son stressed, a law unto himself. The bearded patriarchs are, however, more than father-figures. They will surely put most readers in mind of the Inquisition, particularly when Josef K., like Vivaldi in *The Italian*, is visited by two men dressed in black, who are reminiscent of its agents. The 'interrogation chamber' and the 'great organization' at work behind the court point to the Inquisition, and in the context the 'Rumpelkammer' points to the *Folterkammer* (torture chamber) in which the Inquisition broke its victim's body and spirit. In referring (in ch. 3) to 'red-hot pincers', one of the Inquisition's favourite instruments of torture, used in witchcraft (heresy) interrogations and in the ghastly preliminaries to executions, Kafka makes explicit the allusion to one of the most villainous documents composed before the twentieth century, the notorious *Malleus*

---

[28] 'Ghosts', *Collected Poems of Emily Dickinson* (N.Y & Avenel, N.J.: Gramercy Books, 1982), 208.

Maleficarum of 1486. If Kant's account of the workings of the conscience explains the legal fiction on which *Der Proceß* is based, the *Malleus Maleficarum* shows that Josef K.'s 'diabolical' guilt has a whole further dimension, to which we now come.

7.2.2. The Process of Justice

The spelling of the word *Proceß* gives it a doubly alien, unexpected look, taking its meaning so far away from the civil/criminal 'trial' implied by the normal modern spelling *Prozeß* that 'Trial' becomes a mistranslation (it should be *Process*, which, especially in Scots English, discloses all the relevant meanings). Instead of the older spelling of *Process*, Kafka uses the spelling, *Proceß*, that was the preferred one in 1910,[29] but which is, historically speaking, a transitional and indeed bastard form. To modern eyes the word should be either *Prozeß* or (until the end of the nineteenth century) *Process*. The form of the word which Kafka uses is thus both historically and orthographically correct and yet at the same time, especially when seen in retrospect, something of an anomaly, a medieval (Gothic) form alienated by being given that final ß. Kafka could have used the modern form, *Prozeß*, which was also available (as spelling of second choice) in 1910, but has preferred not to do so, presumably because as a then new-fangled spelling it would have lacked the (Gothic) connotation(s) that he valued. He evidently thought long and carefully about the meanings of the word and those he wished to foreground, including the historical connotation that is slowly revealed, and on the processes, proceedings and procedures involved, all implied in his title.

It was in August 1913, a matter of months before beginning work on the novel, that he read Gustav Roskoff's *Geschichte des Teufels* (see BF 444f.). For him the revelation was not so much what Roskoff writes about the Devil/devils, with much of which he was already sufficiently familiar, as what he writes, at such length,[30] about the *Malleus Maleficarum* or *Hexenhammer (Hammer of Witchcraft)*, which showed the power of contemporary belief in the Devil in that those who denied it were deemed heretics. The word 'Proceß' denotes something remarkably like the 'Process of Justice' described in the Third Part of the *Malleus Maleficarum*, that is, 'A process of justice, how it should be conducted, and the method of pronouncing sentence'.[31] What is in question in this novel seems to be an imaginary process of justice, based on a

---

29   F. E. Petri, *Handwörterbuch der Fremdwörter in der deutschen Schrift- und Umgangssprache* (Munich: Melchior Kupferschmid, 1910).

30   Roskoff, II, 225-292.

31   *Malleus Maleficarum*, tr. M. Summers (London: The Pushkin Press, 1948), 194-275. All quotations refer to this edition. The more commonly available Folio Society edition is incomplete and excludes much of what is in the present context the most interesting material.

conflation of Kant's metaphorical court of justice or 'supernatural assize' with the process described in the *Malleus Maleficarum*.

In this process-at-law the Judge is Conscience, the offence 'heresy', and the penalty death. By 'heresy' is meant failure to observe the religion of the father, for a heretic is 'one who follows new and false opinions' and heresy 'a form of infidelity',[32] as a result of subjection to devils, from which Kafka believed himself, and showed Josef K., to suffer. The vicious, diabolocentric ethos of the Old Testament, on which that of the Inquisition was based, had no time for so-called 'dreamers of dreams' (*Deut.*, XIII, 5-11), meaning heretics, who, it was thought, should be put to death. Erich Heller wrote more specifically, with reference to *Das Schloß*, and in the context of an overly religious interpretation of that novel, that

> [K.] is a kind of Pelagius believing that he 'can if he ought', yet living in a relentlessly predestined world. This situation produces a theology very much after the model of Gnostic and Manichaean beliefs [...] The castle of Kafka's novel is, as it were, the heavily fortified garrison of a company of Gnostic demons, successfully holding an advanced position against the manoeuvres of an impatient soul [...] The correspondence between the spiritual structure of *The Castle* and the view of the world systematized into Gnostic and Manichaean dogma is [...] striking.[33]

It is tempting to think in such terms, particularly if *Der Proceß* in part involves Kafka condemning himself for his heresy; after all, does not Amalia in *Das Schloß*, in rejecting the world of physical reality, appear to be a true representative of the 'Manichaean disposition'? However, the fact remains, as Heller himself went on to acknowledge, that 'There is [...] no reason to assume that Kafka had any special knowledge of these ancient heresies'.

On the other hand there is every reason to think that the concept of 'heresy' had, for Kafka, ironical quotation marks about it, and that it simply denoted departure from the dogmatic world-view of his father, who, like the Jewish Yahweh, and like Klamm in *Das Schloß,* was as it were God and Devil in one. What the father thought of as his own 'orthodoxy' was in reality, according to his son, hide-bound, pig-headed dogmatism, peculiar to himself: he believed what he believed because it was himself who believed it. In doing so, he was believing in himself. All this means, in the context of *Der Proceß*, that the whole imaginary 'process of justice' is a 'legal fiction', a term (corresponding to what Schopenhauer calls Kant's 'judicial form'), from which Kafka surely drew general inspiration in planning the novel, which is used repeatedly in the *Malleus Maleficarum*.[34] It was to the *Hexenjagd* (witch-hunt) as described in the *Hexenhammer (Hammer of Witchcraft)* that Kafka was slyly alluding when he made Josef K. refer to 'diese[s] Gericht, das fast nur aus Frauenjägern besteht' (this court which consists almost entirely of woman-hunters). This time Kafka deliberately

---

32 *Malleus Maleficarum*, 198f.
33 Erich Heller, *The Disinherited Mind* (Cambridge: Bowes & Bowes, 1952), 175, 177.
34 *Malleus Maleficarum*, 201, 203, etc.

uses the literal term *Frauenjäger,* rather than the more usual but, in the present context, less telling, figurative term *Schürzenjäger,* which is, however, taken literally when Titorelli 'jagte hinter ihr [der Buckligen] her, packte sie bei den Röcken' (chased after her, grabbing her by the skirt). In saying that the Court consists almost entirely of woman-hunters, Kafka is, in his literal, tongue-in-cheek way, identifying the court with the one whose diabolical procedures are described in the *Malleus Maleficarum.*

Like the Court, the Inquisition was attracted to guilt (in the form of heresy), which it sought out and destroyed. Even suspicion of heresy resulted in immediate arrest. The particular process to which Josef K. sees himself being subjected is the second of the three methods of initiating a Process in the *Malleus Maleficarum:* by denunciation or calumniation ('one person denounces another without producing any proof, 'very little proof [being] required [...] since it takes very little argument to expose a person's guilt'.[35] Although I translated the word 'verleumden' in the first line of the novel as 'to take a person's name in vain', it can equally well mean 'to denounce or calumniate'. This is the procedure attributed to the Inquisition in earlier Gothic novels: 'You know an enemy has nothing to do but lay an accusation of heresy against any unfortunate and innocent individual, and the victim expires in horrible tortures, or lingers the wretched remnant of his life in dark and solitary cells'.[36]

For the most part those accused of witchcraft (the *Malleus Maleficarum* simply says 'witches', which proves my point) deny their guilt, which 'engenders a greater suspicion than if they were to answer that they left it to a superior judgment to decide whether there were [guilt present] or not',[37] which is precisely the Priest's argument when he counters K.'s protestations of innocence with the words 'that's what the guilty always say.' The Third Part of the *Malleus Maleficarum* arguably gave Kafka nothing less than an historical model and analogue for the working of the 'law' in *Der Proceß* and *In der Strafkolonie,* in both of which there is no more question of a not guilty verdict than there was in virtually all witchcraft trials. If he hadn't already got it, it also gave him the charge. The Criminalcodex of the *Malleus Maleficarum* [38] is full of concepts that are relevant to Josef K.'s 'case', including *Aberglaube* (superstition), *Beisitzer* (member of the court), and *Geständnis* (confession); if the accused wishes to defend herself (or himself, for the text mostly uses the masculine) an *Anwalt* or *Advocat* (both words mean lawyer or advocate) is appointed, whose job it is to conduct the accused's case 'as well as may be [...] but not to the detriment of justice.'[39] For good measure Kafka provided Josef K. with both an *Advokat* (Huld) and, in a fragment of the novel, an *Anwalt* (Hasterer), not that he was doing or showing Josef

---

35 *Malleus Maleficarum,* 208.
36 Shelley, *Zastrozzi,* ed. Behrendt, 81.
37 *Malleus Maleficarum,* 212. See G.Roskoff, *Geschichte des Teufels,* 2 vols (Leipzig: F. A. Brockhaus, 1869), II, 269.
38 Roskoff, II, 263-292.
39 Roskoff, II, 273 .

K. any favour (*Huld* in German) in providing him with an advocate who is shown sitting in a corner because he is a *Winkeladvokat*, that is, not a real advocate at all (but a symbolical one).

The three possible outcomes listed by Titorelli are reminiscent of the 'three methods of procedure provided by the law'[40] and, more especially, of the 'three kinds of sentence'[41] in witchcraft (heresy) trials. The parallel, already close, becomes even closer when in the *Malleus Maleficarum* the Judge or Inquisitor is enjoined never to acquit, but merely to suspend proceedings temporarily:

> Let care be taken not to put anywhere in the sentence that the accused is innocent or immune, but that [the case against him] was not legally proved [...]; for if after a little time he should again be brought to trial, and it should be legally proved, he can, notwithstanding the previous sentence of absolution, then be condemned.[42]

Clearly 'real acquittal' was no more available to those accused of witchcraft than it is to Josef K. What is provided for in each case, by the same kind of legalistic double-think, is precisely the 'temporary acquittal' or 'delaying tactics' (the word 'Verschleppung' refers to the burden which has to be dragged around in the meantime, personified in 'Block') of Titorelli's exegesis. Even the principle underlying the *Malleus Maleficarum*, and indeed the *Vehmgerichte* and the Inquisition as such, is applicable to Josef K.: 'once the accused confesses, he has judged himself.'[43] The sentence is carried out immediately: Josef K.'s execution will follow directly upon his confession, which Kafka, with characteristic logic and irony, has him make on the way to execution.

It is difficult to overestimate the significance from Kafka's point of view of Roskoff's analysis of the phenomenon with which subjection to the Devil was long associated, witchcraft. Kafka's definition of women as 'snares waiting to drag man down into the merely finite' (J 123) not only coincides with the view of woman as 'the mainspring of sensuality', which underlay the persecution of women for witchcraft, the procedures for which were codified in the *Malleus Maleficarum;* it almost certainly derives from the *Malleus Maleficarum* itself, in Part I (Question 6) of which the idea of woman as a snare is analysed,[44] and the conclusion reached that women are 'a snare set by demons' for men.[45] Kafka's definition of woman is doubly disturbing, but also doubly revealing, because it means that he was seeing her both as 'unclean' (cf. the extraordinary diary-entry for 14 August 1913, in which he wrote that

---

40 *Malleus Maleficarum*, 205.
41 *Malleus Maleficarum*, 235.
42 *Malleus Maleficarum*, 235.
43 Roskoff, II, 344. In German and Austrian law the onus is on the accused to prove his innocence.
44 *Malleus Maleficarum*, 47. No one reading Roskoff's account of the *Malleus Maleficarum* could doubt the truth of Janouch's account in this respect.
45 Quoted from Michael Kunze, *Highroad to the Stake*, tr. W. E. Yuill (Chicago & London: University of Chicago Press, 1987), 344.

'To live as ascetically as possible, more ascetically than a bachelor, is the only way in which I could endure marriage') and as witch, she-devil or *instrumentum diaboli*. On the other hand, it was his own sense of 'uncleanness', and his sense of persecution, that led him to identify with the witch. The disturbing similes used in *Der Proceß* in relation to Frl. Bürstner ('Scrubber' exactly conveys the ambiguity in English) and Leni - the pungent smell and the webbed hands - are reminiscent of the *odor diabolicum* and the *stigma diabolicum* respectively. No less striking is the way in which Josef K., taking leave of Frl B., 'kissed her first on the lips, then all over the face, like some thirsty animal lapping greedily at a spring of longed-for fresh water. Finally he kissed her on the neck, right on the throat, and kept his lips there for a long time', because it points to vampirism (discussed in the next chapter), and therefore to the 'cannibalism' of which Kafka accused himself, this being projected on to Josef K. The present vampiric kiss prefigures another, when Leni later kisses Josef K.

Kafka knew from Roskoff[46] about the ways in which supposed witches were tortured, and given that the way in which her hands are described identifies Leni as a vampire and hence a witch, her webbed hands may put the reader in mind of the popular *Hexenprobe* (manner in which supposed witches were put to the test) of 'swimming'. Kafka knew that being 'swum' (*anglice* drowned) in a river (cf. the fate of Georg Bendemann in *Das Urteil*, who is likewise guilty of disobedience, heresy in the present context) was, in effect, one of the penalties for witchcraft, and that it was commonplace for parents to condemn their children to death by implicating them in the witchcraft of which they were themselves accused (again, cf. *Das Urteil*, for the son's values are no more those of the father than the father's are those of the son).

The Inquisition's procedures, as codified in the *Malleus Maleficarum*, presented Kafka with a model for the workings of the Law: the principle on which his Penal Colony operates, that 'guilt is always beyond doubt', is precisely that of the *Hexenhammer (Hammer of Witchcraft)*, which so ordered the trial that the accused persons had virtually no chance of being acquitted, for if they did not plead guilty at the outset, they were 'put to the question' (tortured) until they did. This is, in effect, the truth to which Josef K. is led by Titorelli. The artist tells him that 'In the codex of the Law [...] it is [...] laid down [...] that the innocent shall be acquitted [...] Now, my experience is diametrically opposed to that. I have not met with a single case of definite acquittal', which is equally applicable to the Criminalcodex of the *Malleus Maleficarum*. If ever there was a trial of which it was true to say that 'Becoming involved in such a case means losing it before it has even begun' (*Der Proceß*, ch. 6), it was the trial for witchcraft as heresy (cf. Josef K.'s view of 'Glaube' [faith] as 'Aberglaube' [superstition]),[47] in which, as in *Der Proceß*, the court, after employing

---

46 *Geschichte des Teufels*, II, 276-283.
47 *Aberglaube* is a perversion of *Glaube*, as *Aberwitz* is of *Witz*.

'all the machinery of the law' (ch. 6), 'conjures up, out of nothing at all, a great fabric of guilt' (ch. 7). The very different contexts do not affect the ominous logic and the process of attrition which ends in the acceptance of guilt not because it is present,[48] but because there is no alternative (I am, therefore I am guilty; being guilty, I must no longer be). In his punitive fantasies Kafka therefore seems to be equating the victims of the Law with those of the Inquisition and to be identifying with the Witch, who was, like himself, the 'scapegoat of humanity', believed to be able to change human beings into animals,[49] as he himself did in *Die Verwandlung* and elsewhere. In the background, of course, is the idea of writing as 'service to the Devil': I write, therefore I am guilty.

Kafka's reference to red-hot pincers, which probably reflects his reading of Roskoff - the *Hexenhammer* usually speaks of 'the ordeal of red-hot iron'[50] - stands out because of the characteristic wording ('the man cried out as if K. had gripped him with red-hot pincers rather than with two fingers'), which means that in a real, symbolical sense this is what happens, so that Kafka is visualizing himself being tortured, in the person of the student, for his lack of allegiance to his father's values and for the 'dissolute behaviour' of which his father disapproved. An earlier detail in the same chapter (ch. 3) of the novel probably derives indirectly from Roskoff's account of witchcraft trials and the tortures involved: the court-attendant (K. as he is not, but should be) has a dream in which the student (K. as he is) is 'held down, just above floor level, his arms stretched out, his fingers spread, his bandy legs forced into a circle, and splashes of blood all around'. The fact that this dream prefigures K.'s death confirms that it is for his heresy that he (K.) is condemned and is throttled (in the 'civilized', Northern countries of Europe witches were normally garotted before being burned) while at the same time being ritually stabbed in the heart, a detail which is explained presently. For an illustration of the torture to which the student is subjected one would have to turn to early books on witchcraft; Kafka's description suggests that he envisaged the student being broken on the wheel. The student represents the 'dissolute behaviour' of Josef K., who is obliged to study the law throughout the novel; he is accordingly seen as a monster ('Scheusal') of lechery.

The machinery of 'justice' of the endlessly hierarchical court system finds its appropriate instrument and symbol in the torture-machine with its 'bed' to which the victim is strapped in *In der Strafkolonie.* On one level this is a reference to the day-bed in the 'penal colony' of his parents' apartment on which Kafka spent so much time, but there is more to it than that. The *Malleus Maleficarum* spoke of 'engines of torture'

---

[48] Cf. Nietzsche: 'Although the most intelligent judges of the witches, and even the witches themselves, were convinced of the guilt of witchcraft, the guilt, nevertheless, was not there' (*The Joyful Wisdom*, tr. Thomas Common [Edinburgh & London: T. N. Foulis, 1910], 205).
[49] Roskoff, II, 228.
[50] *Malleus Maleficarum,* Part III, Question XVII , in Roskoff, II, 282.

(Folterwerkzeuge, Folterinstrumente), and Schopenhauer remarked that it was salutary to regard the world 'as a place of penance, a penal institution, as it were, a penal colony'.[51] Indeed, Schopenhauer regarded the world as 'the product of our guilt'[52] and humanity as that which ought not to exist since it does so only as a result of sexual indulgence and therefore, in his Buddhistic-ascetic world view, of transgression. This may well be deemed the ultimate Gothic transgression.

7.2.3. The Final Judgment

Also associated with the Court are five further Gothic motifs: darkness, the labyrinth, confined spaces, the locked room, and the desolate landscape. Darkness and the fog of self-obfuscation accompany K. wherever he goes, and are invariably associated with the Court. The streets to and from the Court are as dark and labyrinthine as the workings of the Court and therefore of the shifty, evasive mind which Josef K. finds increasingly burdensome until finally the almost impenetrable darkness in the Cathedral gives way to 'black night' as the full extent of his folly is revealed. It is, however, above all in the most tellingly Gothic symbolism of the novel, that of claustrophobically confined space, that the oppressiveness of his dawning sense of guilt is externalized from the second chapter onwards. The ceiling of the courtroom is so low that those in the gallery need (dream-logic!) cushions to protect their heads, and the *Rumpelkammer* has a similarly low ceiling; K. is crushed against the Examining magistrate's table; Titorelli's studio, Huld's room, and the side-chapel in the Cathedral are likewise as small and cramped as the grave for which Josef K. is all the time heading. The impression created is as unambiguous as it is Gothic.

The *Rumpelkammer* combines the motifs of claustrophobically confined space and the locked room (cf. the decayed set of apartments in *The Old English Baron* that had been locked for years) with overdetermined dream-symbolism. Josef K. is both the man with the lash and his victim in this remarkably Gothic scene, which gains in dramatic impact from being static, like a child's nightmare that will not go away. This literal tableau shows Josef K. envisaging himself being 'put to the question', and accordingly represents his increasing awareness of the infinite danger lurking within what had once seemed familiar and safe. However, the scene represents more than a renewed 'awakening' and a renewed 'arrest', for in German *Rumpelkammer* ('lumber room') has the secondary meaning of 'limbo', appropriate in that Josef K., who has been living in a kind of limbo with the threat of further arrest hanging over him, is about to begin facing up to the fact that his life is threatening to become a hell; Chapter 5 is the halfway stage in the process. The door of the symbolical torture

---

[51] Schopenhauer, *SW*, V, 328.
[52] ibid.

chamber does not need to open for a third time because once it has opened and shut for the second time, Josef K. has resolved to take his case seriously, though without, as yet, realizing the implications of doing so. Realizing that he has a case to answer is the first step in a process that will end in ritual execution.

The wasteland scene ('Heidelandschaft') that the artist Titorelli paints obsessively (another static tableau, it depicts two stunted trees standing far apart in dark grass, with, in the background, a many-hued sunset) is a pastiche of the typical Gothic landscape, 'desolate, alienating and full of menace',[53] with the important difference that the sublime (in the eighteenth century a reflection of the divine), present in the awesome mountains of Gothic à la Radcliffe and referenced on the last page of Kafka's previous novel, is here absent; the colourful sunset has Spenglerian rather than Burkean/Kantian undertones, being less an enigmatic reminder of sublimity than a pointer to the *Untergang des Abendlandes (Decline of the West)*. These 'Heidelandschaften' (there is a pun in German: they are heathen [godless] landscapes as well as heathscapes) are pictures of alienation; the two trees are the Tree of Knowledge and the Tree of Life, compare aphorism 83, which applies to Josef K.'s guilt: 'We are guilty not only because we have eaten of the tree of knowledge, but also because we have not eaten of the tree of life. The condition in which we find ourselves is sinful, irrespective of any actual guilt as such.' Other landscapes and urban landscapes in the K.-novels are for the most part no less desolately 'Gothic' than these god-forsaken 'heath[en]scapes', portraying a terra incognita, the very opposite of the *hortus occlusus* or paradise, although the idea of occlusion loses its otherwise ideal connotation in the Gothic context.

The Cathedral in *Der Proceß* is the natural successor to the ruined abbeys of Gothic convention and is of a symbolical piece with them. It too may be said to be 'symbolic of demonic space where the ritual of man's servitude to lawless power is performed';[54] indeed, these words of a contemporary critic amount to a paraphrase of the dismissive words spoken by Josef K. to the Priest: 'A lie is turned into a universal principle'. K. approaches the Cathedral as a work of art, that is, as a place without a numinous religious centre and as such a spatial symbol of his own lack of belief. For him it is in effect a picturesque ruin representing the superstition of the past, so that his attitude towards it is much the same as the attitude of the early Gothic novelists to the ruined abbeys that were one of their preferred loci, but with the difference that Josef K.'s target is Judaeo-Christian faith, and beyond it the nature of religious faith as such, whereas theirs was often merely the inquisitional and other excesses of the Catholic church, the Church of England of the time being too pickled in port to be a danger to anyone but itself.

---

53 Botting, 2.
54 Alok Balla, *The Cartographers of Hell* (New Delhi: Sterling Publishers, 1991), 80.

144

In the novel the church (cathedral) is closely linked with the court, as it was in the middle ages in the context of witch-hunting and witchcraft trials. The 'Gothic obscurity of the church' is seen here, as in *The Monk*, both in its literal sense and in the figurative sense of obscurantism. What takes place in the Cathedral, as in the opening cathedral scene in *The Monk*, is pure theatre, with the telling symbolical difference that in Lewis's novel 'all Madrid' is present at Ambrosio's sermon, whereas in Kafka's only Josef K. and his alter ego (the Priest) are present, and that whereas Ambrosio's reprobate days are ahead of him, Josef K.'s are all but over. The dramatic dialogue between Josef K. and the Priest is reminiscent of Sade's 'Dialogue between a priest and a dying man' to the extent that Josef K.'s symbolical death follows immediately on the Parable of the Doorkeeper and its exegesis, which ends in his rejection of what he thinks of as religious superstition. What Robert Kiely wrote in the context of *The Monk*, 'the artist in terror novels is most often depicted as the destroyer, the executioner, the gatekeeper, whose victims are confined in the name of order and tradition by the imposition of one will upon another. The artistic process is seen [...] as devil's work',[55] is applicable to the Parable as the work of one who regarded writing as just that, 'Teufelsdienst'. All this is Gothic enough, as is the impassable doorway and the story-within-a-story that is both a part of the Gothic narrative convention (among others) and, within that convention, a paradigm of what Sedgwick has called the 'inside-outside relation', where 'the self is massively blocked off from something to which it ought normally to have access'.[56]

Der Proceß being the exploration of a dreamlike mental process, a serial nightmare, it follows that what happens in the final chapter, which is in line with both our analogues, is also dreamt. Josef K. does not die, but does, in this ultimate punishment fantasy, imagine himself dying in the most humiliating of circumstances. The final chapter of the novel, both in its printed and in its alternative versions, is its most macabre feature. The ending of the novel as printed is both pure Gothic and pure theatre. The deserted quarry is a Gothic enough locality, given what takes place there, but with the important difference that the 'execution' takes place not in some gloomy underground vault, as in the projected ending of *Der Bau*, but in the open air, on the outskirts of what might under different circumstances have been urban normality, with the moon shining down on the scene with 'that simplicity and serenity which no other light possesses'. The quarry is symbolically speaking the source of the obstacles (in German, *die Steine [,die er sich in den Weg gelegt hat]*, stones) that Josef K. has placed in his own way throughout the novel.

---

55 Robert Kiely, *The Romantic Novel in England* (Cambridge, MA: Harvard University Press, 1972), 103.
56 Eve Kosofsky Sedgwick, *The Coherence of Gothic Conventions,* new edn (N.Y. & London: Methuen, 1986), 12f.

The long knife derives from the metaphor *das lange Messer führen* (to brag, literally to wield the long knife), which has been taken literally, and accordingly represents Josef K.'s damnable pride. It is also, in symbolical terms, the knife which Kafka enjoyed imagining being twisted in his heart (diary, 2 Nov. 1911). The hesitation about who is to do the deed is, of course, pure theatre,[57] for like all the figures in the novel, these two gentlemen ('second-rate actors', Kafka teases the reader by calling them) are projections of Josef K. himself. In symbolical terms he therefore kills himself, or rather, since this is a symbolical novel, he punishes himself by envisioning this happening, but lives on to struggle again in *Das Schloß*, hence the neatly folded clothes. That Josef K. is throttled and stabbed in the heart, with the knife ritually turned twice, shows that he is being punished not only for his heresy, but, also and more specifically, for his vampirism, in other words, for his lechery.

There are two alternative endings which, though rejected by Kafka, probably as being less powerful and less challenging than the actual ending, put this in perspective. In the first the condemned man (whom one assumes to be 'Josef K.') is stabbed to death by the executioner either in his prison cell or in his own room (diary, 20/22 July 1916); there is no need for anyone else to be present at this ultimate Gothic *coup de théâtre*. The other, official alternative ending of the novel, entitled (and published separately as) 'Ein Traum', is pure Gothic nightmare. Beginning 'Josef K. was dreaming', this version goes on: 'It was a fine day and K. had decided to go for a walk, but no sooner had he taken two steps than he was already at the cemetery.' There he finds two men standing beside a newly dug grave supporting a headstone; as soon as Josef K. appears, they plant the headstone, whereupon a third figure appears, an 'artist' who is not named but who is highly reminiscent of Titorelli. After this artist has inscribed 'Here lies' on the headstone, there is an embarrassing pause. Moved by the artist's obvious embarrassment after he has written 'J', Josef K. jumps into the grave, his name appears on the headstone, and - he wakes up. Gothic, after all, is fantasy, even when the fantasy is deadly serious. In its way this is as striking an ending as the one Kafka finally adopted, and is more revealing (this may be the reason for its rejection) in that it reminds the reader that the whole process has been a dream. In the event Kafka evidently preferred to complete the circle of the novel on a more enigmatic note.

---

[57] Influence of Kafka's actor-friend Jizschak Löwy?

8. *DAS SCHLOSS*

8.1. Fairytale Motifs

Das Schloß, like *Der Proceß,* follows a common fairytale pattern in that while the opening paragraph bears some resemblance to reality, the protagonist swiftly passes 'through the looking-glass', here represented by the bridge, into an inside-out world of externalized inner reality. We are not told where K. comes from or what he has been prior to his arrival on the bridge that symbolizes his transition to a realm of increasingly challenged consciousness. Kafka goes beyond some versions of the fairytale motif in introducing his hero not at the moment of departure, but at the moment of arrival in a new, alien world. The bridge on which K. is found standing in the first paragraph is tantamount to the 'bridge to the otherworld' of fairytale, except that here the otherworld is internalized. Arriving to take up a post is itself a fairytale motif, and the fact that K. travels from afar seeking to gain entrance to an arguably empty castle is a version of the fairytale motif of the stranger who travels from afar and enters an empty, silent castle.[1] The telephone by means of which contact appears to be established with the Castle is an example of *Requisitenverschiebung* (prop shift) in the modern fairytale.

The enchanted or accursed castle as such is an important motif borrowed from fairytale[2] by Gothic, but *Das Schloß* involves, more specifically, the castle that suddenly appears, standing on a mountain.[3] This is what K. sees when he steps outside following his first night in the village. The Castle has many features that equate it with the 'edifice' of fantasy.[4] In fairytale the enchanted castle may be the Devil's house; in many ways that is what it is for K. More specifically, this castle supposedly inhabited by Klamm, who comes to loom so large in K.'s mind, is reminiscent of the castle-in-the-air of Indian fairytale inhabited by a Giant.[5] Both are possible metaphorical models for Kafka's Castle. In other respects it resembles the magic or accursed castle of folklore and fairytale, being magic in having neither entrance nor exit and in changing its appearance to the extent to which it does. Its ambiguity is

---

[1]   Cf. Lüthi, *The Fairytale as Art Form,* 119.
[2]   Cf. KHM 26, 243; Kurt Ranke (ed.), *Folktales of Germany,* tr. Lotte Baumann (Chicago: University of Chicago Press, 1966), 54-5.
[3]   'All of a sudden they saw the castle standing on a mountain': see 'The Girl Who Married the Devil', in Ranke, 43.
[4]   See Clute and Grant, *The Encyclopedia of Fantasy,* 309f.
[5]   Stith Thompson, *Motif-Index,* G162.

itself a fairytale feature, for it combines the Castles of Light and Darkness of fairytale. The Castle of Light, representing a lofty, spiritual goal, often appears and disappears like a mirage, and is usually set on a height. All this applies to Kafka's castle, which, although veiled in mist and darkness when he arrives, is, on the following morning, revealed 'clearly defined in the sparklingly clear air', the covering of fresh snow seeming to emphasize its identity as a Castle of Light. In the novel, unlike in fairytales, the castle does not suddenly appear in the path of the wanderer; on the contrary, it is so shrouded in mist and darkness as to appear non-existent, the irony being that in symbolical terms it really is non-existent, so that it is its appearance in the full light of day, as an apparent Castle of Light, that is truly misleading. The darkness in which it is hidden associates it with the Castle of Darkness representing a fearful challenge and symbolizing evil and death. Such a castle contains a treasure to be wrested from dark powers within it. That the symbolism of darkness prevails, suggests that this is also the 'castle of no return' of fairytale: the will to salvation, symbolized by the castle, may be there, but there is no sign whatsoever of salvation as such, just every sign of the triumph of chaos and darkness, in other words, of death.

The figures in *Das Schloß* resemble those in fairytale in extending all the way from Count to stable-lad. Like fairytale figures, they are figures without substance, inner reality or history; they lack any relation to past and future. Even Klamm, a figurative ogre who looms so large in K.'s thinking, is a shadowy figure who in his inscrutability and intangibility retains the aura of otherness of the fairytale. K.'s attempts to obtain from this ogre-like figure the boon of certainty are reminiscent of the fairytale motif of attempting to capture the ogre's treasure. The 'maiden from the castle' is reminiscent of the same figure in Icelandic fairytale (which Kafka seems to have known well), who gives the hero directions on his quest. The 'maiden from the castle' also involves an echo of the Bluebeard tales, as does the sinister Sortini, one of Klamm's personae, and the story of K.'s violation of Klamm's sledge, too, contains the basic elements of the Bluebeard story, that is, a forbidden chamber, an agent of prohibition and punishment, and a figure who violates the prohibition; the idea of K. pigging up (in German, *versauen*) Klamm's sledge (coach) may have been suggested by Andersen's 'The Pigs', and more especially by the illustration entitled 'The Pigs at home in the Old State Coach', which probably gave Kafka his starting-point for the incident. K.'s 'assistants' (as they are normally called in English) are caricatures of the 'helpers' (which 'Gehilfen' also means) of fairytale, here subverted into useless, comic figures. Barnabas is the 'bringer of good news' of fairytale, subverted into a bringer of unreliable, ambiguous news.

The episode in Chapter 11 of *Das Schloß*, when a large black cat bounds in in the middle of the night, giving K. 'the biggest fright he had experienced since his arrival in the village', is reminiscent of the two big black cats who bound in towards midnight in Grimm's 'Märchen von einem, der auszog das Fürchten zu lernen' ('Tale of one who

148

set out to learn how to be afraid'). In Grimm the incident takes place, suggestively enough, in an enchanted castle. The black cat, in folklore the witch's familiar, stands for her (cf. Gisa, whom K. calls 'eine böse, hinterlistige Katze' [a sly, deceitful cat]). Amalia's garnet necklace may have been suggested by the miller's daughter's necklace in 'Rumpelstilzchen' (KHM, 180), the reason for the reference, if intended, being the fact that the tale embodies the 'impossible task' which is at the heart of Kafka's view of life in general and of this novel in particular. The three versions of Amalia's story (as told/seen by Amalia, Olga, and their father) are reminiscent of the three tales told by the Queen in 'Sneewittchen'. In the background, in the Bürgel episode, is the fairytale motif of resisting sleep for an impossibly long time (39 days, 7 years, or whatever). The way in which K. falls asleep at precisely the wrong time links him with the villain of fairytale, while the way in which he was to have been cheated by death at the end of the novel involves the reversal of the common fairytale motif of deceiving death by disguise, shamming, or substitution.

While it clearly does not lack fairytale features, *Das Schloß* as a whole is closer to nightmare, and therefore to Gothic, than to the fairytale as such, although elements of the two forms are intertwined, for when the tale of wonder is deprived of its wonder, what remains is the tale of terror. The way in which K.'s life slips further and further beyond his control is Gothic through and through.

8.2. Gothic Readings
8.2.1. Castle in the Air

Kafka's last novel, *Das Schloß* was written in 1922, although an early fragment ('Verlockung im Dorf': T 389) went back as far as June 1914, that is, to the time when he was writing *Der Proceß*. Published posthumously in 1926, this fragment, which, like the later 'Variante des Beginns' does not figure in the novel as such, is a fairytale version of the beginning: 'One summer evening I came to a village in which I had never been before.' When Kafka came to write *Das Schloß*, he began writing it in the first person, only to change this later. As these first-person, 'fairytale' beginnings indicate, the protagonist, K., is again a part-autobiographical figure. In effect he is an older, refocussed and therefore altered version of Josef K., relating to Kafka in partly different ways. *Das Schloß* is a reformulation of *Der Proceß* with different emphasis as self-definition is now challenged by feelings less of guilt than of nonentity and worthlessness.

In order to underline his point that one cannot hope to understand things from the outside, Schopenhauer wrote 'In that case one would be like a man walking round a castle, looking in vain for an entrance'.[6] On one level this gave Kafka his starting-point, but his Castle, as the enigmatic remainder of a metaphor whose first term has been suppressed, is not only a thoroughly Gothic one; it is also an 'air-built vision',[7] a 'castle-in-the-air', for Kafka, like Scythrop (Shelley) as described by Peacock in his spaghetti-Gothic *Nightmare Abbey* (ch. 2), 'built many castles in the air, and peopled them with secret tribunals'.[8] What makes K.'s Castle different is the fact that it represents his self. It is his own castle (cf. Br 20: 'Many a book works like the key to unknown rooms of one's own castle'), his inner citadel, the key to the lock of which (*das Schloß* in German; the lock and missing key is yet another piece of Gothic machinery) is in his hands alone, if he can but find it (*schließen* means not only to close, but to conclude or deduce, meanings we shall see to be relevant; in German *Schloß* [Castle, lock] and *Schluß* [conclusion] are related). The Castle therefore cannot be approached from outside, which K. is necessarily shown trying to do in the novel, although the fact is misleading, for in truth he is trapped inside it in the sense of being trapped within his own mindset, his delusion of significance. The Gothic motif of trying to escape from the castle-prison, inverted on the literal level, applies on the figurative level.

Klamm, who comes to symbolize the Castle in K.'s mind, is similarly non-existent in any objective sense: in Czech *klam* means 'delusion, fallacy, error, deception', each term more relevant and, from K.'s point of view, negative than the one before. Klamm's name therefore carries the idea of deception, delusion, beguilement. All appears to be *klam a mam* (*Lug und Trug*, lies and deception; cf. Klamm and Momus). The question is whether Klamm is real. His name implies that he is is not, but there is no certainty when the name is Deception. The fact that Kafka, in his manuscript, twice wrote Klam, and then changed it into Klamm,[9] confirms the meaning of Klamm's name, and is also as good an illustration as any of the fact that one of his main reasons for making amendments to his text was to disguise his meaning. He needed to express and thereby exorcize his inner demons without exposing them too openly to prying eyes.

K. in his new guise is the mysterious stranger and wanderer of Gothic convention, the accursed wanderer of fantasy, although the Country Doctor of 'Ein Landarzt' is a better example of the latter type. The length of K.'s journey is stressed, as is the 'fact' (it is not a fact at all, but a fiction) that he lost his way several times and only arrived in the village 'by mistake', an ominous inversion of the fairytale formula 'as if by magic'. In the alternative opening of the novel, which Kafka cancelled, K. had booked

---

6   *Arthur Schopenhauer's sämmtliche Werke in sechs Bänden*, ed. Eduard Grisebach (Leipzig: Reclam, n.d.), I, 150
7   Shelley, *Zastrozzi*, ed. Behrendt, 81.
8   Cf. Ben Jonson: 'Alas, all the castles I have, are built with air' (*Eastward Ho*, II, ii, 226)
9   Franz Kafka, *Das Schloß*, ed. Malcolm Pasley (Frankfurt a. M.: S. Fischer, 1982), Text, 82f; Apparatus, 191.

a first-floor room known as 'Das Fürstenzimmer' (an indication of the size of his ego before being deflated), which in the event turned out to be far from princely. Once K. has arrived, the novel is, on the face of it, about his attempts to have his appointment as 'Landvermesser' ('land-surveyor') confirmed. If one remembers that the Castle is in reality not a 'great Castle', but a little town, and thus tantamount to a village, and that the verb *sich vermessen* means 'to make a wrong measurement, to misjudge' (there is also the simple verb *vermessen* ['to survey'] and the adjective *vermessen* ['presumptuous']), it will be clear from the outset that there is again much more to this novel than meets the eye, and that ideally the eye needs to be reading it in German, for much of the meaning of this novel too is buried in German secondary meanings, puns (e.g. 'unterrichten', to teach, also has the connotation of acting as a lower judge *[Unterrichter]*) and metaphors which Kafka takes literally (e.g. *mit jemandem Schlitten fahren* [literally, to go sledging with someone], to haul someone over the coals; *etwas an den Nagel hängen* [literally, to hang something on a nail], to give something up; *bei sich in die Schule gehen* [literally, to go to school on one's own], to learn from one's mistakes) and then develops in a formally realistic narrative which is in reality the very opposite of realistic in the anticipated sense. The anticipation is the reader's; for Kafka reality is unrealistic and inward. What this means is that *Das Schloß* is less straightforwardly or superficially 'Gothic' than it seems, and a great deal more sophisticated, especially in a linguistic way, than any Gothic novel. Late Gothic here shades into high modernism.

Rambling, mysterious, ominous, this Castle, if castle it is, possesses, to an exemplary degree, the phantasmagorically shifting outline of the archetypal Gothic castle, its features, like those of Montoni's castle in *The Mysteries of Udolpho*, 'lost in the obscurity of evening'. In accordance with the spirit, if not the letter, of Gothic, the Castle is - apparently, arguably, symbolically - not a castle at all. The reader is told that 'if K. had not known it was a castle, he might have taken it for a little town', which is a glorious piece of misinformation, for K. knows no such thing; he is merely under an impression which practically everything shows to be mistaken. Phantasmagorically, its outline shifts as K. appoaches it, so that it appears to be now a castle, now a kind of glorified village, and now simply an hallucinatory image, a shimmering mirage or castle-in-the-air *(Luftschloß)*. Alternatively, it can be seen not as a glorified village, but as a run-down town, the tatty remains of the once-celestial city of medieval art, in which case K. as 'land-surveyor' might be compared to the 'measurer' of the New Jerusalem's outer walls as depicted at Prague's Burg Karlstein (Karlštejn),[10] but for the fact that K. is not a land-surveyor or measurer, but a mismeasurer, and even that only in a symbolical sense. Either way, the 'suggestive

---

[10] Cf. Hyde, 128.

obscurity'[11] of the Gothic novelist has never been put to better use. The reader is put in mind of a passage in Schopenhauer's 'Paränesen und Maximen' (Admonitions and Maxims): 'Our experience of life is like that of the traveller who finds that, as he goes forward, objects assume different forms from those they exhibited from a distance, changing, as it were, as he approaches them'.[12]

As in Gothic, the castle is dilapidated, its tower in particular scarcely tower-like. The village, where the castle authorities do their business, so that it is just as much a castle (cf. that corridor full of doors in the public house, so reminiscent of a prison and therefore of Gothic) as the castle is a village, has its equivalent of the tower in the form of a church that turns out to be only a chapel. The village school has 'a look of great age' because in a symbolical sense it goes back to the Renaissance and its undermining of patriarchal authority in the form of the church. The school is linked to the Castle via 'Schwarzer' - cf. Karl R.'s nickname (Negro) at the end of *Der Verschollene*, the diabolical connotations of that name, and the Priest in *Der Proceß*, who is also a *Schwarzer* (Catholic priest), although he is not so dubbed in the text - and, of course, via K. himself, of whom all these figures are projections. K. is the one who needs to learn (cf. aphorism 22: 'You yourself are the task. There is no other pupil in sight'). Castle and village are either image and counter-image, or identical one with the other, according to the perspective that continues to shift throughout the novel, which means that no one view of the Castle totally precludes another, and that there can be no certainty, only ever greater uncertainty. That the Castle is not only K.'s, but Kafka's, is shown by the crows swirling round it: because his name *(kavka)* means 'jackdaw' in Czech, Kafka was in the habit of using black birds (ravens, crows, blackbirds) as an emblem and cryptic self-reference. The crow is moreover said to be 'the devil's bird',[13] and the raven too conceals further meanings: colloquially *Rabe* means a young offender, in which sense it is said to derive from Czech *rab* (in German, *Knecht*, groom, labourer, the status to which K. is finally, and appropriately, reduced). There is a highly appropriate, and quite invisible, further meaning involved, too, for *kavka* also means a dupe or gullible person, just the sort of person to be taken in by someone whose very name, Klamm, proclaims him to be a figment or phantom.

Like the typical Gothic castle, K.'s Castle is the major locus and focus of the plot, 'decaying, bleak and full of hidden passages',[14] and is associated, like the old régime in the penal colony, with the feudal/patriarchal past, the age of superstition. The bureaucratic administrative forms associated with the Castle are, implicitly, as hollow and void of meaning as those practised in the Penal Colony following the death of the

---

[11] Tomkins, 257.
[12] Schopenhauer, *SW*, IV, 462.
[13] R.H.Dana, Snr, in *Paul Feltham* : see his *Poems and Prose Writings*, 2 vols (N.Y.: Baker and Scribner, 1850), I, 310.
[14] Botting, 2.

Old Commandant. Given the nature of the Castle and the identity of Klamm they could not be otherwise. With its wanderer hero, *Das Schloß* also points back to the last great early Gothic novel, Maturin's *Melmoth the Wanderer*. Like it, *Der Proceß* and *Das Schloß* dwell, one on religious superstition, and the other on the spiritual emptiness of the post-Christian world; both novels, in other words, are imbued with religious feeling of a kind, although it is a fugitive, self-doubting feeling, not to be identified with any particular religion claiming to validate it.

If the Castle could be taken at face value, it would be true to say that 'The unapproachable and unfathomable nature of law and authority is presented, in *The Castle*, as the looming, dark and distant edifice of Gothic terror',[15] for this Castle seems, like that of Udolpho, to be a 'figure of power, tyranny and malevolence'.[16] Evidence of the feudal past, with which the Castle is linked by its phantom owner, Graf Westwest, appears to be further provided by the treatment of Barnabas's family by the 'Castle-authorities'. In short, the Castle seems to be the seat of just the sort of arbitrary, autocratic patriarchal power that in Grosse's *Der Genius* controls even people's private actions. The designation of the 'Mädchen aus dem Schloß' by whom K. is captivated is reminiscent of Grosse's *Die Dame vom Schloße* (in *Des Grafen von Vargas Novellen,* 1792). Kafka's *Schloßbehörde* (castle-authority) thus appears to locate itself, loosely, in the German Gothic tradition, and Schloß Westwest to be the locus of seemingly arbitrary power of Gothic convention, although the convention is reversed in that K. is, on the face of it, attempting to get into the castle (a fairytale motif), not escape from it (a Gothic one). In reality he needs to escape from his obsession with it, so this Gothic motif too is internalized.

Like the 'road [to Montoni's castle] winding round the base of a mountain' in *The Mysteries of Udolpho*, the Village has just one street twisting its way round the Castle. More to the point, however, is Schopenhauer's 'walking around a castle' simile, for this village road seems never to get any nearer to, or further away from, what one may therefore be wrong in thinking of as its goal; more certainly it represents a vicious circle, leading nowhere. The 'sense of ruined structure, lost connections, and closed routes'[17] is inescapable. The obvious inference is that the Castle is the centre of the Village, and Castle and Village identical, for, as K. is told, 'This village belongs to the Castle, anyone living or spending the night here, is living or spending the night as it were in the Castle.' That 'as it were' is a transparent attempt to beguile the reader.

In seeking access to the Castle, K. is seeking validation of his existence, hence personal empowerment, but whereas the conventional motif of escape from the Gothic castle is about personal empowerment through liberation, K., as his creator's surrogate, seeks, at least subconsciously, the empowerment that comes from

---

15 Botting 160.
16 Botting, 68.
17 Hyde, 134.

knowledge and above all from self-knowledge. The Castle is the symbol both of everything he seeks, as Faustian a stronghold as Vathek's Tower, and the symbol of all that prevents him from attaining it; it is the citadel of the self from which he is alienated by radical self-doubt and therefore the very reification of the ambiguity in which Gothic is clothed.

Apparition-like in being now there, now not there, and in presenting now one face and now another, this Castle marks the ascendancy of the irrational over the rational, of dream over 'reality', of dream logic over what normally passes for logic. In all of this it may be thought to symbolize the ascendancy of the Gothic. It represents what ought to be order, yet is not, and is haunted by figures, foremost among them Klamm, who seem to represent order in K.'s mind, but are in truth merely phantoms representing his mind's disorder. Although these figures exist only as figments of his imaginative fears, those fears are so strong that it could be argued from this point of view too that K. is all the time 'im Bereich des Schlosses' (within the castle; 'within the limits of his own castle' in the phrase used, in the literal sense, by Harriet Lee of Kruitzner). In being unable to escape from his obsession with the Castle, K. is symbolically trapped within it, both insofar as it represents a fixation on his part and insofar as it is at the same time the embodiment of those negative attributes of fear and doubt that lie behind that fixation and prevent him from escaping from it.

That the Castle lacks not only the 'gate, whose portals were terrible even in ruins' of Gothic convention, but any door as such, again brings it close to the enchanted castle of fairytale. It is the symbolical opposite of the Hotel Occidental in *Der Verschollene* - to which it is linked via the name of its owner, Count Westwest - with its myriad doors. In terms of Gothic convention as described by Sedgwick, it is the 'massive inaccessibility' of the Castle that is its most Gothic feature, for here indeed the self is blocked off from something to which by reason it ought to have access.[18] That something is itself. Whether the process is defined in the positive terms of achieving individuation or the negative ones of escaping from a state of alienation, ultimately makes no difference, for there is no way of reaching either goal. Either way the key to the Castle is a magic that no longer exists, a serenity that K. so signally lacks.

Like the Castle of Otranto in Walpole's Gothic folly, Schloß Westwest is the controlling fiction of *Das Schloß*. It governs the protagonist's every act; his mind is haunted by it. Indeed, what Frank has written of the Gothic castle as such:

> The Gothic castle itself becomes the novel's principal character, a superhuman personality [...] the Gothic building possesses the human characters [...] surrounds them with [...] identity crises [...] the [...] castle [becomes] a metaphoric embodiment of the precarious structure of the mind.[19]

---

18 Sedgwick, 12f.
19 Frederick S. Frank, *The First Gothics* (New York & London: Garland, 1987), xxiiif.

is arguably more applicable to Kafka's Castle than to the castles of early Gothic. The point, first made by Montague Summers,[20] has been glossed by Michael Aguirre in words that could be a description of Kafka's Castle and indeed of Pollunder's country house:

> the Gothic castle is 'alive' with a power that perplexes its inhabitants or visitors. It tends to have an irregular, asymmetrical shape; its geometry is uncanny, whether because of an actual distortion of the whole or because part of it remains unknown [...] This [...] distortion yields mystery, precludes human control.[21]

Kafka's Castle has many Gothic features, but the comparison with Castle Dracula, made in the final section of the present chapter, shows that it is only partly Gothic. In some ways it has more in common with Shelley's air-built castles, and with Bunyan's Doubting Castle, than with any ostensibly more solid Gothic edifices.

That K. first sees the castle 'in the air' is a sure indication that it is an 'airy fabric of fancy',[22] as unreal as every such edifice, but at the same time as real, and, to K., as psychologically necessary, as every obsession. The Castle is Klam(m). Haunted by the idea of the mysterious Klamm and increasingly identified with him, it is an example of what Mircea Eliade terms 'sacred space', that is, space set aside for encounters of the mystical kind, encounters with the *mysterium tremendum*, the presence of which appears to be suggested by a strange, unearthly humming on the telephone line (another example of prop shift), although this could equally well be a fault on the line or a matter of K. 'hearing things' as the labyrinth of the inner ear misleads him, or part of the web of misunderstanding that is so sedulously spun round the reader.

K. receives two mysterious messages purporting to come from Klamm, but the K. with which they are signed, aping his own initial, is close enough to X, the sign of the unknown, to aggravate the doubt in his mind. He may appear to see Klamm when he peers through the keyhole, but his eyes deceive him into 'seeing' what he wants to see; what he cannot see is how his own mind is deluding him. Klamm is the equivalent of the Castle: both he and it exist only in the sense of being figments of K.'s imagination, apparitions, fixations. In Gothic and in *Das Schloß* there is a similar underlying question: are apparitions 'real', or are they projections of a psychic disturbance in those to whom they manifest themselves? Klamm may be defined in many ways. Thus he is (i) a ghostly apparition haunting the 'Castle' in K.'s mind, no more real than the average Gothic ghost, yet as real as every fixation or figure of nightmare, (ii) K.'s diametrically opposed alter ego, but also his super-ego, for he is empowered in the way in which K. would be empowered, the very embodiment of everything K. lacks and for which he searches in vain, and (iii) K.'s devil or Gothic lower self, his id or

---

20 *The Gothic Quest*, 410.
21 Aguirre, 92.
22 Charles Maturin, *Fatal Revenge* (Far Thrupp: Alan Sutton, 1994), 4.

shadow, and as such the embodiment of all that prevents him from attaining what he seeks.

It is the fact that *Das Schloß* closely resembles the typical Gothic 'demonic quest-romance, in which a lonely, self-divided hero embarks on insane pursuit of the Absolute',[23] that has spawned so many religious misinterpretations of the novel. In truth the Castle represents not only the absolute certainty that K. seeks, which in the end turns out to be a deadly truism, but also the absolute uncertainty by which he is possessed. Insofar as Klamm is the Castle, he must also be Graf Westwest. Insofar as he is the Castle, he must also be K., in whose mind alone the castle exists. In the manuscript of the novel Kafka, on several occasions,[24] wrote Kla's instead of K.'s; while obviously a mistake, it reveals the secret identity of K. and Klamm, who is described as the head ('Vorstand', cf. *Verstand*, understanding, reason) of the 'X. Kanzlei' (Department X) of the Castle, and as such the very source and quasi-guarantor of the certainty that K. seeks. This department is a mysterious one, for X is, in Roman numerals, the sign of the unknown (cf. Latin *clam*, secretly, and German *klam[m]heimlich*, on the quiet, which derives from it), suggesting that Klamm represents the unknown and indeed the unknowable. The very fact that Klamm's name is Delusion means that the certainty that K. thinks he could obtain from Klamm is itself an illusion. That the other 'secretaries' are identical with Klamm can be shown linguistically: German *Sekretär* = Czech *tajemník* → *tajemne* (secret) → Latin *clam* → Czech *klam* → Klamm.

Klamm is an obsession based on *Angst*, the fear of insignificance, of life, of death. Even so he is an ambiguous figure: does he signify that it is a delusion on K.'s part to think that he can find the meaning of his existence anywhere except within himself? Or that his life has no given meaning, and therefore no meaning whatsoever? The former meaning is certain; the latter cannot be discounted. K. thinks he has been appointed land-surveyor, but in truth he has not, and the reality/unreality of Klamm and Castle alike follow from that initial misapprehension. Besides, what is 'reality'? Was it not above all in his preoccupation with precisely that question that Kafka revealed his kinship with Hoffmann and the proximity of his work to the *Kunstmärchen* ?

The meaning of the illusory figure of Klamm in K.'s mind resides in his ambiguity. On the one hand he is an inscrutably patriarchal, even divine-seeming figure, K.'s 'god', though more a *deus absconditus* than a real presence; on the other he is even more clearly K.'s personal devil or demon, for it is a diabolical notion that one should go outside oneself for what can only be found within oneself or not at all. The Devil, be it remembered, was believed to be able to assume any form in order to lure human

---

[23]   Thompson, in *The Gothic Imagination*, 2.
[24]   Franz Kafka, *Das Schloß*, ed. Malcolm Pasley (Frankfurt a. M.: S. Fischer, 1982), Text, 243, 254, 291; Apparatus, 324, 332, 368).

beings on to self-deception and thence to self-destruction. It is only in his negative guise of K.'s devil that Klamm has anything to offer K., and that is simply the certainty of uncertainty, a diabolical, self-deceiving protraction of the situation and state in which K. has found himself since crossing that fateful bridge on the first page of the novel, precisely the state with which Josef K. was unable to live.

Kafka's Castle is naturally a deal more complex than its remote historical precursor, the Castle of Otranto, for it exists only in K.'s mind and is accordingly as much his construct as he is its. It is the Other to which K. cannot attain because he is already effectively imprisoned within it in the guise of his alienated, self-doubting self. *Das Schloß* is about self-image *(Selbstdefinition)* and therefore, like so much of Kafka's work, and so much of Gothic (including Dostoevsky), about identity, notably the identity of the man who has no *raison d'être* and therefore no self-respect,[25] but also the identity of the author, who, as a writer ('surveyor') surveying his life's work, fears that his judgments may be misjudgments and his works mere hollow constructs. That these are Gothic themes is shown by *Die Elixiere des Teufels*, although the fact must not blind us to the many significant differences between Kafka's novels and Hoffmann's most powerful and most Gothic work, not least among them the fact that at the end of *Die Elixiere des Teufels* Medardus has risen above what he was at the beginning of the novel, whereas at the end of Kafka's novels the protagonist has signally failed to do so.

Das Schloß is in line with Gothic convention at its most cerebrally refined in including within the narrative an inset novella or story-within-a story-within-a story à la Maturin. Within the main narrative is the story of Barnabas and his family, and within that the story first of the fire brigade fête, and then of Amalia's Secret and Fall. The first of these is a fascinating, somewhat over-determined interlude, reminiscent of the Naturtheater von Oklahoma, which is probably based on a fête that Kafka witnessed in the Bohemian village of Zürau. It is the story, again a parable, of the fire brigade fête on 3rd July, Kafka's birthday. The occasion was to be marked by the 'Übergabe der [neuen] Spritze' (literally, the handing over of a new fire engine [or hose]; but what no translation can ever reveal is the fact that 'Spritze' is a slang term for a girl, so that it also refers to the demanded handing over of Amalia to Sortini). At this ceremony Castle and Village come together for the first and last time in the novel. The symbolical season is summer, the setting a riverside meadow outside the Village which contrasts so strongly with the wintry wilderness that is, otherwise, all that K. knows in the seven days of this reverse Creation, as to appear positively paradisal. That is the whole point. The meadow here stands for Eden (Canaan, the promised land), the river is the river Pison (Gen. II, 11); the 'Spritze', now a phallic symbol

---

25 Like Shelley's Wolfstein, K. cannot face the thought that he is 'a being useless to himself and to society' (*Zastrozzi and St Irvyne*, ed. Behrendt, 109).

symbolising Sortini's lust, is the Serpent, for although Amalia does not succumb to Sortini, she does eat of the tree of knowledge: her eyes are opened and she knows good and evil.

If the setting of this ceremony is reminiscent of the Paradise myth in Genesis, it has further points in common with another form of the myth in Ezekiel (XXVIII, 12-19), viz. the 'stones of fire' (cf. the fireworks here), the music of tabrets and pipes (cf. the trumpets here), and the precious stones of the iniquitous Tyre (cf. Amalia's garnet necklace, by which Sortini is attracted, and all the discussion of the iniquity involved). There is plenty of evidence that the meadow beside the river outside the village represents a symbolical Paradise that is about to be lost, for the scene is reminiscent not only of the Fall of Man, but of the Apocalypse and the Fall of Babylon, with the fire engine as the 'great red dragon' and the trumpets as the seven trumps of doom. The latter, presented to the fire brigade by the Castle, are stressed by Olga, who is telling the story. She speaks of the 'entsetzlicher Lärm' they make, the word 'entsetzlich' (figuratively, horrible [din]; but literally, lawless, contrary to the Law) revealing Kafka's meaning. He hated noise, which he thought of as 'wüster Lärm' (terrible din; but *wüst* also means licentious). The noise here therefore connotes *Wüstheit* (licentiousness), and is such that one would have thought the Turks had arrived, although even the Turks are not unambiguous, for the word 'Türken' implies, by extension, that the episode is made up (*einen Türken bauen* means to concoct a cock-and-bull story). The typical subjunctive formulation, on the other hand, means that the Turks (who occupied and traumatized part of Austro-Hungary in the sixteenth and seventeenth centuries) are symbolically present in the hordes of licentious Castle-servants, previously identified as demons. The scene is reminiscent of the one that greeted Karl Rossmann in the Nature Theatre, when he tried out the tune of a drinking-song on Fanny's trumpet. The trumpets in the Nature Theatre produced, alternately, angelic and satanic sounds; those presented to the local fire-brigade by the 'Castle' produce similar sounds, ecstatic yet satanic. It is an appropriately ambiguous sound to be heard in this re-enactment of the Fall and ritual celebration of the Castle Mysteries which makes it as clear as may be that the subject is again original sin or the corruption of Man, the theme of many an earlier Gothic interlude. It was shortly after this that Sortini (an alias of Klamm) showed himself in his true colours when he jumped over ('sprang über') the shaft of the (horse-drawn) fire-engine. The reader cannot afford to overlook *(überspringen)* the significance of the episode ('Deichsel', shaft → *Deixel*, Devil). Kafka even has Sortini sit on the shaft in order to show, in the manner of dreams, that he is the devil in qu estion.

The story of Amalia's Secret is, on one level, an elaborate story of transgression with a difference in that the real transgression is not the one for which Amalia's father wishes to accept the blame, but a transgression against Amalia, a gross abuse of power on the part of the ambiguously named Sortini (alias Sordini), who seems a pretty conventional Gothic villain in the mould of Radcliffe's Schedoni in using his arbitrary patriarchal power in an attempt to possess himself of the courageous Amalia. When interiorized, however, the story is a study of guilty conscience, in which what counts is not the fact but the sense of guilt. Each of Kafka's novels has its figure of the almost obligatory Italian of Gothic convention (Giacomo; the Italian; Sortini/Sordini, Vallabene), but Kafka again (assuming his awareness of it) puts a spin on the convention by ostensibly making Olga, whose name means that she is to be seen as saintly for giving herself to the Castle menials, into the heroine of the story, which relates to the main narrative as the Parable of the Doorkeeper did in *Der Proceß*. Olga's story is indeed relevant to that parable. Josef K., in *Der Proceß*, is unable to prove his innocence because he is guilty; Amalia's father, for his part, is unable to prove his guilt because he is innocent. In his prime he once carried Galater out of the blazing Herrenhof at a run (cf. the Devil as strong man; insofar as Galater is another alias of Klamm/Sortini, and therefore of the Devil, his superhuman strength seems, on this occasion, to have been projected on to Amalia's father). As for his daughters, they are symbolical types representing not so much the fortunes of vice and misfortunes of virtue, as the pros and cons of yielding to fate (Olga) and struggling against it (Amalia). Each is both right and wrong: the crass moral inversions of Sade are avoided, but the by comparison subtler antinomies of Gothic are still unresolved. On the face of it, they both represent the Gothic heroine suffering at the hands of a corrupt and tyrannical patriarchal power, as well as corresponding to the opposing sisters/pairs of opposites of Gothic and fairytale convention, their counterparts in the main narrative being Frieda and the 'girl [maiden and mother] from the castle', who in terms of aphorism 79 represent profane and sacred love respectively. However here too there is a point beyond which the Gothic analogy ceases to apply, for the context in which the story of Amalia and Olga is told and set is Gothic only on the surface. Beneath the surface the machinery of Gothic is used to power a more individual sort of craft.

At the end K. was to have been told that he had not in fact been appointed land-surveyor, but was free to remain in the village until his death, which was then to have taken place. Left incomplete, though not inchoate, all three of Kafka's novels were thus to have ended, like so many of his tales, in the final alienation of death. This, it could be argued, is their most Gothic feature of all, for the prison-house of Gothic fiction houses not only patriarchy and the self, which caused Kafka more problems than most, but, beyond that, mortality: all those ever-shrinking enclosures, physical and metaphysical alike, foreshadow that ultimate Gothic locus, the charnel house or grave, of which K. said to Frieda, in a remarkably open, Gothic-Romantic way: 'I dream of a grave, deep and narrow, where we could clasp each other in our arms as with iron bars, and I would hide my face in you and you would hide your face in me, and nobody would ever see us any more' (ch. 13). *Das Schloß* therefore ends with the bottomless pit, the chaos from which the world came and to which it is now returned in what has been well called a 'cosmogony in reverse',[26] a point which serves to underline the metaphysical weight of what, if less weighty, might well have been thought of as Kafka's Gothic.

8.2.2. Graf Westwest and Count Dracula

The most obvious of the intriguing intertextualities between *Das Schloß* and *Dracula* concerns their castle-heroes. The land-surveyor K.'s initial impression of Schloß Westwest, which changes as his perspective changes, can be compared with the conveyancer Jonathan Harker's first impression of Castle Dracula:

> a vast ruined castle, from whose tall black windows came no ray of light, and whose broken battlements showed a jagged line against the moonlit sky [...] In the gloom the courtyard looked of considerable size, and as several dark ways led from it under great round arches it perhaps seemed bigger than it really is. I have not yet been able to see it by daylight [...] through these frowning walls and dark window openings it was not likely that my voice could penetrate [...] the walls of [the] castle are broken; the shadows are many, and the wind breathes cold through the broken battlements and casements [...] doors, doors, doors everywhere, and all locked and bolted [...] The castle was built on the corner of a great rock, so that on three sides it was quite impregnable [...] the clear line of Dracula's castle cut the sky [...] We saw it in all its grandeur, perched a thousand feet on the summit of a sheer precipice [...] There was something wild and uncanny about the place. We could hear the distant howling of wolves [...] the sound [...] full of terror.

Of K. it may be said, as of Harker, that 'when he [...] crossed the bridge, the phantoms came to meet him'.[27] Castle Dracula is, in more senses than one, the Gothic castle to end all Gothic castles - vast, ruined, with broken battlements and locked doors, doors everywhere, as in the Irish fairytale of the otherworld king whose palace has one hundred doors, and as in each of Kafka's novels (in symbolical terms it follows that Kafka's Castle too must have doors everywhere, but also, paradoxically, that it has no door anywhere), shrouded in darkness.[28] Its location on the summit of the sublime of terror takes the reader back to the ghastly end of Lewis's Ambrosio. That Schloß Westwest too is veiled in mist and darkness helps to emphasize its most Gothic feature, that phantasmagorically shifting outline which makes it appear now a great castle, now a sprawling village; it too has the broken battlements of its kind. In neither castle is there any sign of life. The main difference between the two edifices is that the perpendicularity of Castle Dracula is emphasized, whereas in the case of Schloß Westwest it is its rambling, horizontal, earthbound, secular nature that is stressed. Castle Dracula does at least recall the Gothic tower/spire of which it is the ultimate

---

[26] Politzer, 248.

[27] The words from *Nosferatu* (1922, the year of *Das Schloß*) are quoted from Prawer, *Caligari's Children,* 108.

[28] 'Death hath so many doors to let out life'. (John Fletcher [with Massinger], *The Custom of the Country,* II, ii, 164, 203, 267.

perversion, although its dilapidated condition speaks for itself. Kafka's Castle, on the other hand, is not only implied to be an illusion; it is not a castle at all, just a mirror image of the village, more *fau[x]bourg* than *bourg*, though that does not by any means imply that it is not a Gothic edifice. The Herrenhof public house (based on the Herrenhof café in Vienna, popularly known as the Hurenhof [whorehouse]) is, in symbolical terms, the real castle, for it is there that castle business is conducted, so that a Freudian reading of all those doors cannot be precluded. Although it is usual to call Schloß Westwest 'Kafka's Castle', it is really K.'s castle: it stands in him and for him, its door (if door there is) that never opens as personal to him as the Door that never shut in his lifetime was to the man-from-the-country in the parable that anticipated and summarized so much in the novel that followed it.

Dracula is about the evil count of Gothic convention (Dracula's name means 'son of the Devil'; he is, in Wilhelm Hauff's phrase, one of the metamorphoses of Satan), who in *Das Schloß* has become no more than a ghostly memory, for Graf Westwest, the supposed owner of this castle-in-the-air is never seen and does not exist in any useful or tangible sense, his role as the *seigneur* insisting on his supposed *droit* being taken over by Sortini.[29] His name, like every other name in Kafka's work, can be made to reveal meanings, though whether these meanings, ghosts of a ghost, are to the point, can never be told with certainty. Thus the Count's name suggests (i) all those other counts in the Gothic novel and, more generally, in the history of the West, particularly if G(raf)West(west) is construed as meaning *g'west (gewesen)*, which would imply that he is a has-been, the representative, with the Old Commandant of the penal colony, of the *ancien régime* in a range of senses, (ii) the idea of the decline of the West (Oswald Spengler's *Der Untergang des Abendlandes* appeared shortly before *Das Schloß,* in 1918-22) and the invasion of the West by the East, which begins, we are told, at Budapest, and (iii) the identity problem of the westernized (assimilated) Jew. More particularly, Westwest invites comparison with the name Westenra in *Dracula.* West, emphasized by reduplication in Westwest, refers to the West, where Eastern Jews are aliens until they are assimilated (colonized) by the West, whereupon they are alienated from their roots. All this is a way of emphasizing that K.'s Castle is the site of his identity problem. Lucy Westenra's name, by contrast, refers to a reverse colonization, the idea of a Westerner being taken over (colonized, vampirized, raped) by the East.[30] As Stephen Arata has said, 'The Late-Victorian nightmare of reverse colonization is expressed succinctly [when] Harker envisions

---

29 Freud writes of 'the *droit du seigneur* which Count Almaviva tried to exercise over Susanna' in *The Marriage of Figaro* (*The Interpretation of Dreams*, 209).

30 See Stephen Arata, *Fictions of loss in the Victorian fin de siècle* (Cambridge: Cambridge University Press, 1996), 107-132, esp. 115-126.

semi-demons spreading through the realm, colonizing bodies and land indiscriminately.'[31]

While one novel reverses the other, they share a discourse that concerns their respective authors. On Kafka's side the story begins with *Der Verschollene*, in which Onkel Jakob (formerly Jakob Bendelmeyer, now Senator Edward Jacob, who is thus known literally by his Christian name), unlike Karl R. at that stage, is the westernized (or assimilated or colonized or alienated) Jew, or indeed any human being, who has allowed himself to be taken over by the Other or, in symbolical terms, who has allowed himself to be vampirized, as Karl was by Johanna, who almost choked him in the process. Karl, like Onkel Jakob before him, goes west, although the English metaphor does not exist in German, as does K. in heading for Schloß Westwest. In symbolical terms the West is, of course, the domain of the Devil.[32] Now behind the K.-novels in particular is Kafka's difficulty in identifying and defining himself: as a German-speaker he is in a small minority in Prague; as a Jew he is in a minority among the German-speakers; unorthodox, he is in a minority among the Jews; denied by his father, he is an outcast at home; as a writer he is in a minority among the human race. Defined in such a negative way, he might well have problems with his self-image. This is, however, only to emphasize the parallel with *Dracula.* Although *Dracula* is, on one level, about the reverse colonization feared by the Late Victorians, one also needs to remember that for Stoker, with his Irish cultural consciousness, living in London was, with the partial exception of language (although both men's accents will have marked them out as men apart: Kafka spoke German with something of a Czech accent, Stoker had an Irish accent), comparable to Kafka's experience of living as a stranger in his 'native city' of Prague. Stoker was less self-aware than Kafka, but for him too his own cultural and national identity was potentially problematical. In many ways the Jew living in Prague and the Irishman living in London were in a similar position, their only choice that between two forms of alienation.

We have already seen that Karl's first thought on seeing Klara in the first re-enactment of his seduction in Chapter 3 of *Der Verschollene* was 'Die roten Lippen, die sie hat' (what red lips she has), remarkably close to Jonathan Harker's thought on first seeing the three young vampires in Castle Dracula: 'I felt in my heart a wicked, burning desire that they would kiss me with those red lips.' It is tempting, given the added allusions to vampirism in *Der Proceß*, and the parallels between *Das Schloß* and *Dracula*, to associate the stoker of *Der Verschollene* with Bram Stoker and his novel, in which ships (*Demeter, Czarina Catherine*) also feature; in each case we have phantom ships with the Devil in the hold. It would, however, be fanciful to do so, for

---

[31] Arata, 115.
[32] J. E. Cirlot, *A Dictionary of Symbols*, 2nd edn (London: Routledge & Kegan Paul, 1971), 369.

Bram Stoker has nothing at all in common with Kafka's stoker, although Dracula does. Slovaks and Rumanians receive unflattering mention in both novels, but this is the incidental product of their setting. The stoker, a Devil-figure in German, represents Karl's alienated, rejected ('monstrous') self, the devil in him who caused him to succumb to Johanna Brummer, a succubus figure with a laugh 'like a witch', and can therefore be compared to Dracula ('son of the Devil'). Karl's box (echoed in the Stoker's 'sea-chest', also 'Koffer' in German) and Dracula's coffin, which is often referred to as his box, both represent themselves, their selves; when Dracula's coffin is rudely opened and his heart penetrated by Morris's bowie knife, he is paid back in his own coin for the rape of his victims.

Sex is a problem not only in *Dracula*, but in *Der Verschollene* and, more to the point, in *Der Proceß*, where Josef K. is presented as a latent vampire. At this stage the reader needs to know that Kafka identified with the vampire (see BV 190): he imagined his father thinking of him as one of those 'vermin which [...] suck [their victims'] blood [...] to sustain their own life'. In the first chapter of *Der Proceß* Josef K. first kisses Frl. B., with all the rabid thirst of a vampire, to which the highly unusual simile draws attention, 'right on the throat, and [keeps] his lips there for a long time'; then in the guise of the student Bertold he kisses the wife of the Court-Attendant 'loudly' on the throat, and, finally, is himself 'kissed and bitten on the throat' by the vampiric Leni (a descendant of the nineteenth-century vampire woman from Le Fanu's Carmilla to the daughters of Dracula), whose middle fingers are webbed exactly like a bat's wing, which consists of a web of skin stretched between elongated fingers ('eine hübsche Kralle' indeed), after he has kissed those fingers. Finally, he 'dies' like a vampire when a long knife is 'thrust into his heart and turned twice', not only a 'Gothic' enough death,[33] but one which confirms that Josef K. has been a vampire (or 'cannibal', to use Kafka's term). That the knife is a butcher's knife points back to Kafka's paternal grandfather, and thus confirms that it is by patriarchy that Kafka sees Josef K., like Georg Bendemann and Gregor Samsa, being destroyed. It cannot be coincidence that each of the three sexual encounters in the novel is associated with a vampire-image, and that one of these is identified as such. Was Kafka here betraying, or, more likely, signalling, his knowledge of *Dracula*? The nature of Josef K.'s 'death' makes it likely that Kafka had *Dracula* in mind when he used those vampire-images in *Der Proceß* .[34]

Kafka's work can be compared with vampire Gothic on two related grounds. If vampirism stands for decadent/perverse sex, as thought by Nietzsche, who

33 See Soldan/Heppe, *Geschichte der Hexenprozesse*, ed. Max Bauer (Hanau/M.: Müller & Kiepenheuer, 1911, repr. n.d.), Vol II, between pages 398 and 399, for a woodcut illustration, dating from 1509, of the various forms of punishment and execution current in the middle ages, one detail of which shows a man, lying on his back, being stabbed to death by the executioner.

34 That he knew of Sade, is clear from Janouch (88), who quotes him as saying that 'Marquis de Sade [...] ist der eigentliche Patron unserer Zeit.'

commented that the suppression of sex in the name of morality only led to its return in hideous disguises, including 'uncanny vampire form',[35] Kafka was in two minds about sex as such, regarding it, at times, as perverse, hence the 'censored' vampire-images when Josef K. kisses Frl. B. and the court-attendant's wife. At other times, as when K. makes love to Frieda in the third chapter of *Das Schloß*, the vampire-image is not present, although the idea of enchantment is. Sex, which he construed into uncleanness, is, as we have seen, the basic reason for Kafka's self-condemnation, and his work is also linked with vampire Gothic by the 'cannibalism' motif, of which sex is an important part.[36] A strict vegetarian, he contrasts 'cannibalism' with asceticism and with civilization (see, for instance, 'Schakale und Araber' and 'Ein altes Blatt'), and blames himself, at times bitterly, for what he thinks of as his own cannibal impulse. It was for his latent 'cannibalism' ('Throw your whip away or I will eat you', he had said) that the original victim in *In der Strafkolonie* was being tortured,[37] and it was his latent cannibalism that the student revealed in *Der Proceß* (ch. 3) when he snapped at K.'s hand with his teeth. An alternative version of *Ein Hungerkünstler*[38] features a cannibal; the better known version more tamely features the opposite, a starvation-artist, a master-ascete who enjoys punishing his body for its latent 'cannibalism'.

[35] Prawer, *The Uncanny*, 14.

[36] As Marina Warner has said, 'In myth and fairy tale, the metaphor of devouring often stands in for sex' (*From the Beast to the Blonde* [London: Chatto & Windus, 1994], 259).

[37] On this whole question, see J. M. S. Pasley, 'Asceticism and Cannibalism: Notes on an Unpublished Kafka Text', *OGS*, 1(1966), 102-113.

[38] First published by Pasley, ibid.

9. FAIRYTALE AND GOTHIC TALE

9.1. *Das Urteil*

There are, of course, fairytale motifs and features in some of the best known shorter pieces as well as in the novels. Thus Georg Bendemann's father in *Das Urteil* appears at one point as an ogre ('my father is still an ogre' [i.e. my father is still the ogre he appeared to be in my childhood]), the Stoker in *Der Verschollene* is similarly described as 'riesig' (gigantic), as is Green; and Brunelda, as an intensification of Johanna Brummer, is necessarily depicted as an ogress. In fairytale, ogres (often *Kinderfresser[innen]* [devourers of children] in the original) are frequently associated with cannibalism (and thence with sex), and Kafka, via Georg Bendemann, is probably thinking both of his father's physical stature and of his father's father, who was not only 'a giant of a man', but a butcher by trade. The ascetic, vegetarian son certainly associated his own father with 'cannibalism' in a range of figurative, symbolical senses. The father of *Das Urteil*, who condemns his son to death, acts the part of figurative *Kinderfresser*, as does the father of *Die Verwandlung*, who is instrumental in his son's death. In the former, the father's murderous hatred of his son is projected on to the son, who momentarily allows his giant-killer heritage to reveal itself when he wishes that his father would, like Humpty-Dumpty, have a great fall and break in so many pieces that no one could put him together again. In fairytale the size of the ogre is a reflection of the magnitude of the fear of the person who encounters him, which in turns reflects their own size at the time; in *Das Urteil* the fact that Georg sees his father as an ogre therefore means that his oedipal problem goes back to childhood. Kafka, whose fear of his own father is the ultimate reason why Georg sees his father as an ogre, imagined in vain a situation where he would one day be his father's equal; he went on 'that would, admittedly, be like a fairytale' (BV 185).

There is more to this classical, dreamlike delineation of a destructive love-hate relationship than the ogre motif at its centre, but the fairytale motif serves to focus the relationship, thus ensuring that the central problem is not obscured as the real-life relationship between Kafka *père et fils* is fictionalized. What makes the story dreamlike is the fact that the three key figures correspond to mental image or perception (the father as seen by the son, the son as seen by the father, the son the father would have preferred) rather than to external 'reality'. A high degree of fictionalization or poetic elaboration was needed to enable the study, at the heart of which are the ogre-figure and the Humpty Dumpty motif. In itself the relationship between father and son owes more to Gothic than to fairytale: the murderous abuse of paternal power and the motifs of disinheritance and usurpation are straightforwardly Gothic. The story anticipates the later twentieth-century Gothic fairytale in thus combining Gothic and fairytale motifs.

9.2. *Die Verwandlung*

Most literal and memorable of the many Gothic-and-fairytale-style metamorphoses in Kafka's work is that of Gregor Samsa in *Die Verwandlung*, the story that has long since supplanted Richard Marsh's *The Beetle* of 1897 as the prime example of what Dorothy Scarborough dubbed 'entomological supernaturalism'. Marsh's story, described by the publisher of a reprint edition as 'possibly the most vile creation in English fiction', involves a priestess of Isis who haunts the world in the form of a loathsome scarab. From that little known example of horror literature dating from the Gothic revival of the 1890s it is a far cry to Kafka's differently realized but no less chilling study of Samsa (a projection of himself as solitary bachelor), who awakens to a disastrous collapse of his self-image and self-esteem to the point where he finds that he has become a bug, *Ungeziefer*, in the original meaning of the word something so unclean as to be unsuitable for ritual use. Kafka, who described himself in his earliest diary [T 18] as being 'no better than an *Ungeziefer*', saw himself as a scapegoat for humanity. Metamorphosis is one of a number of motifs shared by Gothic and *Märchen*, but the particular form of change undergone by Gregor Samsa brings Kafka's text closer to the folk fairytale, in which the transformation of man to beetle is known,[1] as is self-transformation, while the transformation of man to insect is commonplace.[2]

Kafka has in effect taken the fairytale motif of transformation as punishment and applied it to self-punishment: Gregor's transformation, though unexplained, evidently flows from the self-blame to which Kafka was so prone. Gregor Samsa's metamorphosis as the result of a wish voiced by his precursor Eduard Raban in *Hochzeitsvorbereitungen auf dem Lande* corresponds to the idea of metamorphosis as the result of a wish in the Grimms' 'Die sieben Raben'. Raban (another of Kafka's self-projections, cf. Czech *rab*, slave, and Kafka's view of himzelf, in the *Brief an den Vater*, as a slave in the house of a master) expressed the wish that he might be transformed into a maybug or whatever in order to avoid marriage, the state for which Kafka longed, but from which he instinctively shrank. The present story is the expression and exploration of that fear. Like Oscar Wilde's *Dorian Gray*, *Die*

---

[1]   See Stith Thompson, *Motif-Index*, D184.1.
[2]   Stith Thompson, *Motif-Index*, D180.

Verwandlung is 'structured around a "wish-come-true" device',[3] but with the wish in question voiced in a pre-text or precursor text. If Dorian Gray's picture is 'an ideal reproduction of himself, self as perfect other', Gregor Samsa's assumed self-image is the opposite, for the Beetle, like Frankenstein, is his creator's other in the more usual negative sense. He is, however, not 'another being than himself, with his reason intact',[4] but, as in fairytale, another body. That wished-for diminution is, at it were, an inversion and subversion of Goethe's fairytale 'Die neue Melusine',[5] in which the dwarf Melusine grows in size in order to attract a husband; Goethe's *Kunstmärchen* was itself a (sub)version of the medieval legend of the supernatural wife Melusine. Kafka's tale, like so much of his work, thus has ancient roots, although, as usual, it moves well away from them. *Die Verwandlung* is as it were a double reversal of the Grimms' 'Froschkönig' in that (i) the metamorphosis takes place immediately before the story opens, and (ii) it is a metamorphosis for the worse. Those who are changed into loathsome creatures in fairytale, usually by 'witches' (sc. the ill-will of another), are normally changed back when the evil-doer is punished and order restored, whereas in Kafka's work it is, on the bourgeois face of it, disorder that is established. From Gregor Samsa's point of view, on the other hand, it is a higher order that finally triumphs.

Die Verwandlung is, in a number of different ways, a variation on the classic theme of 'La belle et la bête', which also features the 'poor old father', from whom Kafka's father-figure differs in that he thrives when no longer challenged by his son. In fairytale the metamorphosed male is often liberated by his sister (or lover); in *Die Verwandlung* this does not happen, for the story is no fairytale, but Kafka refers to the motif and indeed to the brother-sister incest which is a feature of Gothic and folktale alike. Politzer noted that Gregor's name corresponds to that of Hartmann von Aue's Gregorius, who 'committed an act of incest and atoned while suffering a miraculous metamorphosis',[6] and while this is potentially misleading, a blind alley of the kind that Kafka deliberately incorporated into his work in order to distract the distractible, he did note in passing that sister-love, avoiding the complications of marriage, was (as Gregor calls it) a pretty dream, that is, a fairytale of the kind the present tale denies. The way in which Gregor 'covers' the image of the woman in the fur coat shows that he is not simply a model bachelor, while the contrast between the furs by which the woman is protected from exposure, and the hard elytra which fail to protect Gregor from patriarchy's deadly blow, speaks for itself.

In showing Gregor Samsa transformed into an 'ungeheures Ungeziefer' (huge bug), Kafka is emphasizing that he has become not only a bug, but an uncanny, monstrous

---

[3] Jackson, *Fantasy*, 112f.
[4] Jackson, *Fantasy*, 30.
[5] *Wilhelm Meisters Wanderjahre*, ch. 16.
[6] Politzer, 77.

one, in other words, a monster or ogre as well, a double transformation. This has come about as a result not of some conventional enchantment, but of the opposite, a radical disenchantment with self, for Gregor Samsa's transformation, though unexplained, appears to result from radical doubt about his identity and even gender, given his unwillingness to marry (both *Käfer* and *Brummer* mean young woman, cf. the Freudian meaning of elytrum; contrast Cz. *samec*, male → Samsa), and thus the ultimate in self-loathing and self-rejection. In Jungian terms it represents the takeover of the personality by the personal unconscious or shadow. The beetle-form ties in with Kafka's identification with women in general and with witches in particular as fellow-victims of patriarchy. In folklore beetles may represent witches, as well as having vampiric and therefore 'cannibalistic' connotations. Nosferat was said to visit people by night in the form of a beetle.[7] Given that Kafka also identified with the vampire, Samsa's self-loathing is presumably rooted in his 'vampirism' or 'cannibalism', that is, in his unclean behaviour. There is more than cheerful vulgarity in the cleaner's reference to Gregor as an 'old dung-beetle'.

In typically Kafkaesque manner the word *Ungeziefer* is the nodal point of a nexus of meanings. In general terms it denotes a 'bug', a word with similar connotations in English; more specifically it means a kind of cockchafer or May-bug.[8] In the story's precursor text, *Hochzeitsvorbereitungen auf dem Lande*, Eduard Raban wishes he could be transformed into a great beetle such as a *Hirschkäfer* (stag-beetle) or *Maikäfer* (May-bug). This wish becomes, as it were, father to Samsa's metamorphosis, which thus comes about not causelessly, but as the realization of a latent desire.[9] Samsa's room, his home and symbol of *das Heimliche*, comes to represent *das Unheimliche,* but its uncanny size and emptiness are also a reflection of the world outside, in which grey sky and grey land merge into one another as presence and absence, life and death, become indistinguishable. This metamorphosis, as a process which converts Samsa into so much waste matter, 'pulling him towards entropy',[10] is in the final analysis the life process itself, which is merely dramatized and speeded up. Reduced to the naked creaturely condition, Samsa slowly forgets his lost humanity. Forfeiting speech and sight, he suffers a typically Gothic loss of control on his way to being destroyed by paternal power: *Die Verwandlung* is complemented and completed by the *Brief an den Vater,* in which Kafka imagines his father likening him to a blood-sucking 'Ungeziefer', but then makes it clear that this is really how he, the son, views himself.

'Samsa' is not only a visual imitation of Kafka; it also contains within itself the ideas of celibacy (Czech *sám*, alone, lonely, oneself) and of gender identity (Czech

---

7   Ernest Jones, *Nightmare, Witches and Devils*, 47.
8   Cf. 'The May-Beetle Dream' in Freud's *The Interpretation of Dreams*, 289-92.
9   Cf. Jackson, *Fantasy,* 160.
10   Jackson, *Fantasy,* 160.

168

samec, male), while the word *Ungeziefer* also has the further highly relevant meaning of *Schmarotzer* (parasite), this connecting with the *Brief an den Vater*, in which Kafka imagines his father pondering his son's 'parasitism' (in German he uses the word 'Schmarotzertum', see T 24). On top of all this an *Ungeziefer* is, by extension, *ungeheuer(lich)* (monstrous), a pint-sized monster (*Ungeheuer*), and therefore *nicht geheuer* (uncanny). The word *Verwandlung*, which denotes the metamorphosis of a crysalis into an adult bug, here stands for Gregor Samsa's emergence as the parasite his super-ego/father had concluded him to be; much of the detail of the piece links with the *Brief an den Vater*. Given that in Counter-Reformation art St. Gregory is associated with scenes of souls in purgatory, Samsa's given name can be read as a reference to the purgatory in which he lives. It is important to remember that the beetle (scarab), a scavenger which contributes to regeneration by devouring the detritus of the physical world, is traditionally an emblem of rebirth/regeneration (in early Christianity it became, under Egyptian influence, a symbol of resurrection), for in a symbolical sense Samsa devours his own lower self; the flat, dry, wafer-like 'thing' that remains at the end is as it were his higher, ascetic self (cf. the similar ambiguity in the ending of 'Ein Hungerkünstler'), so that in a sense he has defeated the material world, not been defeated by it.

At the time of writing *Die Verwandlung* Kafka had not read Roskoff, but when he read this satanology in August 1913, he will have been struck by Roskoff's paraphrase of what is said in the *Malleus Maleficarum* on the subject of tranformation, which makes it clear that, unless divinely ordained to punish or correct sinners, it is the work of the Devil, the implication being that Samsa is not only parasitical, but diabolical. If Kafka went on, as he appears to have done, to read the text of the *Malleus Maleficarum*, he will have been no less struck on reading that 'Whoever believes that it is possible for any creature to be changed [...] into any other shape or likeness [...] is [...] an infidel and worse than a pagan' (i.10). Thus the transformation of Gregor Samsa too seems to go back to Kafka's perception of himself (as a writer) as a devilish person.

Die Verwandlung has been placed in the context of *Märchen* at least since 1952, when Clemens Heselhaus declared it to be an 'anti-fairy tale' showing the world 'as it ought not to be',[11] a form of words which in effect related it to the English Gothic context in the persons of Bage and Godwin. Heinz Politzer took issue with Heselhaus, arguing that Gregor Samsa's 'commonplace character' - the fact that he is neither 'an enchanted prince languishing in the shape of an animal for his redemption' nor a 'legendary pauper' - meant that the concept of the fairytale did not apply to him.[12] More important, in my view, is the question of how the tale's relationship to fairytale

---

[11] Clemens Heselhaus, 'Franz Kafkas Erzählformen', *DVjs,* 26(1952), 356.
[12] Politzer, 80.

is best defined. Is it an anti-fairytale, a fairytale in reverse, a subverted fairytale, or what? Volker Klotz, in his standard history of the European *Kunstmärchen,*[13] took it as an example of what he called the 'pervertierte(s) Märchen', on the grounds that while it contains many fairytale features, the meaning of those features is reversed ('umgepolt'). Pawel, without defining the term, called it a 'poisoned fairy tale'.[14] Basic fairytale features include Gregor Samsa's supernatural transmogrification into a gigantic bug and the lack of surprise with which he reacts to this dire event (one of Hans Andersen's tales, it should be said, involves a beetle who learns to take things as they come), but also the ideas of death by poisoned (in this case, poisoning) apple, which links the tale with 'Sneewittchen', and of brother being saved by sister, which for a time seems to apply, until Grete changes from saving sister to witch, for this is a tale of multiple transformations, two of them affecting Gregor and one each affecting Grete and their parents. Clearly the story reverses the metamorphosis common in folklore and myth, in which, typically, the spell is broken at the appropriate time: in Kafka's story the spell takes ever tighter hold as Samsa's sense of guilt and self-loathing intensifies.

However, although it references several well-known fairytale motifs, *Die Verwandlung* is self-evidently no fairytale. It differs from fairytale in the way in which Gregor dwells on his transformation, the way in which he initially finds it so difficult to control his newly discovered body, the way in which Grete turns from saving angel into avenging fury, and - last but not least - the way in which the apple lodged in his body kills Gregor (unlike Snow-White, who is saved by love). The black magic of Gregor's transformation is countered by no white magic, and it is the very fairytale motif of the poisoned apple that kills him in the end, for the folk-fairytale reminiscences are accompanied by the black logic of Gothic and the everyday world.

In pelting Gregor with apples, Herr Samsa is playing the part of Cain in a Jewish apocryphal version of the Biblical story according to which Cain threw stones at Abel until he hit a vital spot.[15] In an Irish folktale Cain was slain not by a stone, but by an apple. It is ironical that it is the father in the story who represents Cain, for it is the real-life son's self-image as Cain that underlies this story which combines fairytale motifs with the spirit of Gothic, only to transcend and move away from both in its autobiographical fantasy. The apple which lodges in Gregor's body, causing inflammation and finally death as it rots, may represent Felice Bauer, who inflamed the spiritual wound of which Kafka was prone to speak, but it surely also represents the genetic seed implanted by the father (cf. the saying *der Apfel fällt nicht weit vom Stamm* [it's in the blood. Czech: *jablicko nepadlo daleko od stromu*, like father, like

---

13   Volker Klotz, *Das europäische Kunstmärchen* (Stuttgart: Metzler, 1985).
14   Pawel, 279.
15   *Funk & Wagnall's Standard Dictionary of Folklore, Mythology and Folklore*, ed. Maria Leach (London: New English Library, 1975), 180.

son]). Resurrection, as represented by the Egyptian scarab (dung-beetle), sometimes given a human face, is not in question in Kafka's text, although Gregor does finally achieve a form of negative transcendence as he sheds his materiality, and his story has, of course, achieved immortality.

9.3. *Ein Landarzt*

Another famous text incorporating fairytale motifs, *Ein Landarzt* belongs to type AT500-559 of tales involving a supernatural helper, but veers sharply away from fairytale as such. The horses which appear, as if by magic, at the beginning of the story correspond to all those supernatural horses or magic steeds *(Wunschrosse)* of folktale that help the hero to fulfil all his wishes. In Propp's terms they are 'magical agents'. Here the motif is subverted, in that the otherworldly horses carry the doctor away from the object of his desire, leaving him totally frustrated and, at the end, an accursed wanderer figure, so that the magic, if any, is black. The horse symbol as such has already been discussed (6.2.1). Kafka describes the doctor's steeds as 'unirdisch' (implying that they are uncanny and symbolical) rather than 'überirdisch' because on one reading what they enable the country doctor to do is to obey the 'Fehlläuten der Nachtglocke', this being paralleled by the way in which the parish priest, apparently possessed by some *Reißteufel* (a person who wears their clothes out very quickly, but literally a devil prompting someone to tear things up), rends his vestments, though here we are in the realm of linguistic speculation rather than fairytale. The horses' appearance from a disused pigsty is a subverted reminiscence of the appearance out of a hazelnut of the coach, horses and coachman to take Cinderella to the ball. At the same time the doctor corresponds to the 'wild rider' of Gothic.

Kafka's starting-point was a Polish legend about a doctor who initially despaired of healing his patient, but was successful at the second attempt.[16] This he changed to a doctor who first despaired of finding anything wrong with his patient, but then tried again so purposefully that he found him (and himself) to be incurable.[17] Fairytale motifs outside the story help to put it firmly in the fairytale context which it proceeds to unravel; they include, among others, the doctor who loses a horse for the sake of the truth (in our text it is the loss of his original horse that leads the country doctor to the truth), the doctor who is urged to cure himself before doctoring others, and the doctor who is scorned because he is unable to cure himself.[18] The doctor traditionally embodies the altruism that is typical of the fairytale hero, but Kafka's protagonist, who fails in his self-imposed task, is no saver of lives or souls, let alone a *salvator rosae* -

---

16 See H. Binder, *Kafka-Kommentar zu sämtlichen Erzählungen* (Munich: Winkler, 1975), 211.

17 See James S. Whitlark, 'Kafka's "A Country Doctor" as Neoromantic Fairy Tale', in *The Shape of the Fantastic*, ed. O. H. Saciuk [New York: New Greenwood, 1986], 47.

18 Stith Thompson, *Motif-Index*, J551.3, J1062 and J1062.2.

he can, when not distracted, diagnose mortality, but he cannot cure it. His patients expect miracles, but these days there are no more miracles than there are fairytales with their miracle cures and wound-healing balms, let alone supernatural horses. Even the doctor's motivation and moral imperatives are unclear: is he driven by altruism, or by the desire to get back to Rosa as quickly as possible?

At the beginning of the story he discovers, in quick succession, the two magic steads (named Brother and Sister, a positive open sesame of folk-fairytale motifs)[19] that will carry him to his patient and to the discovery of his own mortality. Just as he cannot save his 'sister' from the lust of the vampiric, cannibalistic stable-lad whose teeth leave their ominous imprint on her cheek, so she cannot save her 'brother' from tragic knowledge. At first the doctor can find nothing wrong with his patient because his main concern is to return to Rosa before it is too late, but then his own wound (conscience) opens, he looks again and, as if by magic, it appears that his patient has a festering wound in the region of his thigh. As Andrew Webber has said, at this point Kafka 'projects into his tale that archetypal image of the Gothic uncanny, Füßli's *[The] Nightmare*', one version of which hung in Freud's consulting room.[20] In a succession of overdetermined images the doctor is reduced to the naked human condition by the village elders and placed in bed beside the patient whose wound is his own: 'rosa', it stands for Rosa, and is reminiscent both of the 'deep wound' of legend and of the folktale motif of the wound that breaks open while the lover is in bed with his mistress (N 386), as the doctor would be. At the end the doctor, bereft of his symbolical fur coat, is left exposed to the elements and the apparent meaninglessness of life. He may have found, as if by magic, the horses he thought he needed, and the wound he at first thought his patient did not have, but in the end magic fails him utterly.

Though starting off with multiple fairytale resonances, *Ein Landarzt* moves further and further away from fairytale as such, which it subverts at every point. It is accordingly less 'Gothic fairytale' than 'anti-fairytale'.

9.4. *In der Strafkolonie*

The latent cannibalism expressed by the captain's batman (the sacrificial victim of the torture-machine in the Penal Colony) when he says 'Wirf die Peitsche weg, oder ich fresse dich' ('Throw away your whip, or I'll eat you up') - an extraordinary wording - goes back to the words spoken by the wolf to the miller in the Grimms' 'Der Wolf und die sieben jungen Geißlein' (The Wolf and the Seven Little Kids'): 'Wenn du es nicht thust, so fresse ich dich' ('If you don't do so, I'll eat you up'). Cannibalism looms larger

---

[19] Stith Thompson, *Motif-Index,* P253.
[20] Andrew J. Webber, *The Doppelgänger* (Oxford: Clarendon Press, 1996), 334.

in Grimm's fairytales than English readers may realize, for what is translated as 'ogre' is often 'Menschenfresser(in)' (cannibal) in the original. The connexion between nightmare, fairytale and Gothic is brought home when one reads, in the Grimms' famous 'Von dem Machandelboom' ('The Juniper Tree') that 'My mother she killed me, / My father he ate me', the point, which Kafka must have associated with the idea of the family hunt with himself as prey, underlined by the figure of 'Der Kinderfresser' in a sixteeth-century broadsheet engraving by Hans Weiditz.[21] One need look no further than Grimm's fairytales as a source for the idea of 'cannibalism' in Kafka, which goes way beyond Grimm, however, as it develops into a very personal motif.[22] Kafka uses the term as the symbolical opposite of asceticism. That it is a Gothic motif is shown not only by *Melmoth*, but by an earlier and more lurid German novel from the *Räuberroman* (novel of banditti) branch of the Gothic family:

> My companions and I had deviated so far from the natural norm that we ate the flesh of those we had murdered, provided they were young and healthy [...] Strong, good-looking youths were slaughtered as a matter of course, and the young women we had enjoyed were roasted and devoured.

This perverse and gruesome nonsense, clearly intended to offend the reader, is to be found in *Der Schwarze Jonas* [23] by Ignaz Ferdinand Arnold (ps. of Theodor Ferdinand Kajetan Arnold), a grisly Gothic tale which involves one of the three types of ogre in the *Kinder- und Hausmärchen:* 'The second group consists of social deviants; among them are the robbers and highwaymen who waylay young women, murder them, chop up their corpses, and cook the pieces in a stew.'[24] Stith Thompson has shown just how common a folktale-motif cannibalism is.[25] In Kafka's hands it overlaps with vampirism.

The ultimate patriarchal control-mechanism is the torture-machine of *In der Strafkolonie*. Established by the Old Commandant (the embodiment of the fairytale figure of the issuer of commandments), and described by Kafka with the precision that is his stylistic hallmark, it is reminiscent of Poe's Pendulum, and, more specifically, of a similar torture-cum-execution machine in an early French Gothic novel by Jacques-Antoine Reveroni de Saint-Cyr, *Pauliska, ou la perversité moderne, mémoires récents d'une Polonaise* (published anonymously in Paris by Courcier, in

---

21   Reproduced in Marina Warner, *No Go the Bogeyman* (London: Chatto & Windus, 1998), 5; also, ch. 2 ('My father he ate me') as a whole.
22   See Jacques Geninasca, 'Conte populaire et identité du cannibalisme', *Nouvelle Revue de Psychanalyse*, VI (1972), 215-30.
23   Ignaz Ferdinand Arnold, *Der Schwarze Jonas. Kapuziner, Räuber und Mordbrenner* [Erfurt: Hennings, 1805], ed. H. P. Foltin (Hildesheim & New York: Olms, 1972), 249. I am grateful to Alan Menhennet for drawing this to my attention.
24   Tatar, *The Hard Facts of the Grimms' Fairy Tales*, 139.
25   Stith Thompson, *Motif-Index*, G10-95.

1798),[26] which includes a description of such a machine that is remarkable both in its own right and as a precursor of Kafka's demonstrably Gothic torture-machine:

> Pauliska, innocent and guilty at once, activates the machine which will kill her saviour and engrave on his chest the words *death and damnation to traitors* [page 94]. As in Kafka's *Penal Colony* the machine inscribes the law and [with it] death on the human body; and it no more responds to the wishes of those who have transgressed than it does in his case.[27]

Kafka's machine, like Saint-Cyr's, was almost certainly inspired by the Inquisition and the machinery by means of which it 'regulated' the torture of those suspected or accused of heresy.

Schopenhauer summed up the Inquisition and all its works when he said that the most appropriate symbol of Christianity was the instrument of torture. The whole Inquisition was an elaborate machinery for punishing disobedience, the idea that underlies Kafka's punitive fantasies. The torture-machine of *In der Strafkolonie* surpasses anything else in the 'horrid' tradition; nothing is more in the black spirit of Gothic than the scientific-legalistic, Poe-like way in which the workings of the machine are described. *In der Strafkolonie*, written in October 1914, interrupting Kafka's work on *Der Proceß*, belongs together with that novel. Both are punishment fantasies reflecting aspects of his life in what he called the 'Marterlabyrinth' (torture-labyrinth) of Prague, and, more especially, his feelings of guilt vis-à-vis his father (his starting-point for the tyrannical Old Commandant), which often caused him to torture himself mentally in a quite unnecessary way.

That is ultimately why he wrote to Milena that 'torture is very important to me, I am concerned with nothing but torturing and being tortured' (*BM*, 244). He was referring to the tubercular throat that was killing him and the coughing which was torture for others to hear (what must it have been like for him to endure?), but the words have a far wider resonance in the context of the self-flagellation of this tormented ascetic with what he felt to be the guilty desire for a normal human relationship, from which he knew himself to be excluded by his creative nightlife. And all this is on top of the Gothic connotations of the subject. The sprawling, dilapidated 'Palastbauten der Kommandantur' are closely connected with the Castle of Kafka's third novel, for a 'Palast' is a 'Burg', which is in turn 'Schloß'.They are identical with the ruins of the Law, between the stones of which Kafka - who described himself as a 'Ruinenbewohner' [T 16] - saw the blood oozing. This is a strikingly Gothic cluster of images. The mental torture endured by the part-autobiographical protagonist of *Der Proceß* is more obviously internalized than the physical torture endured by the erstwhile supervisor of the torture-machine, but the two are related, as the *Prüglerszene* shows, and both relate, specifically, to the same

---

26 See Michel Delon, 'Machines gothiques', *europe. revue littéraire mensuelle*, No. 659, March 1984, 72-79.
27 Delon, 76.

Gothic problem of 'emancipation from old codes and laws',[28] of which *In der Strafkolonie* is a classic exposition, a Gothic tale with a fairytale motif that merely serves to underline the absence of any *deus ex machina*.

9.5. *Der Bau*

Stories like *Ein Bericht für eine Akademie* and *Forschungen eines Hundes* involve the anthropomorphosis of an animal (here representing Kafka) that is basic to the folktale and literary fairytale alike. *Ein Bericht für eine Akademie* invites comparison with Hoffmann's *Nachricht von einem gebildeten jungen Mann* and Wilhelm Hauff's *Der junge Engländer*,[29] as well as with the Chinese literary fairytale *The Ape Sun Wu Kung*, which Kafka also knew.[30] The dog is, with the horse, the animal that features most in folk literature, where a monkey is mistaken for a nobleman,[31] and the motif of the man transformed into a monkey, reversed by Kafka, is widespread. Also featured is the mole; contexts include those of the mole being killed in its own burrow and of being buried as punishment.[32] Most of the motifs in question are more relevant to Dehmel's *Märchen vom Maulwurf* than to Kafka's *Der Bau*, but it is possible that Kafka was familiar with Dehmel's once widely known fairytale about a dwarf who slowly turns into a mole and is struck blind on completing his self-imposed task of burrowing up towards the light. The subterranean (inverted) castle or *Satansburg* with its forbidden chamber, which may well derive in part from the (upside-down) reflection of the Hradcany in the river Vltava, is part of the Bluebeard complex. The Burrower plays both the Devil and Bluebeard's wife in this piece of underground theatre.

After being projected into the open, expelled from an infantine paradise at the moment of birth, human life consists, as Kafka sees it, of a process of foreclosure, a closing down, a shutting of doors, a series of entrapments in ever more confined spaces, each one a premature and minatory entombment. The open grave into which Josef K. jumps in the alternative ending of *Der Proceß*, and which opens up as if by magic to receive him, is a stark symbol of the end of the process. We have seen that it is the 'traumatic and claustrophobic nature of Gothic experience'[33] that Kafka's novels illustrate with such painful clarity. The claustrophobic space and spatial imagery (cf. *claudere* [to shut] → *schließen* [to shut; to conclude] → *Schloß* [lock; castle] →

---

28 *Der Heizer [...]*, ed. Pasley, 17.
29 See Bridgwater, *The Learned Ape*, passim (esp. 11-15, 18-24).
30 It appears in R. Wilhelm's *Chinesische Volksmärchen* (Jena: Diederichs, 1914) *[The Chinese Fairy Book* (London: Fisher Unwin 1922)]*, which Kafka possessed.
31 Stith Thompson, *Motif-Index*, J1762.6
32 Stith Thompson, *Motif-Index*, K1642 and K581.3.
33 Brown, 297.

Schluß [end; conclusion]) are typically Gothic, every space a potential tomb. So too is the idea of haunted consciousness, that is, of the mind invaded by the demons of fear, self-doubt, guilt or whatever and thereby turned into a prison. For Josef K. and K., as for Karl Roßmann, the present is merely the haunted, haunting awareness of what has been lost. The haunted castle of Gothic convention becomes the haunted castle or house of the mind; the house of the self becomes the house of the guilty self, and as such the abode of dread.

The best example of this is the story *Der Bau*, which takes the reader back to the subterranean vaults (the Czech word for vault, *hrobka*, contains within it the word for grave, *hrob*) in which Gothic subjects are liable to find themselves imprisoned. The difference is that Gothic heroes and heroines are imprisoned there by others, whereas Kafka's mole-like persona, representing the creative artist-constructor trapped in his own construct, its elaborate defences pointless when the threat comes from within, is imprisoned in its own consciousness, the victim of its own fear of death. The word 'Bau' appropriately has the subsidiary meaning of 'glasshouse' in the military sense of place of arrest or confinement, in civilian terms a clink or prison, or, in terms of the *Schloß* metaphor, a lock-up, so that this story too, which is closely related to *Das Schloß*, is a punitive fantasy.

Kafka left keys to this particular story in his letters when he wrote 'I am alternately running around and sitting petrified, like a desperate animal in its burrow when surrounded by enemies' (Br 390), and when he wrote of 'the horrible dark, low, subterranean passages of the story' (BM 48), and again when he wrote in the *Brief an den Vater*, of his troubled relationship with his father, that he had 'spent so many days and nights thinking and burrowing through the whole thing' (BV 178). Another layer in *Der Bau* was revealed when he went on to write, in that same letter, that 'my life consists in [...] letting no danger that I can avert, indeed no possibility of such a danger, get too near [my attempts at independence]' (BV 187f). There is a further autobiographical dimension to the story: the shifting edges of the burrow, which mimic the shifting outlines of the Castle, are a reflection of the fact that at one level of meaning it also stands for Kafka's lungs, continually contracting and expanding, but with contraction gaining the upper hand as he lay dying.

The burrow is of its very nature a *Satansburg* or upside-down castle, an inversion of the Castle and of the attics in *Der Proceß*, but like them also represents the mind or conscious self. Intended as a Citadel of Security, it turns into its opposite, a Castle of Perdition. Once again Kafka's protagonist, and through him Kafka himself, for this is the most personal and metafictional of all his tales, is identified with the Devil. At one point the mole-like creature is likened to a badger; it is given to sleeping (sc. *wie ein Dachs*, literally 'like a badger', figuratively 'like a top'), whence there is a verbal bridge (*Dachs → [Schädel]Dach,* head) to the iconography or spatial architecture of *Der Proceß*. Like Tieck's *William Lovell*, *Der Bau* shows the mind disintegrating under pressure, the challenge to the burrower coming when its mind is invaded by paranoia. *William Lovell* was about the 'progressive disorientation and disintegration of the human mind under the influence of an overcharged imagination'.[34] Kafka's burrowing animal-persona too, though far removed from the late eighteenth-century 'enthusiast', is undone by imagination as it fancies an enemy is burrowing towards it, preparing to assault it in the very stronghold ('Burgplatz' = the 'forbidden chamber') of its underground citadel.

There may be an echo here of the German folk fairytale in which dwarfs are said to live in an underground castle,[35] which in turn opens up the whole symbolical world of dwarfs, whose folkloric uncleanness involves a concept of fundamental importance for Kafka. Normally *Burg* has a highly positive, even divine connotation (cf. 'Ein feste Burg ist unser Gott' [A safe stronghold our God is still]), but here the connotation is inverted, evoking the *Satansburg* of Hell, for it is a very Hell in which the burrower, like the Devil, lives. Lovell was afraid that external agency in the form of a malevolent demon would drag him down into the abyss.[36] Kafka's frantic burrower lives in the abyss, the demon Death burrrowing away within him. It is as if Kafka's persona is being hunted down by his shadow. The Gothic figures of Death and the Devil fuse here, as do the motifs of pursuit and incarceration: Kafka's major heroes are pursued by their consciences, externalized as in a dream in the guise of another figure, and are effectively trapped in a world of inadequacy and guilt from which there is no escape. That from which one cannot escape is, in the final analysis, the grave. Kafka here gives the Gothic motif of live burial a twist by having his Burrower bury himself alive; in doing so he is recognizing that he had himself done the same thing by burying himself in his work.

Der Bau is also a notable example of the labyrinth metaphor that dominates Kafka's work. As such it can be related not only to the Cretan Labyrinth,[37] but to the inner and outer labyrinths of Gothic convention; representing 'one's own labyrinth' (BM 28), the convolutions of a mind under intolerable pressure, it is a symbol of radical alienation, the long labyrinth of interior darkness. In early Gothic the subterranean and the labyrinthine normally corresponded, but in Kafka the Gothic convention is once more internalized, with the subterranean replaced by the subconscious, and the labyrinthine passages by the labyrinthine workings of the mind, for the labyrinth, as part of the inner ear, is also a gateway to the mind. Implicit in the labyrinth metaphor is the Gothic motif of the 'false path', to which Kafka's myth of the true way may be compared, for to every true way ('wahrer Weg') there must be a false way, a *Holzweg* or *Irrweg* (wrong track) or *Abweg* (moral error). It is human not

---

34 Blackall, 158.
35 Stith Thompson, *Motif-Index*, F 451.4.1.2.
36 Blackall, 154.
37 See Kafka, *Der Heizer [...]*, ed. Pasley, 24.

only to err, but to do so specifically in mistaking a false path for the right one. Kafka's novels are, of course, labyrinthine in more senses than one. As tortuous, fragmented narratives they embody and relate tortuous mental processes, externalized as the tortuous workings of a bureaucratic authority. The labyrinth is present not only in the sense that Kafka's personae are unwittingly trapped in the very labyrinth whose centre they seek, but also in the labyrinthine logic pursued with such legalistic precision. Language, the house of being, thus turns into a maze and a trap, and since there is, ultimately, no way out of this labyrinth of language, verbalization, which once represented salvation, now spells entrapment. Nor, as critics have repeatedly discovered to their cost, is there any certain way into it from the outside, so that here too what may seem to be the true way is liable to turn out to be a false one, with the unwitting critic trapped in a snare carefully set by the author, for Kafka not only disapproved of critics honing their egos at the author's expense, but tried to make sure that they paid for their hubristic endeavour. Shelley did something similar in *Zastrozzi*, though in more of a clever-schoolboy way.

Der Bau is, then, not only a classical labyrinth-text and as good an example as any of Kafka's internalized Gothic; at the same time it is both a modern *Kunstmärchen* and a *Metamärchen* in the sense of a *Märchen* that is about itself, that is, about the creative act, its ramifications, consequences, and price.

10. POSTSCRIPT

Lüthi's remark that 'Great literature of all ages has borrowed from fairy-tale motifs and often exhibited an imaginativeness not unlike that of the fairy tale'[1] applies, above all, to writing, like Kafka's, with a strong element of fantasy and myth. This quality often goes back to a childhood love of fairytale. Kafka, like Dickens before him, was made as a writer by the fairytales he read with such delight from early childhood onwards. Brod described his work as being informed by 'märchenhafte Erfindung', that is, by an imagination attuned to fairytale and an inventiveness honed by it. More recently Pawel has written of Kafka's 'enduring fascination with these profoundly ambiguous collective dreams and nightmares, fed by sources painfully close to Kafka's own creative inspiration'.[2] If he loved the genre, Kafka hated the word *Märchen* because it denoted a world of magic no longer credible and hope no longer available, and was therefore in the final analysis a source not of imaginative delight, but of sorrow. That 'there are no fairytales these days' was a matter of profound regret to him. It was, in particular, the loss of innocence that he regretted.

With hindsight, it was inevitable that he would be captivated by the fairytale, for here, in limpid, visually memorable form, were tales of universal wisdom and applicability, teaching, as it were in passing, the virtues of truthfulness and patience, the need for hope and the wisdom of fear. In psychological terms they showed the young Kafka that even the most personal of his problems were as old as mankind and therefore capable of resolution, an insight from which he derived much-needed creative solace. In addition to showing how surface simplicity could be combined with profound, elusive meaning, they showed the young writer how to transcend the subjective and personal, something which, otherwise, would have been a problem for him. They even gave him a model for the counter-metaphor that became his stock in trade. And, to cap it all, they were entirely compatible with the dream-world in which he lived.

Kafka's literary constructions inevitably include bricks borrowed from 'models' of various kinds, of which the fairytale is arguably the most important. Even writers as wholly original as Kafka locate themselves with reference to the work of other writers, his attitude towards whom, like his attitude towards his own work, tends to be deconstructive. But for his love of Hans Andersen, Dickens and Dostoevsky, say, his work would have been different. It is no chance that the writers whom he regarded as

---

[1] Lüthi, *Once upon a Time*, 21.
[2] Pawel, 74.

blood relatives (Andersen, Dickens, Dostoevsky, Hoffmann) themselves combined Gothic and fairytale in their work. Dickens, in particular, deploys in his 'Wirklichkeitsmärchen'[3] motifs and devices that derive from the Gothic of Ann Radcliffe, with which he grew up, as does Dostoevsky, and Andersen is the author of a little known novel on the Wandering Jew of Gothic, *Ahasverus* (1848). Klotz argues that Kafka develops what Hoffmann, Andersen and Dickens began in their 'Wirklichkeitsmärchen', which is obviously true, but being impressed and influenced by the fairytale to the extent that Kafka was, is not the same as being a writer of fairytales, which he was not and never could have been.

His relationship to fairytale has been well epitomized by Donald Haase, who observes that in order to portray his alienated protagonists

> Kafka adapted the dreamlike conditions of the fairy tale with an ironic twist. Whereas fairy-tale characters are at home in the magical landscapes they inhabit, Kafka's blend of the irrational and the realistic disorientates his confused characters and alienates them from the very society they are trying to join. By inverting the classical fairy tale and playing with its motifs, Kafka created what has been called the anti-fairy tale, which questions the certainties and optimism of the classical genre.[4]

That Kafka inverts and subverts the fairytale (rather than perverting it, as Volker Klotz has argued), can hardly be doubted, but whether this makes his works 'anti-fairy tales', as Clemens Heselhaus first maintained in 1952, remains an open question, for the fact is that the works in question have much in common with fairytales, and that Kafka's characteristic 'Entstellung von Märchenzügen' is only one among many forms of 'Entstellung' that he uses. Essentially deconstructive though it is, his work is far more than that. Specifically, there is more to his work than the idea of unwriting fairytale. His tales are more than anti-fairytales.

Nor is it only a matter of the 'Entstellung' of fairytale motifs and types, for there is more to Gothic and fairytale, and to the close relationship between them, than motifs and character types. The parallel between them extends to the structure or pattern of 'functions' which they also have in common. Hannelotte Dorner Bachmann,[5] in applying Propp's morphology of the fairytale to the Gothic novel (in the form of Walpole's *The Castle of Otranto*, Radcliffe's *The Italian*, and Lewis's *The Monk*), has shown that the early Gothic novel took its basic structure directly from the fairytale, so that it can be described as a more developed and sophisticated form of fairytale. Notwithstanding the fact that fairytale reveals its structure on the surface of the text, while the Gothic novel conceals its fairytale structure,[6] she concludes that Propp's

---

[3]   Klotz, 340.
[4]   In *The Oxford Companion to Fairy Tales*, ed. Zipes, 274.
[5]   Hannelotte Dorner-Bachmann, *Erzählstruktur und Texttheorie. Zu den Grundlagen einer Erzähltheorie unter besonderer Berücksichtigung des Märchens und der Gothic Novel* (Hildesheim: Olms,1979), esp. 357, 359, 396.
[6]   Hannelotte Dorner-Bachmann, 119, 395-9, 445.

structural model not only applies to the fairytale, but, being more or less identical with the structure of the Gothic novel, is also fundamental to this as a form of 'fairytale-novel'.

However, despite containing many and varied fairytale elements, none of Kafka's novels is adequately described as a *Märchenroman*. *Der Verschollene*, it is true, includes a surprisingly large proportion of fairytale 'functions', and in that sense is close to fairytale, but this does not make it a fairytale novel, for its mock-fairytale structure is filled with an admixture of Gothic motifs, and what characterizes the novel is the resultant tension between fairytale wish fulfilment and Gothic disillusionment. In *Das Schloß*, K. sets out, like the fairytale hero, to seek his fortune, here in the form of the boon of certainty which amounts to the treasure to be wrested from the ogre, Klamm, and in crossing that fateful bridge on the outskirts of Westwest, enters a baffling otherworld that is enchanted in the sense of being a law unto itself. The Castle-without-an-entrance and its ogre-personification owe much to fairytale, but the fact remains that, as Haase concludes, K. 'does not progress like the conventional fairy-tale hero from the peasant village to the castle, but remains dislocated between these fairy-tale extremes without achieving a happy end'. Disenchantment in the sense of liberation from the spell or curse (here, of alienated self-awareness) never comes, a fact which serves to make the fairytale motifs and echoes of the novel doubly disenchanting (in the sense of disillusioning) for the reader. When all is said and done, *Das Schloß* is closer to Gothic than to fairytale, and the same is true of *Der Proceß*. The Parable of the Door-Keeper may be a literary fairytale, and Josef K. comparable to the *Unheld* (anti-hero) of the folk fairytale, his arrest reflecting the way in which the folk fairytale expresses internal feelings through external events, but in this novel the fairytale elements are swamped by Gothic ones, for it is the product of Kafka's unhappiest period and, as such, is closer to nightmare and thence to Gothic. In brief, his novels combine the iconography, spatialities and localities of Gothic with an admixture of disenchanting fairytale motifs within an overall format that is personal and symbolical.

His shorter texts, which range from Gothic-plus-fairytale to Gothic Fairytale to *Metamärchen*, also show that generalization is unwise, for they vary from *Die Verwandlung*, in which the fairytale elements are overshadowed by Gothic ones, to *Ein Landarzt,* which is, exceptionally, an anti-fairytale in the sense of subverting fairytale at every point, to *Der Bau*, which is both a modern *Kunstmärchen* and a *Metamärchen,* as well as being a prime example of Kafka's internalized Gothic. The more short texts that are taken into account, the more numerous the ways in which they relate to fairytale. What many of them have in common is the fact that they define themselves by their relationship to fairytale.

In his work Kafka reacts to fairytale and Gothic in much the same way, by going beyond and subverting them. He had a deeper, more direct knowledge of fairytale than of Gothic as such, but many of his favourite writers stand in the Gothic tradition, some of them, as we have seen, standing in the line of succession to both conventions.

If the parallels between Kafka's novels and the Gothic novel are legion, there are also many significant differences between them. Whereas the typical Gothic narrative moves towards the discovery of the danger lurking within or beneath the familiar and safe, Kafka starts with that discovery, working inexorably towards its consequence, typically the death of the person concerned. In each of his novels and stories the situation of the protagonist is more precarious and problematical than he (or very occasionally she, e.g. the circus-rider in 'Auf der Galerie') thought, and worse is always to follow, for what in early Gothic appeared exceptional, or at best equivocal, has in Kafka become the norm: 'Physical immolation, dismemberment, live burial, loss, death, metamorphosis, entropy, are no longer equivocal images, as they were in Gothic fiction. Kafka, in the wake of Dickens, Dostoevsky and Poe, makes them the norm, fantasies structured around the Oedipal drama'.[7] In the high Gothic first wave of the modernist revolution, the times were seen as lawless and out of joint, although it was possible, with luck and maybe at the last minute (as in the fairytale from which Gothic learned so much), to escape from incarceration, death, or whatever, back into normality. A century later things are very different, for in the meantime the exception has become the norm: the world is turning into an uncanny prison without bars, and freedom, the ideal of the early Gothics, is fast becoming meaningless, unreal, the stuff of legend (compare Titorelli's legends of real acquittal).

The problematical relationship between inner and outer worlds in Gothic, stemming as it did from the conflict between an ever more complex and eventually overburdened subconscious on the one hand, and a hostile and/or chaotic external world on the other, is given a new spin in Kafka's novels, where the subject's manifold selves are externalized to look like independent figures and events in a hostile real world, but in truth represent the tensions, slippages and misunderstandings to which we are all subject in our efforts to understand ourselves. What looks like the 'external world' is, even in *Der Verschollene*, where Kafka was only beginning to develop his characteristic style and novel-technique, already well on the way to being an externalization of an inner world of self-conflict, self-doubt, self-misunderstanding, and so on. As such it is a form of virtual reality going beyond the less problematical, because less challenged, fantasy of the earlier Gothic romance. In these novels, as, incipiently, in *The Mysteries of Udolpho*,[8] the real and the unreal change place. What was once real, and now becomes unreal, is not particular moments, but the external world as a whole, the world outside of the mind, which accordingly becomes unsure

---

7   Jackson, *Fantasy*, 162.
8   Terry Castle, 'The Spectralization of the Other in *The Mysteries of Udolpho* ', in *The New Eighteenth Century: Theory, Politics, and English Literature*, ed. F. Nussbaum & L. Brown (N.Y. & London: Methuen, 1987), 231-253.

as to whether it is faced by reality or by a will-o'-the-wisp, dream or phantasmagoria. What was once unreal, and now becomes real, as it was already beginning to do in Radcliffe's novels, is the imagery of the subconscious mind. Kafka naturally goes much further than she and her contemporaries do, but it is in a direction to which they first pointed. It needs to be remembered, in this connexion, that Kafka's creative lifetime, like that of the early Gothic novelists, was preceded and accompanied by philosophies that taught that the world exists only in the mind, of which it a projective construct. One of his favourite philosophers, Arthur Schopenhauer, who was at his most influential at the turn of the century, taught precisely that in language that is as compellingly lucid and as concrete as Kafka's own .

The most distinctive, non-Gothic feature of these novels is the fact that they are autobiographical in a way and symbolical to a degree in which most Gothic novels are not. The figures in them are masks or personae of the author-narrator and his protagonist, something which, otherwise, only applies to Gothic of the most cerebral (Brockden Brown) or naive (P. B. Shelley) kind. The Gothic novel, although a romance, generally works as a novel works, and is in that sense all exterior; what it generally depicts is an imaginary exterior reality, a fantasized version of the outside world. Kafka's novels, while they may seem to do this, are in truth all interior, all interplay between projections of the essentially autobiographical hero. To read them otherwise might make them seem more Gothic, but it would also be to misread them. This is not to say, however, that Kafka's three protagonists are simply so many versions of the author at different ages and stages. While they are all the time more or less Kafka-like, always relating to him in one often hermetic way or another, in important respects they are the very opposite of Kafka. Where most Gothic novels have surface, Kafka's novels have depth. In terms of 'perpendicularity', they go beyond and transcend Gothic, as they cannot fail to do, being separated from what may be thought their distant precursors by two centuries of radical developments in metaphysics, physics, psychology and theology. The more they transcend or exceed Gothic, the less Gothic they become. We have seen that they transcend their fairytale starting-points and motifs in much the same way. Kafka's quasi-Gothic world is mobile in the sense that his protagonists carry it around with them, their mind like the Wandering Jew's existence, a prison without an exit short of the final habitation which they (unlike him) dread. The subterranean vault is replaced by the subconscious, that subterranean vault of the mind, personified most obviously and most alarmingly in the 'Prügler' (man with the lash) of *Der Proceß,* and reified most suggestively in the Burrow.The question is, of course, whether the subterranean vaults of Gothic are replaced, in Kafka, by a degothicized subconscious, or whether they themselves stood for the subconscious. Given the work of men like Saalfeld, Fuseli and Gotthilf Heinrich von Schubert, I would argue that the latter meaning was always latent.

The 'concern with ultimate questions and lack of faith in the adequacy of reason or religious faith to make comprehensible the paradoxes of human existence', which Hume found in the Gothic novel,[9] is certainly present in Kafka. The only question is the extent to which this too was actually present in Gothic, which will depend on the models considered. The Gothic 'quest for the numinous' still applies, albeit with the important historical proviso that in Kafka the numinous has become inaccessible if not downright problematical, existing, as it does, more in Kafka's own obstinate belief in the presence of something indestructible in himself, than in any evidence of its existence in the novels. In the Parable of the Doorkeeper it exists as a kind of enigmatic afterglow or ghost-image that might equally well be the kind of ghostly emanation that is not uncommon in the Gothic novel.

Otherwise the numinous appears in the negative guise of the uncanny, it being their deployment of the uncanny, among other things, that shows just how closely Kafka and Hoffmann, for instance, are related. While Kafka is ultimately at pains to express his own belief in the divine, which he does *ex negativo* by showing life, in *Der Proceß*, to be insupportable without it (it was, after all, to prove this to himself that he wrote the novel), he is not interested in naive supernatural paraphernalia of the kind often found in Gothic, although there could hardly be a better example of what Maturin called 'the passion of supernatural fear' and 'fear arising from objects of invisible terror'[10] than the emotion felt by Kafka's frantic Burrower. On most definitions the supernatural as such, as opposed to the grotesque and the fantastic, appears to be absent from his work, which shows that there is no relying on the supernatural divine, unless it is at work in the guise of the 'supernatural assize' of the conscience, punishing the slightest deviation from the straight and narrow path of virtue and truth, whatever exactly these may be in the context. In the absence, or apparent absence, of the divine, the validity of subjective notions of virtue and vice is unclear. Josef K. appears to be driven by some form of moral law in condemning himself for his greed and selfishness, but the law, if that is what it is, is his own law, as the Parable of the Doorkeeper shows. There is no evidence for the existence of any overarching, absolute moral (let alone divine) Law, so that the world as experienced by Kafka's negative heroes seems to be one without law or moral coherence. The plurality of devils or demons, in which Kafka had a positively medieval belief, are inner demons, the products, often, of an over-active conscience, not supernatural phenomena in an externally validated form. The Burrower's death, as it approaches, seems to be embodied in a host of imaginary Enemies, but in reality it is all the time at work within him, burrowing its way towards his heart. The difference between Kafka and the early Gothic novelists as regards the uncanny is that in the early Gothics the

---

9   Robert D. Hume, 'Gothic versus Romantic: A Revaluation of the Gothic Novel', *PMLA*, 84 (1969), 282-290.
10 See Dennis Jasper Murphy's Preface to Maturin's *Fatal Revenge*.

uncanny is part of a residually Christian scheme of things, a kind of Christianity without the excesses, whereas in Kafka it has become an enigma, and, as such, is 'unassimilated into any recognizable transcendent or ethical scheme'.[11] Earlier, at the very beginning of the (in literary terms) Gothic period, Young's *Night-Thoughts* (1742-45), had achieved spectacular success in the Germany of the 1760s, when *Nachtgedankenmacherei* (going in for 'night-thoughts') was all the rage, this serving to focus attention on the grave, the terrors of which came to loom even larger when religion was later identified with superstition. Freed from its original context, the uncanny becomes doubly challenging.

While one of Kafka's basic techniques is the externalization or projection of aspects of his protagonist's mind, so that a purely mental process appears as though it were taking place in a 'real' world, or at least a romance one, in terms of his relationship to the Gothic form and convention it is internalization that counts. He internalizes every aspect of Gothic, and in doing so gets rid of some of its coarser and crasser features. In his work, for instance, as in Gothic, sexual passion is a locus of danger; the difference is that Kafka, though he does not avoid it altogether, does not dwell on salacious detail. He is in far stricter control of himself and his medium than most Gothic novelists of the 'Horrid Mysteries' persuasion: not for him the erotic crudities of M. G. Lewis or the aesthetic ones of Karl Friedrich Kahlert, or indeed of Bram Stoker, whose van Helsing (the anagram of whose name proclaims him to be English, though he is described as Dutch) speaks an inconsistently barbarous mixture of supposedly 'German' English and the real thing that illustrates nothing so clearly as the limitations of Stoker's knowledge of German.

One of the major differences between the typical Gothic novel and Kafka's novels is the fact that his language is crystal-clear, his focus incomparably sharp. His aesthetic-linguistic skills go far beyond those of any recognized Gothic novelist, and are perhaps unsurpassed by any novelists except James Joyce and Vladimir Nobokov. His explorations of the metaphors embedded in the German language not only reveal an astonishing linguistic sophistication, but show that his aim was totally different to the aim of the early Gothics. While subversive of the traditional novel as such, in that he writes as the German romantic novelists mostly wrote, as a poet writes, deploying poetic logic, and of all *idées fixes*, his novels are at the same time advanced mainstream novels. The separation of the Gothic novel from the then torpid mainstream novel in about 1790, although its origins went back a generation further, is finally reversed.

As we have seen, the many fairytale motifs, like the related Gothic ones, serve to give his work an appearance that is in some ways profoundly deceptive in that they raise expectations, for a more exciting reading experience, or for a happy ending, or

---

[11]   Prawer, *The Uncanny*, 17.

whatever, that are soon dashed. Although in other ways both sets of intertextual relationship run deep, the Gothic trappings in Kafka's novels not infrequently lie on the surface of the text rather than within its deep structures, and can therefore be particularly misleading to those whose knowledge of the novels necessarily depends on the Muirs' translation, which, admirable though it is, serves, as would every other translation, to show that while he may be read in English, Kafka can only be fully understood in German because the metaphors which he takes literally and develops in that inscrutable way of his are, as often as not, absent in English. Much of the meaning even of such basic words as 'Proceß' and 'Schloß' is also lost in translation, which is simply not in a position to convey the polysemy of Kafka's texts. Also lost in translation is the way in which he signals identity by symbolical use of the second person familiar, or the way in which he reveals a true state of affairs by appearing to throw doubt on it through the subjunctive, or the way in which he appears to be saying one thing, in the plainest possible words, while those very words, as often as not, have another quite different meaning, or indeed several such meanings. The cumulative loss of such signals amounts to a serious loss of meaning.

The manifold parallels linking the arts of the early nineteenth and early twentieth centuries (to say nothing of those linking the late nineteenth and late twentieth centuries, or the last decades of the last six centuries) include those between the Gothic novel and Kafka's novels, for what one sees in Kafka is precisely 'the self [...] dispossessed in its own house, in a condition of rupture, disjunction, fragmentation'[12] that characterizes those eras. The classic images of such dispossession are *Der Proceß* and *Das Schloß*. A structural instability akin to that of Gothic has never been more perspicuously represented than in Kafka's work, where everything is an effect of anxiety or existential dread, it being in their claustrophobic spatialities that these three novels come closest to Gothic. This is the sense in which it is true to say that 'Some of the most disturbingly Gothic images of the twentieth century appear in the writings of Franz Kafka'.[13] These images are not infrequently combined with deadpan humour in a surreal context, for although the subject matter of his novels is invariably deadly serious, the treatment may appear not to be, although analysis usually discloses a serious point that is best made precisely through a comic wording that is more thought-provoking than a more laboured one would be. One of the most memorable images is that of the spectators in the gallery of the courtroom in *Der Proceß*, who place cushions on their heads to protect them from the low ceiling. The reference is to the fear of death, of being 'covered up' (cf. the father's fear of being 'zugedeckt' in *Das Urteil*), and the off-beat, wry humour, which gives the image its memorability and at first seems to defuse it, in fact slowly intensifies the intended reference: the humour is

---

[12] Miles, 3.
[13] Botting, 160.

black. This is typical of the way in which so much of the paraphernalia of Gothic appears in a characteristically Kafkaesque, and to that extent, no longer Gothic form, stripped down to the psychological bare essentials. On the other hand, given that in the Romantic period Gothic writing as such was already being internalized, with gloom and darkness becoming external markers of mental states, Kafka could be said to represent the final phase of Romantic Gothic in an exemplary way. This internalization, intensified in the twentieth century, appears in a peculiarly literal and extreme form in his work.

Something very like that key ingredient of Gothic, its 'atmosphere [...] of evil and brooding terror',[14] is present in Kafka's stories and novels alike, and yet at the same time his style is everywhere so cool, so 'rational', so controlled, that it seems a far cry from, say, the melodramatic, arbitrary violence which abounds in the more lurid examples of Gothic. It is precisely the chill inherent in the wording that creates the terror, for where there is arbitrariness, there remains the possibility of a happy outcome in the form of a *deus ex machina* or happy chance, whereas with Kafka there is no such possibility. His superrealism is diabolocentric, not theocentric, so that the appearance of a *diabolus ex machina* is all too likely, as the opening paragraphs of some of his most famous works show. In seeming to suggest that there can be a Devil without a God, his work is the opposite of Gothic, for when the eighteenth-century Enlightenment tried to produce a God without a Devil, the Gothics reacted against it. Kafka's work shows that by the early twentieth century the Devil has become more accessible, and therefore more real, than the *deus absconditus* who demands an act of faith that has become well-nigh impossible. Such a belief in a personal Devil may well strike readers as anachronistic, but for Kafka it was a fact of life.

Some of the many apparent similarities between his novels and the Gothic disappear or diminish in significance when the novel in question is analysed, since his subversion of Gothic for his own esoterically subjective ends means that his writing is often not so much Gothic as Gothic-like, consisting, like Gothic itself, of course, of 'a series of [...] devices, codes, figurations, for the expression of the fragmented subject'.[15] There is much in the expression of his work that is code-like, although critical opinion still opines that it was not deliberately encrypted in the writing. He worried not only that he had not expressed himself clearly enough, but that he had expressed himself too clearly. Even if there were general agreement as to what they are, none of his works can be said to display all the main features of Gothic, any more than they can be said to include all the features of the folk fairytale as isolated by Vladimir Propp. Collectively, it is a different matter. In a magisterial judgment S. S. Prawer has written of

---

[14] Hume, 286f.
[15] Miles, 3.

Kafka truths [...] which lead one to the [...] conviction that we [...] need works that focus a sense of homelessness, articulate feelings of strangeness and disorientation, keep us alive to the possibility of orders of existence which cannot easily be assimilated in the categories of our waking consciousness [...] hidden aspects of ourselves and our world which we should not be too ready to reject.[16]

In the final analysis such 'truths' are, however, more Kafkaesque than Gothic.

Notwithstanding the last point, Kafka is the greatest literary master of the Gothic form in the sense that what is generally understood by Gothic has never been used to greater effect than in his work, and has never been deployed with greater literary skill. If there is any truth in Elizabeth Napier's thesis that the Gothic novel 'inadvertently raised serious issues, but flinched before them',[17] a somewhat bizarre view that puts its practitioners' competence and integrity in question, Kafka certainly made good any such collective failure of nerve. He at least is desperately honest. His novels combine many of the formal components of Gothic with a philosophical depth and an artistic precision the genre did not always possess. If Gothic texts revise one another, a Gothic reading of Kafka cannot fail to affect our reading of Gothic as such. Thus the absence in it of Kafka's aesthetic and metaphysical virtues could be construed as a weakness, though not exactly a failure, given that few, if any, literary forms have ever been more successful.

In brief, Kafka both fits into and bursts out of the Gothic context. It is the same with fairytale: his work is both fairytale-like and the very denial of fairytale.

---

[16] Prawer, *Caligari's Children*, 280.
[17] Miles, 1. Elizabeth Napier's view is elaborated in her book *The Failure of Gothic* (Oxford: Clarendon Press, 1987).

Bibliography

Aguirre, Manuel, *The closed space: Horror literature and western symbolism* (Manchester: Manchester University Press, 1990)

Altenhöner, F., *Der Traum und die Traumstruktur im Werk Franz Kafkas* (Diss. Münster, 1964)

Angus, Douglas, '"Metamorphosis" and "The Beauty and the Beast" Tale', *JEGP*, 53 (1954), 69-71

Anon., *Die Nachtwachen des Bonaventura* (Leipzig: Insel, 1921)

Arata, Stephen, *Fictions of loss in the Victorian fin de siècle* (Cambridge: Cambridge University Press, 1996)

Beaujean, Marion, *Der Trivialroman in der zweiten Hälfte des 18. Jahrhunderts* (Bonn: Bouvier, 1964)

Béguin, A., *L'Ame romantique et le rêve*, 2nd edn (Paris: Corti, 1939)

Beicken, Peter U., *Franz Kafka. Eine kritische Einführung in die Forschung* (Frankfurt a. M.: Athenaeum, 1974)

Biedermann, Hans, *Knaurs Lexikon der Symbole* (Munich: Droemer Knaur, 1994: *The Wordsworth Dictionary of Symbolism*, tr. James Hulbert [Ware: Wordsworth, 1996])

Binder, Hartmut, *Kafka-Kommentar zu sämtlichen Erzählungen* (Munich: Winkler, 1975

—— *Kafka-Kommentar zu den Romanen*, 2nd edn (Munich: Winkler, 1982)

—— (ed.), *Kafka-Handbuch*, 2 vols (Stuttgart: Kröner, 1979)

Birkhead, Edith, *The Tale of Terror* (London: Constable, 1921)

Blackall, Eric A., *The Novels of the German Romantics* (Ithaca & London: Cornell University Press, 1983)

Boa, Elizabeth, 'Creepy-crawlies: Gilman's *The Yellow Wallpaper* and Kafka's *The Metamorphosis* ', *Paragraph*, 13 (1990), 19-29

Botting, Fred, *Gothic* (London & New York: Routledge, 1996)

Bridgwater, Patrick, *The Learned Ape* (Durham: University of Durham, 1978)

—— *Kafka and Nietzsche,* 2nd edn (Bonn: Bouvier, 1987)

—— *Kafka's Novels: An Interpretation* (Amsterdam & New York: Rodopi, 2003)

Brod, Max, *Über Franz Kafka* (Frankfurt a. M.: Fischer-Bücherei, 1966)

Brown, Marshall, *The Shape of German Romanticism* (Ithaca: Cornell University Press, 1979)

—— 'A Philosophical View of the Gothic Novel', *Studies in Romanticism,* 26 (1987), 275-301

Cersowsky, Peter, *Phantastische Literatur im ersten Viertel des 20. Jahrhunderts* (Munich: Fink, 1983)

Chesser, Eustace, *Shelley & Zastrozzi: self-revelation of a neurotic* (London: Gregg/Archive, 1965)

Chizhevsky, Dmitri, 'The Theme of the Double in Dostoevsky', in *Dostoevsky. A Collection of Critical Essays*, ed. René Wellek (Englewood Cliffs, N.J.: Prentice-Hall, 1962)

Cirlot, J. E., *A Dictionary of Symbols*, 2nd edn (London: Routledge & Kegan Paul, 1971)

Clark, Kenneth, *The Gothic Revival*, 3rd edn (London: Constable, 1962)

Clery, E. J., *The Rise of Supernatural Fiction, 1762-1800* (Cambridge: Cambridge University Press, 1995)

Clute, John, and Grant, John, *The Encyclopedia of Fantasy* (London: Orbit, 1997)

Cornwell, Neil, 'Russian Gothic', in *The Handbook to Gothic Literature*, ed. Marie Mulvey-Roberts (Basingstoke: Macmillan,1998), 199-204

—— (ed.), *The Gothic-Fantastic in Nineteenth-Century Russian Literature* (Amsterdam & Atlanta, GA: Rodopi, 1999)

Delon, Michel, 'Machines gothiques', *europe, revue littéraire mensuelle,* No. 659 (March 1984), 72-79

Dodd, W. J., 'Dostoyevskian Elements in Kafka's Penal Colony', *GLL,* 37 (1983-84), 11-23.

—— *Kafka and Dostoyevsky: The Shaping Influence* (London: Macmillan, 1992)

—— 'Dostoyevsky, punishments and crimes', in *Kafka: The Metamorphosis, The Trial and The Castle*, ed. William J. Dodd (London & New York: Longman, 1995)

Dorner-Bachmann, Hannelotte, *Erählstruktur und Texttheorie. Zu den Grundlagen einer Erzähltheorie unter besonderer analytischer Berücksichtigung des Märchens und der Gothic Novel* (Hildesheim & New York: Olms, 1979)

Eicher, Thomas, *Märchen und Moderne. Fallbeispiele einer intertextuellen Relation* (Münster: Lit, 1996)

Fiedler, Leslie, *Love and Death in the American Novel* (Cleveland: World Publishing Co, 1962; repr. Normal, IL: Dalkey Archive Press, 1997), 106-148

Fraiberg, Selma, 'Kafka and the dream', *Partisan Review*, 23 (1956), 47-69, repr. in *Art and Psychoanalysis*, ed. William Phillips (Cleveland, Ohio: World Publishing, 1963)

Frank, Frederick S., *Guide to the Gothic: An Annotated Bibliography of Criticism* (Metuchen, N.J., & London: The Scarecrow Press, 1984)

—— *The First Gothics* (New York & London: Garland, 1987)

—— *Gothic Fiction. A Master List of Twentieth Century Criticism and Research* (Westport, CT. & London: Meckler, 1988)

—— 'The Gothic *Vathek*. The Problem of Genre resolved', in *Vathek and the Escape from Time. Bicentenary Revaluations*, ed. K. W. Graham (New York: AMS, 1990), pp. 157-172

—— *Guide to the Gothic II: An Annotated Bibliography of Criticism, 1983-1993* (Lanham, Md, & London: The Scarecrow Press, 1995)

Freud, Sigmund, *Introductory Lectures on Psycho-Analysis,* 9th imp. (London: George Allen & Unwin, 1952)

—— *The Interpretation of Dreams*, tr. James Strachey, 3rd imp. (London: George Allen & Unwin, 1967)

—— *Art and Literature*, tr. James Strachey, ed. Albert Dickson (London: Penguin, 1990)

Fromm, Erich, *The Forgotten Language* (London: Victor Gollancz, 1952)

Funk & Wagnalls Standard Dictionary of Folklore, Mythology and Legend , ed. Maria Leach (London: New English Library, 1972)

Garrard, John (ed.), *The Russian Novel from Pushkin to Pasternak* (New Haven & London: Yale University Press, 1983)

Gillespie, Gerald (ed. & tr.), *The Night Watches of Bonaventura* (Austin: University of Texas Press, 1971)

Gothic Fictions: Prohibition/Transgression, ed. K. W. Graham (Ann Arbor: AMS, 1989)

Gothic Horror, ed. Clive Bloom (London: Macmillan, 1998)

Greenberg, Martin, *The Terror of Art: Kafka and Modern Literature* (New York: Basic Books, 1968)

Grimm, Jakob, *Teutonic Mythology*, tr. J. S. Stallybrass, 4 vols (London: George Bell, 1880-88)

Grimm, Jakob & Wilhelm, *German Legends*, tr. Donald Ward, 2 vols (Philadelphia: Institute for the Study of Human Issues, 1881)

—— *Grimm's Fairy Tales*, tr. Margaret Hunt, (London: Routledge & Kegan Paul, 1948)

—— *Kinder- und Hausmärchen,* Ausgabe letzter Hand, ed. Heinz Rölleke (Stuttgart: Reclam, 1997)

—— *Deutsches Wörterbuch*, 16 vols (Leipzig: Hirzel,1854-1960)

Guthke, Karl S., *Englische Vorromantik und deutscher Sturm und Drang* (Göttingen: Vandenhoeck & Ruprecht, 1958)

Hadley, Michael, *The Undiscovered Genre. A Search for the German Gothic Novel* (Berne: Peter Lang, 1978)

Hall, Calvin S., & Lind, Richard E., *Dreams, Life and Literature: A Study of Franz Kafka* (Chapel Hill: University of North Carolina Press, 1970)

Harder, Marie-Luise, *Märchenmotive in der Dichtung Franz Kafkas* (Diss. Münster, 1962)

Hasselblatt, Ursula, *Das Wesen des Volksmärchens und das moderne Kunstmärchen* (Diss. Freiburg, 1956)

Horror Literature: A Core Collection and Reference Guide, ed. Marshall B. Tymn (New York & London: Bowker, 1981)

Horror Literature: A Reader's Guide, ed. N. Barron (New York & London: Garland, 1990)

Howard, Jacqueline, *Reading Gothic Fiction* (Oxford: Clarendon Press, 1994)

Hume, Robert D., 'Gothic versus Romantic: A Revaluation of the Gothic Novel', *PMLA*, 84 (1969), 282-290

Hyde, Virginia M., 'From the "Last Judgment" to Kafka's World: A Study in Gothic Iconography', in *The Gothic Imagination: Essays in Dark Romanticism*, ed. G. R. Thompson (Pullman, WA: Washington State University Press, 1974), 128-149

Ingham, Norman W., *E. T .A .Hoffmann's Reception in Russia* (Würzburg: jal-verlag, 1974)

Jackson, Rosemary, *Dickens and the Gothic Tradition* (Unpublished D.Phil. diss., University of York, 1978)

—— *Fantasy: The Literature of Subversion* (London & New York: Routledge, 1981, repr. 1995)

Janouch, Gustav, *Gespräche mit Kafka* (Frankfurt a. M.: Fischer-Bücherei, 1961)

Jones, Ernest, *Nightmare, Witches and Devils* (New York: Norton, n.d.)

Kafka, Franz, *Tagebücher 1910-1923* (Frankfurt a. M.: S. Fischer, 1951)

—— *Briefe*, ed. Max Brod ([Frankfurt a. M.]: S.Fischer. 1958)

—— *Er,* ed. M. Walser (Frankfurt a. M.: Suhrkamp, 1963)

—— *Short Stories,* ed. J. M. S. Pasley (London: Oxford University Press, 1963)

—— *Der Heizer, In der Strafkolonie, Der Bau*, ed. J. M. S. Pasley (Cambridge: Cambridge University Press, 1966)

—— *Das Schloß* (Kritische Ausgabe), ed. Malcolm Pasley, 2 vols (Frankfurt a. M.: S. Fischer, 1981)

—— *Der Verschollene* (Kritische Ausgabe), ed. Jost Schillemeit, 2 vols (Frankfurt a. M.: S. Fischer, 1983)

—— *Der Proceß* (Kritische Ausgabe), ed. Malcolm Pasley, 2 vols (Frankfurt a. M.: S. Fischer, 1990)

—— *Sogni*, ed. Gaspare Giudice (Palermo: Sellerio, 1990)

—— *Träume*, ed. Gaspare Giudice & Michael Müller (Frankfurt a. M.: S. Fischer, 1993)

Kant, Immanuel, *Critique of Practical Reason*, tr. Thomas Kingsmill Abbott, 3rd edn (London: Longmans, Green & Co, 1883)

Kiely, Robert, *The Romantic Novel in England* (Cambridge, MA.: Harvard University Press, 1972)

Küpper, Heinz, *Handliches Wörterbuch der deutschen Alltagssprache* (Hamburg & Düsseldorf: Claassen, 1968)

Lee, Sophia & Harriet,*Canterbury Tales*, 2 vols (London: Henry Colburn & Richard Bentley, 1832)

Le Tellier, Robert I., *Kindred Spirits: Interrelations and Affinities between the Romantic Novels of England and Germany* (Salzburg: [University of Salzburg] Institut für Anglistik und Amerikanistik, 1982)

Lévy, Maurice, *Le roman <gothique> anglais 1764-1824* (Paris: Albin Michel, [repr.] 1995)

Lovecraft, H. P., *Supernatural Horror in Literature* (Chislehurst: The Gothic Society, 1994)

Lüthi, Max, *Once upon a time. On the Nature of Fairy Tales*, tr. L. Chadeayne & P. Gottwald (New York: Ungar, 1970)

—— *The European Folktale: Form and Nature,* tr. J. D. Niles (Bloomington: Indiana University Press, 1982)

—— *The Fairytale as Art Form and Portrait of Man*, tr. Jon Erickson (Bloomington: Indiana University Press, 1987)

—— *Märchen,* 9th edn, rev. Heinz Rölleke (Stuttgart: Metzler, 1996)

Macnish, Robert, *The Philosophy of Sleep*, 2nd edn (Glasgow: W. R. M'Phun, 1834)

Malleus Maleficarum, tr. M. Summers (London: The Pushkin Press, 1948)

Mayer, Mathias, and Tismar, Jens, *Kunstmärchen* (Stuttgart: Metzler, 1997)

McNutt, Dan J., *The Eighteenth-Century Gothic Novel: An Annotated Bibliography* (Folkstone: Dawson, 1975)

Menhennet, Alan, 'Schiller and the "Germanico-Terrific" Romance', *PEGS*, 51 (1981), 27-47

Miles, Robert, *Gothic Writing 1750-1820* (London & New York: Routledge, 1993)

Miller, Robin Feuer, 'Dostoevsky and the Tale of Terror', in *The Russian Novel from Pushkin to Pasternak*, ed. John Garrard (New Haven: Yale University Press, 1983)

Moser-Rath, Elfriede, 'Antimärchen', in *Enzyklopädie des Märchens*, ed. Kurt Ranke (Berlin & New York: De Gruyter, 1976), cols 609-611

Nolting-Hauff, Inge, 'Märchen und Märchenroman', *Poetica*, 6 (1974), 129-174

——— 'Märchenromane mit leidendem Helden', *Poetica*, 6 (1974), 417-455

Opie, Iona & Peter, *The Classic Fairy Tales* (London: Oxford University Press, 1974)

Otten, Kurt, 'Der englische Schauerroman', in *Europäische Romantik II*, ed. K. Heitmann (Wiesbaden: Athenaion, 1982), 215-242

Parry, I.F., 'Kafka and Gogol', *GLL*, 6 (1952-1953), 141-5

Pasley, J. M. S., 'Asceticism and Cannibalism: Notes on an Unpublished Kafka Text', *OGS*, 1 (1966), 102-113

——— See also under Kafka

Passage, Charles E., *The Russian Hoffmannists* (The Hague: Mouton, 1963)

Paulin, Roger, *Ludwig Tieck, A Literary Biography* (Oxford: Clarendon Press, 1985)

Poggioli, Renato, 'Kafka and Dostoyevsky', in *The Kafka Problem*, ed. Angel Flores (New York: New Directions, 1946)

Prawer, S. S., *The 'Uncanny' in Literature* (London: Westfield College, 1965)

——— *Caligari's Children. The Film as Tale of Terror* (Oxford: Oxford University Press, 1980)

Propp, V., *Morphology of the Folktale*, 14th imp. (Austin: University of Texas Press, 1998)

Punter, David, *The Literature of Terror* (London: Longman, 1980; rev. edn, 2 vols, 1996)

——— (ed.), *A Companion to the Gothic* (Oxford: Blackwell, 2000)

Radcliffe, Mrs, 'On the Supernatural in Poetry', *New Monthly Magazine*, 16 (1826), 145-152

Railo, Eino, *The Haunted Castle* (London: Routledge, & New York: Dutton, 1927)

Rogers, Robert, *The Double in Literature* (Detroit: Wayne State University Press, 1970)

Róheim, Géza, *Gates of the Dream* (N.Y.: International Universities Press, 1952)

Röhrich, Lutz, *Folktales & Reality*, tr. P. Tokofsky (Bloomington: Indiana University Press, 1991)

Rommel, O., 'Rationalistische Dämonie: die Geisterromane des ausgehenden 18. Jahrhunderts', *DVjs,* 177 (1939), 183-220

Roskoff, G., *Geschichte des Teufels,* 2 vols (Leipzig: F. A. Brockhaus, 1869; repr. Nördlingen: Greno, 1987)

Rudwin, Maximilian, *The Devil in Legend and Literature* (London: The Open Court Company, 1931)

Scarborough, Dorothy, *The Supernatural in Modern English Fiction* (New York: Lethe Press, 2001)

Schopenhauer, Arthur, 'Versuch über das Geistersehen und was damit zusammenhängt', in his *Parerga und Paralipomena,* I (Berlin: A.W.Hahn, 1851)

Schubert, Gotthilf Heinrich von, *Die Symbolik des Traumes* (Bamberg: Kunz, 1814; repr. Heidelberg: Lambert Schneider, 1968)

Sedgwick, Eve Kosofsky, *The Coherence of Gothic Conventions* (New York: Arno Press, 1980, repr. New York & London: Methuen, 1986)

Shelley, Percy Bysshe, 'Essay on the Devil and Devils', in *Shelley's Prose,* ed. D. L. Clark (Albuquerque: University of New Mexico Press, 1954)

—— *Zastrozzi and St Irvyne,* ed. Stephen C. Behrendt (Oxford & New York: Oxford University Press, 1986)

Silberer, Herbert, 'Bericht über eine Methode, gewisse symbolische Halluzinations-Erscheinungen hervorzurufen und zu beobachten', *Jahrbuch psychoanalytisch-psychopathologischer Forschungen,* 1 (1909), 49, 102, 344f, 378, 412, 503ff, 513

Sokel, Walter H., *Franz Kafka: Tragik und Ironie* (Munich & Vienna: Langen-Müller, 1964)

—— *Franz Kafka* (New York & London: Columbia University Press, 1966)

Soldan/Heppe, *Geschichte der Hexenprozesse,* ed. Max Bauer (Hanau: Müller & Kiepenheuer, 1911, repr. 1968-69)

Spalding, Keith, An Historical Dictionary of German Figurative Usage (Oxford: Blackwell, 1952-)

Spector, R. D., *The English Gothic: A Bibliographic Guide* (Westport, CT & London: Greenwood Press, 1984)

Spilka, Mark, 'Kafka's Sources for *The Metamorphosis',* Comparative Literature, 11 (1959), 289-307

Stoker, Bram, *Dracula*, ed. Maud Ellmann (Oxford & New York: Oxford University Press, 1998)

Struc, Roman S., 'Categories of the Grotesque: Gogol and Kafka', in *Franz Kafka: His Place in World Literature*, ed. Wolodymyr T.Zyla, (Lubbock, Texas: Texas Tech University, 1971)

Summers, Montague, *A Gothic Bibliography* (London: The Fortune Press, n.d.)

—— *The Gothic Quest* (New York: Russell & Russell, 1964)

Tatar, Maria, *The Hard Facts of the Grimms' Fairy Tales* (Princeton: Princeton University Press, 1987)

—— *Off with their heads! Fairy Tales and the Culture of Childhood* (Princeton: Princeton University Press, 1992)

—— (ed.), *The Classic Fairy Tales* (New York & London: Norton, 1999)

Thalmann, Marianne, *Der Trivialroman des 18. Jahrhunderts und der romantische Roman* (Berlin: Ebering, 1923)

—— *The Romantic Fairy Tale*, tr. Mary B. Corcoran (Ann Arbor: The University of Michigan Press, 1964)

—— *Die Romantik des Trivialen* (Munich: Paul List, 1970)

The Cambridge Companion to Gothic Fiction, ed. Jerrold E. Hogle (Cambridge: Cambridge University Press, 2002)

The Handbook to Gothic Literature, ed. Marie Mulvey-Roberts (Basingstoke & London: Macmillan Press, 1998)

The Oxford Book of Gothic Tales, ed. Chris Baldick (Oxford & New York: Oxford University Press, 1992)

The Oxford Companion to Fairy Tales, ed. Jack Zipes (Oxford: Oxford University Press, 2000)

Thomas, Ronald R., *Dreams of Authority: Freud and the Fictions of the Unconscious* (Ithaca & London: Cornell University Press, 1990)

Thompson, Stith, *The Folktale* (New York :The Dryden Press, 1951)

—— *Motif-Index of Folk Literature*, 6 vols (Copenhagen: Rosenkilde & Bagger, 1955)

Todorov, Tzvetav, *The Fantastic*, tr. R. Howard (Ithaca, New York: Cornell University Press 1975)

Tompkins, J. M. S., *The Popular Novel in England, 1770-1800* (London: Methuen, 1932; repr., n.d.)

Trainer, James, *Ludwig Tieck: From Gothic to Romantic* (The Hague, etc.: Mouton, 1964)

Tresidder, Jack, *The Hutchinson Dictionary of Symbols* (Oxford: Helicon, 1997)

Varendonck, J., *The Psychology of Day-Dreams* (London: George Allen & Unwin, 1921)

Varma, Devendra P., *The Gothic Flame* (Metuchen, N.J., & London: The Scarecrow Press, 1987)

Wagenbach, Klaus, *Franz Kafka. Eine Biographie seiner Jugend 1883-1912* (Berne: Francke, 1958)

—— *Kafka* (Reinbek: Rowohlt, 1964)

Webber, Andrew J., *The Doppelgänger. Double Visions in German Literature* (Oxford: Clarendon Press, 1996)

Wright, Elizabeth, *Speaking Desires Can be Dangerous. The Poetics of the Unconscious* (Oxford: Polity, 2000)

Zipes, Jack, *The Brothers Grimm. From Enchanted Forests to the Modern World* (New York & London: Routledge, 1988)

—— *When Dreams Came True. Classical Fairy Tales and Their Tradition* (New York & London, 1999)